SEX, DRUMS,
ROCK'n'ROLL!

SEX, DRUMS, ROCK'n'ROLL!

The Hardest Hitting Man in Show Business

KENNY ARONOFF

Backbeat
Books

AN IMPRINT OF HAL LEONARD LLC

Published in 2016 by Backbeat Books
An Imprint of Hal Leonard LLC
7777 West Bluemound Road
Milwaukee, WI 53213

Trade Book Division Editorial Offices
33 Plymouth St., Montclair, NJ 07042

Every reasonable effort has been made to contact copyright holders and secure
permissions. Omissions can be remedied in future editions.

Printed in the United States of America

Book design by Michael Kellner

Library of Congress Cataloging-in-Publication Data is available upon request.

ISBN 978-1-4950-0793-4

www.backbeatbooks.com

CONTENTS

CONTENTS

FOREWORD

It is safe to say that of the many paths to becoming a professional musician, none is easy. (At least, before DJs and machine-operators started being called "musicians.") It is said that mastering any worthwhile skill, from athletics to drawing to playing a musical instrument, requires 10,000 hours of dedication.

Just think about that—hundreds of days of one's youth must be sacrificed to practice and study, practice and study. That takes a rare dedication, amounting to *obsession*, and a tremendous outpouring of energy—a gathering of words that starts to lead us toward a description of Kenny Aronoff. Energetic, dedicated, obsessed. Add in talented and well-schooled, musical and hard-rocking, and we are getting closer.

When Cathy Rich and I were planning a tribute record to her father, *Burning for Buddy*, in the 1990s, Kenny was on our list right away. He came in and knocked off his two tracks in short order, working from his homemade notation. You'll read more about that later, but to anyone else the pages looked like a bookie's tally-sheet of scribbles and hieroglyphics. For Kenny it got the job done, and we even had time to record a third track he wanted to try.

Later that year, Kenny was working with another artist at Le Studio in Quebec, near where I have kept a home for over thirty years. He was able to visit my lakeside retreat on a gorgeous summer day, then ride back in my Porsche Speedster—top down, music loud. (Probably *Francis A. and Edward K.*, meaning Sinatra and Ellington, with Sam Woodyard's elegant drumming, a particular favorite around that time.)

During that visit, Kenny and I spent a little time in the studio collaborating on a percussion duet over Steve Ferrone's drumming at the end of "Pick Up the Pieces." I sported a shaved head as well that summer, so we called ourselves the Bald Bongo Brothers. (Kenny said to me, "If you ever see me wearing a toupee, please *shoot* me!" I solemnly swore that vow . . .)

Later, in New York City, Kenny and I performed a longer version of that part at a Buddy Rich tribute concert, with Omar Hakim driving the band.

I believe it was when Kenny was touring with Joe Cocker in the early 2000s that he rode with my longtime bus driver (from 1996 to 2015) Dave Burnette. It was Dave who told me that because Kenny was always flying somewhere on days off to do sessions with other artists, the crew called him "Can-He Earn-Enough?"

But you know he was doing it for love—because he *could*, because he had the *energy*.

There is a condition called "hyperthymia," humorously defined as "having so much energy, doing so many things, and getting so much done—that it annoys other people."

Hold on to that thought for when you get to John Mellencamp's acid comment about Kenny and his "ambition."

As if there is something *wrong* about wanting to play with everybody in the world—and then going out and *doing* it.

As Dizzy Dean said, "It ain't braggin' if you can back it up."

Kenny Aronoff can back it up.

—Neil Peart

INTRODUCTION

Sex, Drums, Rock 'n' Roll!

Playing the drums is an emotional, physical, spiritual, and sexual experience. When done right, there is a fantastic sexual energy between the band and the audience, between the drummer and the band, between the band and the fans out in front of the stage. It's the world's biggest come on.

I've spent my entire life flirting with the audience. It started in my living room and advanced to bars and then arenas and stadiums, and every night I created torrid relationships with the women in the audience (and probably everyone else, too—rock 'n' roll does not discriminate).

But if you are looking for a book where the drummer brags about sleeping with 4,000 women, this isn't the one. Most sex is fleeting, or else why would someone be driven to go to bed with thousands of groupies? I've had my fair share, but this is about something much bigger and hotter. This is about seeing the Beatles on TV and then actually getting to play with them fifty years later, because that is the biggest fantasy to ever come true.

Getting girls to dress up like nurses is easy when you are twenty-five and in a hot band. Staying relevant and keeping the show on the road, not so much. Getting called on the phone every day to do a session with the world's greatest artists is what does it for me. Playing with Sting and Rod Stewart one day, Johnny Cash, Paul McCartney, and Lynyrd Skynyrd the next—that turns me on. Yes, also the women, definitely the women. And when we were young and flying around the world, doors flew open to hotel rooms, orgies, weird scenes, you name it . . . but you aren't going to find giant piles of cocaine in this book either. Drums, not drugs! I'm not judging anyone, but that's what works for me.

I am a fortunate cat. From the first note to the last, in stadiums and arenas for the last three and a half decades (and still going strong), if I had that snare drum between my legs, you could guarantee it was going to be some kind of great night. And after the show I'd send thousands of people home, driven by the power of the beat, to fuck and fall in love. "Sex, Drums, and Rock'n'Roll" is some seriously powerful shit.

—KENNY ARONOFF
Los Angeles, California

SEX, DRUMS, ROCK'n'ROLL!

1

"Hey, I Want to Be a Beatle!"

I was an insanely hyper kid. I had boundless energy from the time I woke up until I fell asleep at night, and I needed outlets that matched my endless energy, so I began running, hiking, playing football, and baseball, basketball, skiing, soccer, hockey, lacrosse, climbing trees, swimming, riding bikes, whatever kids do when they live out in the country, until I finally realized that what I really wanted to do was *hit things with wooden sticks*—which is one way of saying playing the drums in a rock 'n' roll band. Once I sorted that out, there was no turning back. I can only imagine what sort of world we would be living in if I hadn't started playing the drums—I think I would have created all sorts of trouble.

When we were together, my twin brother (identical twins, which meant a *double* dose of all that energy) and I were like an atom bomb. Our parents encouraged us to play outside all the time, just so we wouldn't destroy their house and maybe they could have some peace and quiet. We rarely watched TV because there was nothing exciting to watch on our black-and-white RCA TV set, not up in the Berkshire Hills of Western Massachusetts where we lived, not even with giant rolls of tinfoil clumped onto those ridiculous rabbit ears that everyone had on their old TV sets back then for better reception. We were pretty much at the far edge of any broadcast coming from civilization, so my parents had their LPs spinning on their turntable all the time, playing mostly jazz, classical, and some musicals. They loved singers like Frank Sinatra, Bobby Darin, Ella Fitzgerald, and Sarah Vaughan. They were actually very cool and very open-minded, and very into the arts, music, theater, poetry, dance, painting, all of it.

One night—it was 1964 and I was eleven years old—while I was chasing my brother, Jon, through the house, my mom screamed, "HEY, GUYS! Come to the family room *right now!* You need to watch this!" I figured this was just their way to get us to calm down—to watch the evening news or something equally opiate and dulling for insanely energetic children. I was wrong.

The Beatles were on *The Ed Sullivan Show*. It shut me up all right, but it also created a whole new set of problems.

Watching them play, I was stunned, practically paralyzed. The first song was "All My Loving," which Ringo swung pretty easily, followed by "Till There Was You," which is actually a show tune with a Latin feel. They were still trying to find themselves back then.

But things got crazy: the next song was "She Loves You," as in *YEAH! YEAH! YEAH!,* maybe the greatest lyric ever written, and then they closed the show with "I Saw Her Standing There" and "I Want to Hold Your Hand," total rockers that created complete pandemonium. That was the stuff that launched the revolution.

"*Mom,* I want to be in the Beatles!"

(Silence.)

"I want to play *the drums!*"

(Silence.)

"I want to grow my hair long and dress cool. . . . I want to *be* cool!"

(More silence.)

"I want all those screaming girls wanting me! Mom, I want people going crazy for me playing *rock 'n' roll,* just like the Beatles! I WANT TO BE A ROCK STAR! I WANT TO BE A DRUMMER!"

My mother didn't say anything—she was too busy dancing to the music on TV. She loved the Beatles. My parents were intellectuals, but they weren't square.

Meanwhile, within just a few songs I was obsessed: I was thinking, How am I going to do this? How can I get into that band? Who do I call? Where do I go? What do I do? Growing up in a small town, a million miles away from that dream, how was I going to be *in the Beatles?*

I had to do something. I couldn't just sit around and wait around for it to happen.

When I figured out that I couldn't be in the Beatles, me and a bunch of my friends started a band, our very own Beatles. We called ourselves the Alley Cats, and our theme song was, of course, "The Alley Cat." It was a silly song, but it was being played on the radio a lot in 1964.

Like most parents who wanted their kids to learn an instrument, my mom had started me with piano lessons, but I was drawn to the energy and power of the drums. When I saw the Beatles I hardly noticed the guitars— all I saw was Ringo and his drums.

One day I decided I had enough of those piano lessons, and in an act of rebellion, I ripped up my piano music right in front of my mom and said, "I'm not playing the piano any more. I want to play the drums." It may have been a little bit *more* enthusiastic than that, actually. Enthusiasm bordering on a *riot*. When my mom said she still wanted me to play the piano, I ran around the kitchen table screaming:

"NO MORE PIANO! DRUMS! DRUMS!! DRUMS!!!!! ... *DRUM-MMMMMMS!!!!*"

Drummers are typically either just one step from crazy, or one toke over the line, like Keith Moon, King of the Crazies. We are usually the most energetic guys in the band. There have been a few laid-back drummers, but mostly the drummers I know are dangerous, intense, physical risk-takers, bold and fearless. I know it makes us the brunt of a lot of jokes, but most drummers, unlike guitar players and keyboard players and bassists, tend not to over-intellectualize what we do. And when we start pounding the drums, the adrenaline starts flowing, which makes us even *crazier*. Fortunately, no one has ever tried to stop me.

After seeing the Beatles on TV, I had my ear plastered to the radio all the time and drove everyone crazy, beating on everything and everyone around me as if they were drums. I couldn't afford a full drum set, but I was able to get a snare drum and a cymbal, and I beat on that like an escaped mental patient, as if I were playing a full drum kit, trying to replicate the big beats I heard on the radio, and imagining what it must be like to be RINGO FUCKING STARR with the BEATLES.

I can't explain it fully, but I had a naive vision, or fantasy, that I would one day play with the Beatles. The punch line is, fifty years later, I did get to play drums with the Beatles—Ringo Starr and Paul McCartney, anyway—on a CBS television special celebrating that very night my rock 'n' roll dream was born, when I saw them for the first time on *Ed Sullivan*. I know it sounds crazy, but dreams do come true, and I made it happen. I put it out to the universe, and I worked my ass off. The phone doesn't ring all by itself.

So how did I do it? How does a kid from a town of 3,000 people get to play with the Beatles, with Bon Jovi and Leonard Bernstein, and guys from Black Sabbath and the Rolling Stones? John Mellencamp, John Fogerty, Willie Nelson, Smashing Pumpkins, Bob Dylan, Meat Loaf, and hundreds more? How did I make that phone ring?

I'd like to say it was easy, I simply *willed* it. But that isn't the truth—it was created with hard work and self-discipline, and, of course, the love and passion I had for hitting things with wooden sticks—drumming is one of the few jobs that rewards that sort of behavior.

2

Norman Mailer and Norman Rockwell

I grew up in a little town called Stockbridge. It was a hip place, where community was important and liberal, open-minded ideas thrived. Stockbridge was home to a lot of famous painters, actors, sculptors, playwrights, well-known psychiatrists, famous dancers, lots of musicians, and some well-known ones, like Arlo Guthrie and James Taylor. Stockbridge was three hours from New York City. It was kind of like if you took a slice of the Village in New York City and brought it up into the Berkshires.

When you came out of our driveway and turned right and went one-eighth of a mile down Yale Hill Road, the next house on the left was Norman Mailer's house, author of *The Naked and the Dead* and *The Executioner's Song*. I used to go over there and hang out with his daughter Danielle. I totally had the hots for her, but nothing ever happened between us, mostly because she was just sixteen back then, and if it did, Norman would have kicked my ass from one end of the lawn to the other, or worse. Trust me when I say you didn't want to get on the wrong side of Norman Mailer.

Past Norman's house down the hill was a cottage with a huge water wheel where the actress Eleanor Wilson lived. As a young kid, I used to do her gardening for 25 cents an hour—that's how I paid for my first snare drum and crash cymbal. She was a NYC theater actress who would spend her summers in Stockbridge and occasionally act in the Berkshire Playhouse, which was three-eighths of a mile farther down the hill. This theater is still a well-known summer stock theater where lots of famous actors come to work during the summer. I met many famous actors there, stars like Frank Langella, Richard Dreyfuss, Goldie Hawn, Estelle Parsons, and

Faye Dunaway. They would come to the Berkshires to get out of NYC in the summer and do some old-school acting in a beautiful location. Everyone was super nice and left their attitudes back in New York. It was a great place to grow up.

One summer, when I was twenty-two years old and really coming into my own, I was hired to play drums and percussion for a musical that was being performed at that theater. There was a lot of fucking going on behind the scenes at that theater company that summer, and for some reason I was getting a lot of action. There were lots of very sexy, beautiful female dancers in that musical—and they went crazy for my relentless drummer's energy and rhythm. Maybe now you're starting to see the appeal of playing the drums? No one dances to the guitar player.

—◦—

When my identical twin brother, Jon, and I entered the second grade, our parents thought it would be good to put us into different classes with different teachers to help us develop our own identity, since we were connected in a way that only twins can be.

> **Dr. Jon Aronoff (my brother):** Being an identical twin, my brother and I developed, without any instruction from anyone else, that the Aronoff team was first and foremost. Our identity as a twosome was greater than Jonny and Kenny, it was bigger than either one of us individually, and that we served to honor that, to respect that, to protect that, the integrity of that, and so the currency of everything we did was to maintain this sense of Aronoff twinship. We never violated the code. The twinship was all about team building, it was about collaboration and competition, a lot of things that are essential for boys to become men.

Everyone loved the twin thing, especially Jon and me. We were always popular because of that—people loved seeing us together. Still today, people who know me but don't know I have a twin brother, meet Jon and freak out.

It happens all the time. I have sent Jon into the dressing rooms of artists I work with, people like Joe Cocker, Melissa Etheridge, Bob Seger, John Fogerty, you name it, and they all do a double take. Mick Jagger was *freaked* when he saw us both together.

We used to visit Norman Rockwell, the famous painter and illustrator, when I was in grade school. He lived just out of town. I would watch him paint and he would talk to us, and while my brother was distracting him, I stole his cigarettes. He had these cool pewter boxes that held cigarettes in them, and I would sneak a few at a time to take home to smoke with my brother and sister. It is an odd upbringing when Norman Rockwell is the source of your contraband.

More importantly, if I rode my bike south out of town, I could visit one of my best friends, Tom Gibson. I spent a lot of time at his house in the summer. His family was super liberal and cool, and I guess looking back now, pretty well-off. They had an indoor swimming pool, clay tennis courts, a trampoline, and a small guesthouse that Tom turned into a place where we would rehearse our rock bands and play records as loud as we wanted on his stereo all night long. We smoked a lot of pot and listened to Creedence Clearwater Revival, not knowing, of course, that in thirty years I'd end up playing the drums for their singer-guitarist, John Fogerty. For now I was just rolling joints on his face, on the covers of their albums.

Tom's mom was a big-time psychiatrist who helped pioneer hypnosis for therapy, and his dad was William Gibson, the American novelist and playwright who wrote *The Miracle Worker*, the story about Helen Keller. He also wrote a two-act play called *Two for the Seesaw*. The director of *Two for the Seesaw*—Arthur Penn, who eventually directed *Bonnie and Clyde*, *The Chase*, and *Little Big Man*—lived in our town as well. Arthur eventually built a house up the road from the Gibsons, and his wife, Peggy Penn, acted in the original *Peter Pan* as Wendy.

I would run into all kinds of cool actors and film people at the Gibsons' house. One summer night, it was my turn to come down from the guesthouse and sneak a few beers from the kitchen. I was super stoned and grabbed three beers, hoping to bolt back up to Tommy's rock 'n' roll sanctuary without getting snagged. But just as I had the beers in my hand ready to go, Mrs. Gibson invited me to say hi to her guests, namely Faye Dunaway, Anne Bancroft, Mel Brooks, and Frank Langella, all eating dinner and laughing and having a great time. They were probably stoned—they didn't really care about kids swiping a few bottles of beer.

3

"Purple Haze"

In 1964, the same year I saw the Beatles perform for the first time on *The Ed Sullivan Show*, I made my parents take our family to see *A Hard Day's Night* in a small movie theater called the Mahaiwe in Great Barrington, Massachusetts, a small town three miles south of Stockbridge. I was already rehearsing on the weekends with the Alley Cats, but after seeing *A Hard Day's Night* I was even more crazed to be in the Beatles, or at least be in a rock 'n' roll band *like* the Beatles, with everyone going crazy for us, especially the girls.

Back in the early '60s, the AM radio stations we listened to (FM wouldn't happen for a few more years) played a wide variety of musical styles, so you could hear the Beatles, and later the Rolling Stones and Jimi Hendrix, but also Ray Charles, James Brown, Elvis, and novelty songs like "The Alley Cat," all on the same station, WBZ-AM out of Boston. Even better, there were very few commercials, more music, and great hep patter from the DJs playing the music. You got to know the DJs, and they were stars in their own right. It was a glorious time; they played everything you wanted to hear, all sorts of stuff that really opened up my mind. You never had to change the channel.

The song "The Alley Cat," by someone with the unlikely name of "Bent Fabric," had been a big hit. We did our version featuring our most talented band member, John Sauer, on piano. He played it flawlessly. We rehearsed at his house in his living room on the weekends, when we weren't playing with John's cool electric HO Model racing cars.

John and the other two musicians were one year older than me. Jeff

Hodges played bass, Steve Harris played guitar, and everyone sang but me, and because I could only afford an old wood snare drum and one cymbal, I stood up and played.

Eventually I traded that snare drum for some weed, and then bought a louder snare drum, a metal one made for rock music, but I still couldn't afford a whole kit, not yet.

A funny thing is that the guy who traded me the pot for the drum called me thirty-five years later and said he was going to put it on eBay as "Kenny Aronoff's first drum," so I bought it back. I originally paid $20 for it, but I paid $400 to get it back. No drugs exchanged hands.

My first drum was a six-lug snare drum that made the drum ring a lot (ten-lug snares are more common), which was perfect for jazz, but I wanted a tighter sound for rock 'n' roll, so I used a piece of very thin fabric my mom gave me—I took off the bottom drum head and stretched the fabric across the drum, then put the head, counter hoop, and snares back on.

When I got it back, it still had the original bottom head on it, with the same piece of fabric, which to me was very sentimental and made it well worth the dough.

The first gig I ever played was with the Alley Cats, and, of course, we played "Alley Cat," but we also played some Beatles and Beach Boys songs. Because we only knew about five songs, we played our entire set *twice*, which still only took about twenty minutes, but I was immediately addicted to playing the drums in *front of people*. This was my rock star fantasy coming true, making people sing and dance along with my beat. And of course, again, I had no idea where it was all headed.

> **Ellie Aronoff (my mom):** Stockbridge is a big summer town because it's located two miles from Tanglewood, and in the summer, Tanglewood is open, so you get the whole Boston Symphony for eight weeks, and Kenny was a part of the Tanglewood Music Center Orchestra working with the Boston Symphony Orchestra members. He was a timpanist and a percussionist and wore a tuxedo when he performed.
>
> I'm a New Yorker by background, and the kids' dad, Arthur, was from

New Jersey. I met him up here by accident—Kenny's father was a paper chemist, and moved to the Berkshires to work in a paper mill, and for a New York City girl, that was quite an adjustment, but we ended up having the best life. Kenny and his siblings were raised in a great big ten-room house that was built back in 1848, started out as a farmhouse, and then had wings that were added on. When we first moved into this house, we had very little money, but we worked very hard together and built it up, and I think the kids saw that, and that's how they grew up. Those children had probably the best father anybody could have, he was a wonderful man. Kenny's brother, Jon, who is a clinical psychologist, said to me just the other day, "I think Dad was the best-adjusted man I have ever met."

Nina Aronoff (my sister): We were reminded all the time that we were a *family,* and that we took care of each other. We came from a certain kind of Jewish family that is very oriented towards children, and to education, and to culture. My mother was extremely creative. One of the great strengths she brought to being an elementary school teacher was this idea that there was always something you could create out of the moment. So to have that as a norm in the environment you grew up in is really a gift, that's a privilege to have that, because you learn to draw on your own resources, and you also learn to think that *it's possible to change the moment.*

My parents took me to see a lot of famous jazz musicians perform at a local venue called the Music Inn, way out in the woods in Lenox, Massachusetts, three miles north of Stockbridge. It was an intimate place, perfect for jazz, and I saw a lot of modern jazz legends play live there as a child, from Dizzy Gillespie and Stan Getz to Dave Brubeck, Charles Mingus, the Modern Jazz Quartet, and even Ray Charles, to name a few. These men were the last of a race of giants. No one has replaced them.

I also grew up during an amazing time in rock history: I got to see the Who perform *Tommy* at Tanglewood, the first year they performed *Tommy* in America. I was in the second row with my twin brother. Keith Moon saw us and flipped out because he thought he was seeing double. That night,

Jethro Tull and It's a Beautiful Day opened for them. I saw Iron Butterfly when "In-A-Gadda-Da-Vida" was a huge hit. I saw Miles Davis open up for Santana, and both were at the peak of their careers, same with Joni Mitchell, James Taylor, Sly Stone, Janis Joplin, and the original Jefferson Airplane, whom I eventually toured with in 1990.

As a young kid getting started on the drums, I was trying to imitate everyone. I was a self-taught drummer, because there were no drummers around teaching drum-set lessons, and definitely not *rock* drumming. That drumming style was too new, and really looked down on by "professional music teachers," so I just taught myself. I remember trying to learn the drum beat to Ray Charles's hit "What'd I Say?" which was the coolest beat, that crazy Latin thing just tearing up the ride cymbal with so much energy and flair. I could totally relate to that. I tried to play the drum beat to Mitch Ryder's "Devil with the Blue Dress," which had a killer, tough, funky beat. Johnny "Bee" Badanjek was the drummer in Mitch's band, the Detroit Wheels, and he was absolutely fucking awesome.

My dad had a huge jazz collection, and I tried playing along with Miles Davis and John Coltrane records in my later teens, trying to imitate the great jazz drummers like Elvin Jones, Philly Jo Jones, Art Blakey, Gene Krupa, Louis Bellson, and Dave Brubeck's drummer, Joe Morello, who used to do a drum solo with his hands on the kit like John Bonham did on "Moby Dick" with Led Zeppelin. From all of that jazz I learned a lot about technique, improvising, listening, dynamics, and how important it was to swing all the time, no matter what you were playing.

There was so much amazing new music coming out. The post–World War II world was changing radically, the culture was beginning to open up, and as a kid, I had been very lucky to see some heavy musicians and bands playing all styles of music. But it all started with the Beatles. Seeing them was when the world changed from black and white to color.

Dr. Jon Aronoff: I remember two teachers said the same thing to me, and one was Mr. Beacco in high school, who was so frustrated with my hyperactive brother constantly drumming and banging his hands on his desk, doing crazy drum rolls. Kenny was just an entertaining person all the time, and Mr. Beacco would get so pissed off that I think he did rack my brother's knuckles on a couple of occasions. This was back in the early '60s when teachers could wrap a student's hands if they were misbehaving in class. I remember in Sunday school one of the teachers smacked Kenny across the knuckles with a wooden ruler. I've had both teachers since tell me, "Oh my God, I could have ruined his career by breaking his fingers!"

When I was fourteen years old and I heard "Purple Haze" on the radio for the first time, it blew me away. That was another "it" moment for me.

The Beatles were happy, nice and safe, and parents liked them (this was still pre-LSD). They were *accepted*. Jimi Hendrix, on the other hand, was heavy, deep, powerful, dangerous, scary, and very sexual, but not *too* dangerous, because his voice was kind. But his music felt and sounded like being high on something. You could feel that from his music. How did he do that? How could he do something so different and fresh from the Beatles? Hendrix represented a new social movement. He fused rock, R & B, the blues, and jazz together, and it reached out to everyone in druggy waves of sonic bliss.

I got my first Jimi Hendrix album, *Are You Experienced?*, for Christmas in 1967, and I'll never forget it, because it snowed eighteen inches on Christmas Eve. On Christmas Day we got the fireplace going, and everyone was hanging out downstairs in the living room listening to classical and jazz music, reading quietly, while I was upstairs in my room taking a couple hits off a joint and cranking *Are You Experienced?* over and over again on my turntable, all day and all night, while building model airplanes. My parents kept having to come upstairs every so often banging on the door for me to turn it down, but I was mesmerized. I actually got to go see the Jimi Hendrix Experience perform live, just one hour from Stockbridge, in Troy, New York. It was when *Axis: Bold as Love* had just been released, and it was like a religious experience—the four of us who saw the concert were so blown away, no one talked for ninety minutes on the way home.

I just identified with the soul and the whole vibe of the Jimi Hendrix

Experience, and specific to my instrument, I identified with Jimi's drummer, Mitch Mitchell, because I grew up hearing so much jazz—Mitchell was basically a jazz drummer, improvising a lot and turning it into rock. It brought both worlds together for me, and I always identified with him.

It also kind of fucked me up—years later, when I went for my first big audition and got the gig with John Mellencamp (or John Cougar, as he was known at the time), I had a very different idea of what it meant to be a rock drummer. Playing with Jimi Hendrix offered a lot of freedom—explosive fills, odd meters, flashy rolls, and extended techniques. Mitch was kind of like John Coltrane meets the Who, and it was fabulous and inspirational, but it could only truly exist in that very specific situation—playing in a band in the 1980s struggling for radio hits, not so much. But we'll get to that. I had a lot to learn.

As we got a little older and graduated from stealing Norman Rockwell's cigarettes, we would have these little parties at classmates' houses, and would raid their parents' wine cellar, and some kids would be smoking pot, the usual stuff. I remember being at one of these parties one weekend around that time, and that night everyone was dancing to the Mamas and the Papas' "California Dreamin'," which was a great song to slow-dance to. I remember making out with a chick for the first time at one of those parties. It was a big moment. I even made a try for second base: my hand touched some breast, but a bunch of Kleenex fell out of her bra. Girls used to do that all the time—they called it "stuffing." I have no idea why she didn't stop me.

At one point during one of those parties, while everyone was dancing to "California Dreamin'" or some other dreamy slow song, something came over me and I ripped that 45 off the turntable and put on "Purple Haze." Of course I did—I was a maniac drummer and there was only so much of this *slow* dancing I was willing to put up with. Of course everyone suddenly stopped and started yelling at me, like "KENNY? What THE FUCK are you DOING?" which makes a lot of sense now looking back. What an idiot I was! I blew everyone's groove and everyone's chance to make out and get their own handful of Kleenex. That was another lesson I was going to have to learn. But calm was never my thing.

I got upset because I thought no one understood how cool Jimi Hendrix was, so I left the party with a bottle of very old French wine, probably worth a small fortune, that I had found in the wine cellar at the house that the party was at. I went wild, running around the neighborhood, ripping down street signs, feeling all alone and misunderstood. I recently went back to visit my mom in the big house in Stockbridge where I grew up, and found in the barn one of the street signs I had torn down that night. I still have it: GRAVESLY TERRACE. I had ripped that fucker down in a kind of protest of everybody not understanding me and Jimi Hendrix. It was a souvenir of my rebellion.

Many years later, I got to meet Mitch Mitchell, probably my first drumming hero, after Ringo, anyway. I had just recorded two songs with the Buddy Rich Big Band for a Buddy Rich tribute record that Neil Peart from Rush produced. It was a real drummer's thing. It was a huge honor. You should look it up on the Internet, there is a video of it, and I don't look like I do now—I was still suffering in the cool department, trapped in some post-hippie/pre–hard rock abyss where I looked like a cross between Mick Fleetwood and Annie Hall. I'd have that cured soon enough.

When Mitch saw me, he pointed at me like as if to say "I know you," I sheepishly approached him, in awe, to tell him how much he had influenced my life as a drummer, and before I could say anything, he said, "I know something about you that most people don't know," and I said, "Huh? What's that?!" and he told me, "You know how to *swing*, Kenny."

At this point, my career was rolling along and I was famous for being a hard-hitting, four-on-the-floor drummer. It blew my mind when he said that to me. He explained that he heard my recordings with the Buddy Rich Big Band—not something a lot of rock fans had ever heard. It was one of those amazing moments in life, that feeling of validation by someone you admire. Actually, in this case, more like idolized. Playing with the guys from the Beatles years later was amazing. This was pretty close.

4

Ground Zero

From ages sixteen to eighteen, my brother and I played in bands and would rehearse seven nights a week in our barn from 8 p.m. until midnight. Our daily routine was school, then after-school varsity sports (we were on the varsity soccer team, lacrosse team, and ski team), dinner, homework, and then band practice until we dropped. When I wasn't doing any of that, I just practiced like a fiend.

> **Dr. Jon Aronoff:** I remember one time when Kenny was twelve, he said, "Jon, I'm going to the barn, and I'm going to do a drum roll for an hour," and after he started playing, I would check in with him every fifteen minutes, and he did it for an hour! That was the most amazing thing, to drum-roll for an hour. People have died doing less.

On weekends, we jammed all day and into the night, unless we had gigs to play. There were always guys in the band that were older than us, and they had Volkswagen hippie vans or trucks to move gear when we had shows. We were playing in bars when I was as young as thirteen, and I loved it when older women hit on me. It was exciting, but also a little scary, because they knew things that I clearly did not.

My dad encouraged me and my brother to use his station wagon because he felt we were actually safer driving ourselves than being with older guys in their vehicles, who might be drinking or smoking pot during and after the shows. My parents always felt that my brother and I were safer as a team. They were sort of right, but not completely—Jon and I always had a deal, whoever was the least fucked up drove, and the other guy had to stay awake and keep an eye out for cops or deer jumping out in front of us or anything else. We were always a team.

We always seemed to destroy our parents' cars by stuffing way too much gear into them, not to mention that sometimes we had crazy road races after these gigs on windy dirt roads, through the woods, up and down small mountains, into corn fields and out again, on the highways, all over the place. I get chills thinking about how lucky we are to be alive. I am so lucky I didn't kill myself, or anyone else. I mean shit like that happened to someone every year. "Did you hear Donny finally went too fast around Dead Man's Curve, car spun out on the ice, and he's dead, and Barbara broke her leg and got 50 stitches in her head?" Crazy stuff like that.

Rock 'n' roll was more than just music to me, it was my emotional philosophy, a cool *fuck you* to uptight people and their square approach to life. Rock 'n' roll was creativity, anything goes, and it was as dangerous as you wanted it to be. I partied, but I didn't do acid or heroin like some of my friends. I was wild, but responsible. I took chances, and sometimes went too far, but there was always a voice in my head trying to reason with me, and that may have saved my life a few times.

◄○►

My parents may not have known just how powerful a force rock 'n' roll had become in my life, but they were happy that music was consuming me—they could see my passion for music developing, and they were always encouraging of hard work and artistic exploration.

Two of my grandparents came from Russia, pre–Russian Revolution, around 1907, and the other two came from Romania and the USA. They were so grateful, honored, and relieved to leave their countries to come to America and start a new life. They felt fortunate that in the United States there was freedom of speech, and the freedom to do so much more here than where they came from. And they believed that the only way their children would make a better life than what they had was to study, graduate high school, go to college, get a degree, get a job, work your ass off, raise a family, and have *their* kids go through the same process and continue the American dream.

My dad and mom did exactly that: they were perfect examples of the American dream. Back then there was no such thing as self-entitlement. Being lazy, or not trying, earned you exactly *nothing*. If you didn't study, you got a bad grade, and more importantly, you *earned* that bad grade. If you didn't work hard, you didn't make the team. If you wanted to be successful, you had to work hard, period. There were clearly defined winners and losers. If you didn't win, you *lost*. You didn't get a medal for participating, you went home. I'm glad my parents taught me that. These days I worry about kids being patted on the head just for getting in the game. Winners should get the trophies, and losers should strive to be the winner next time. That's the way it works in the real world. I don't believe in coddling. Coddling is for babies.

During my sophomore year of high school, I noticed my buddy Tommy Gibson was suddenly getting better on drums, and I asked him, "What are you doing to get better?" and he told me he'd been studying with the principle percussionist from the Boston Symphony Orchestra, Arthur Press. He told me I should start taking lessons, and that's exactly what I set out to do. I would catch a bus from our town and go about two hours to Newton, just outside of Boston where Arthur lived, and take a lesson for two to four hours once a month on orchestral snare drum, timpani, and mallets. Throughout the summers, when the Boston Symphony Orchestra moved to their summer location at Tanglewood, three miles from my house, I'd have a lesson with Arthur every week at my house for one hour. He took me to new places, musically and mentally, even though we were studying mostly classical music. It helped me with my approach to learning new things on my drum set, and in life in general. He taught me how to open my mind. He was kicking my ass and teaching me to become more disciplined, more focused. He taught me not only to practice more, but to practice *correctly*, and not waste time. He gave me a better understanding of music, and the kind of hard work it was going to take to make it. He set me on a new path.

—◀o▶—

The night before I took the bus for my first lesson with Arthur, I went to a party in a field on top of a mountain with a bunch of junior and senior guys who played football and soccer, and a lot of hot cheerleaders. As a teenager I was just as much a jock as I was a musician, and I didn't have too much trouble fitting in. I had so much energy and testosterone flowing that playing sports and music at a very high level felt completely natural to me.

So there I was, drinking the night before my first lesson with Arthur Press, trying to be cool with the cheerleaders, and wound up showing up to my very first lesson with a vicious hangover. Well, as I quickly discovered, Arthur Press took his business very seriously. He'd come from the same generation as my folks had, a first-generation American who came to this country with his grandparents and parents, and it was impressed on him in no uncertain terms that he was not here to fuck around. His parents wanted him to become a lawyer or something business-related, but he worked his ass off, went to the Juilliard School of Music, and eventually became the principle percussionist of the Boston Symphony Orchestra.

And as a teacher, he was no nonsense. The first question he asked me after I introduced myself, was: "What have you prepared for me today?" I'd never heard those words come out of anyone's mouth before, and being a teenager, I asked the wrong question in response, "What do you mean?" So he said, his patience already being tried, "Have you prepared a mallet piece for me?"

The next thing I asked him was what mallets were, because I had no idea. He was used to kids from Boston who attended the New England Conservatory of Music and were already going full-tilt on marimba, vibes, timpani, orchestral snare drum, and were very serious percussionists. I was in rock bands and wasn't at that level yet. I hadn't ever thought about that stuff because I was so into rock 'n' roll.

So after I told him I didn't play mallets, he asked me if I'd prepared a timpani piece, and when I said "No," I was really starting to freak out, and he finally said, "Well, what *do* you play, Kenny?" When I told him drums, to my relief, instead of kicking me out of his house before our first lesson even started, he said, "Well, let's go down to the basement and listen to you play the *drums.*"

He put on "Spinning Wheels" by Blood, Sweat & Tears—which is actually a pretty funky song—and luckily I'd already been playing it because I was in the habit of putting records on at home and drumming along with them.

About twenty seconds into the song, he pulled me off the kit, pointed to a practice pad, and said, "We're going to start from the beginning. . . ." So that first day, on the pad, he started teaching me everything starting with how to hold the sticks, and we worked on technique and reading music for the snare drum. Ground zero.

Sometimes, I'd go to his house and have a four-hour lesson with him because I was so determined to get better. He made me cry one time because I wasn't prepared properly, and he was frustrated that I wasn't taking his lessons seriously enough. He'd start yelling at me and pushed me pretty hard just to make a point. It was intense. There was no hand-holding, this was boot camp, and it was great for me. Arthur lit a fire under my ass, and it has never become dull or gone out. I just became relentless.

Ellie Aronoff: We were pretty strict about our kids doing their homework and kept after them when they got home from school so they got their schoolwork done first, but that almost seemed like it backfired on us, because then once he'd finished homework, it was practice, practice, practice all night, and we had to listen to it. It was no fun—it was a good thing we had a big house. Eventually, his setup at home was: we had a whole set of drums and two timpani in the living room, and a big vibraphone in Kenny's bedroom, not to mention the barn. It took over the whole house, and he kind of got out of some jobs because he was so busy practicing. It was constant, and his dedication was inspiring. He *never*, ever let up and dropped it, ever, once he got into it.

Nina Aronoff: Kenny's drums definitely took over the house. I've got kind of permanent Post-Percussive Stress Syndrome. Because of years of listening to piano practice, drum practice, marimba, timpani, and all that stuff, when I hear people doing scales and practicing their instruments, I start to twitch a little bit.

◄o►

By the time I was getting ready to go to college, I was very determined to study music, and my mother held Arthur Press's opinion in enough esteem that she actually went and asked him bluntly, "Do you think this boy can do anything with music, do you think he's developed enough?" And Arthur told her, "He's not good enough to get into Juilliard, New England Conservatory of Music, or Indiana University School of Music, because the programs are so intense, and that's not Kenny. Kenny likes sports and girls *and* music, so maybe he should pursue a liberal arts education with a heavy emphasis in his major on music," which was smart advice at that time.

My mom and I started looking at colleges, and we visited schools like Brandeis, which was way too academic and serious for me. I remember sitting in on a class and I fell asleep. Turns out they didn't want me either, so we visited a couple other schools around Massachusetts that were a little stuffy, and eventually landed at University of Massachusetts, which had a music program, plus a really great lacrosse program. They were ranked in the Top 10 in the country at that time, and I was a *smoking* lacrosse player—I was one of the top-scoring high-school attack men in Western Massachusetts, so coach Garber at UMass knew who I was.

I had two practice sessions as a freshman at UMass and got my ass kicked so fucking hard I dropped lacrosse.

5

From Vietnam to Indiana

Even though it was a freewheeling time, growing up in the '60s and early '70s and as a teenager just off to college, you still lived with the dark cloud of the Vietnam War hanging over you every day. It was on TV every night, on the covers of every newspaper every day, on the cover of *Time* and *Life*. It was in our music: from Creedence Clearwater Revival to the Beatles, Jimi Hendrix to the Who, and everywhere in between, the angst and frustration of the counterculture raged. As a seventeen-year-old in 1970, I had the fear of opening the mailbox after school every day when I was checking for college acceptance letters that I was going to get a draft notice instead.

Our birthday—my twin brother, Jon, and I—is March 7, and we came up in the last draft *just* as we'd both gotten into college, which meant if we got drafted, we could possibly be going to war instead of school.

The war was almost over, but the USA was still sending troops to Vietnam. I'd seen a lot of guys come back from my high school who'd been drafted and made it home, but they were ruined: Zombies, missing limbs, emotionally and mentally a mess. It wasn't just that I was worried about losing an arm, I was worried about dying before my life had really even gotten started.

My mom was freaking and was pretty much ready to move us up to Canada. My father was somewhat more accepting of the situation. He was a World War II veteran, a navigator in one of those bombers that helped kick Hitler's ass and finish the war. He was a hero.

I wasn't against our armed forces; I was against the fucking war. It didn't make sense, and the casualties didn't seem to ever serve our country's purpose in anyway.

The way the last draft worked was a lottery—President Nixon would randomly pick a number written on something that looked like a Ping-Pong ball, out of a bowl or container, with a date written on it. That was a birthday, and if it was yours, congratulations, you just won a trip to Vietnam. The entire country would watch on television, scared and praying it wasn't them or one of their kids.

The first number drawn was March 6, and, wow, that was close, the day before our birthdays. But the next number was, holy shit, March 7! Which meant we were going to have to show up for an Army physical to see if we were fit for military service, and then, if you didn't have some hard core reason why you shouldn't go, you were most likely going to boot camp, and then shipped off to Vietnam.

There was no way we were going to Vietnam to fight a useless war, so we started the process of trying to see if we could get out of the draft with some legitimate medical reasons. I had horrible allergies at that time in my life, and twice a year I had to take some serious antibiotics and other medicine to deal with heavy sinus infections, and my brother was still recovering from having knee surgery from playing sports. So we had our fingers tightly crossed. It had actually gone so far that I went to see the Army doctor and was about to get cleared for a rifle and a pair of combat boots.

I'd brought all my medical paperwork with me to my Army physical, covering what I was allergic to, plus I had sent copies ahead as they had requested. I remember walking to the bus at 6 a.m., eating every kind of food I was allergic to, so I would sound and look like I was in bad shape. It was fall and I already had serious problems with ragweed, so it was real obvious, to me at least, that I was not the best candidate to become a soldier. I rode the bus with a bunch of farm boys who were all gung ho about signing up and killing some commies. They scared the shit out of me.

When we finally got to this big convention center where they were set up to do the physicals, I wound up being first in my line because my last name begins with an A. When they rattled off "Kenny Aronoff," they pulled me into a room with three guys in white lab coats, and one of them asked me, half-yelling, "Where does it say here on all these papers that you should not serve in the military in Vietnam?"

He was flipping through all my paperwork acting angry and pissed, trying to scare me, and it was working—I was freaking out. I thought it would be easier than this.

"What's wrong with you, boy? What are your illnesses that keep you from serving our country and fighting against these Communists? Show me where on all these pages where it says you can't serve in the military. What's wrong with you, boy?"

I actually froze for a second and couldn't remember that I had allergies, but I finally managed to blurt out, "Well, I have allergies," to which one of them replied, "You got allergies, huh? Where does it say here that you have allergies?" The next guy said, "What else you got?" So I told him I'd screwed up my knee playing soccer, and he told me to shut the fuck up.

I thought I was going to Vietnam. There was a long pause, and then he said, "Listen, son, you got enough shit here on these fifty pages to get this whole building kicked out of the Army. Now get the fuck out of here!"

I was escorted out by one of those lab-coat guys—he was actually a cool guy who didn't seem like he wanted to be there either. He told me that the guy who was yelling at me was pissed off because he has to stamp each page in my file twelve times. Me getting out had created more work for him. Oh well.

My brother didn't have it as easy during his physical: they made him go through a rigorous physical for most of the day before they let him walk.

When I got let go, even though it was only around 8:30 in the morning, I was so excited that I went to a liquor store, bought a case of beer, and started hitch-hiking my way back home. I got picked up by a three-hundred-pound redneck, a good ol' boy who took a definite interest in my beer. "Hey, buddy, what are you doing with all that beer at 8:30 a.m.?" When I replied, "Celebrating," and he asked me what over, I lied and said

I was heading to see my girlfriend, because he looked like he would have beat the crap out of me if I'd answered honestly.

–◦–

Most of these kids auditioning for the UMass music program had played in their school marching bands and orchestras for as much as eight years, where I had basically said, "Fuck that, I'm too cool for this shit! I don't want to play with squeaking clarinets and stupid marching band music! I want to be a rock star!" I wanted to be on *those* stages.

So why did University of Massachusetts School of Music accept me? When I auditioned for Peter Tanner, head of the Percussion Department at UMass, I was beneath the skill level of a lot of my fellow percussion students. But, in spite of any skepticism he might have had, he told me that he was impressed with my insatiable drive to be a *great* drummer and percussionist. He could see my ambition shining through, and thought, I can turn this guy into a *champion*. He saw that I was not fucking around.

So the plan was for me to study with Peter for four years, and that first year, my freshman year, I really did get my ass kicked. They were not fucking around either.

I never worked harder, but that made me even more determined and instilled in me the very true belief that you *never* make it, you are always *trying* to make it. Not long into my first year of college, I had to prioritize my life and make the commitment to being the best musician I could be. Dreaming wasn't going to do it.

As a teenager from a small town, I didn't see any way I could make it as a *rock* drummer. There were no teachers or mentors for that yet, so I went to *music* school, and along with timpani, mallets, orchestral snare, and percussion, I studied music theory, music literature, conducting, piano, sight-singing, played in orchestras and percussion ensembles, jazz bands, and also studied a bit of English, math, physics, genetics, and mythology, which, though no one told me at the time, was the blueprint for rock 'n' roll.

◄o►

In order to be accepted into a music program as a percussionist, there were specific requirements: you had to prepare written pieces on a mallet instrument (vibes or marimba), orchestral snare drum, timpani, and sometimes multiple percussion, unless you were declaring yourself a jazz major, in which case you could audition on a drum set. UMass didn't have a jazz program for drummers yet; I would become a "performance major in classical music."

There were technical requirements that you were asked to perform on all instruments—scales, arpeggios, and sight-reading for the mallet instruments. Rudiments and sight-reading on the orchestral snare drum was required, and tuning, rolls, precision with dynamics, articulation, and sight-reading music on timpani—it was brutal.

I played a violin étude on marimba that I had prepared on my vibraphone at home, and after I finished, Peter asked me to play some scales and arpeggios. He gave me this crazy test to check my pitch and understanding of intervals, and asked me to play "A" above middle "C" on the marimba, then sing a perfect fifth above that note. Then he asked me to sing a third below that note, then a second above that note, and finally hit the note on the marimba and see if that was the same note I was hopefully singing. Then it got even harder, because he put some music in front of me and told me to sight-read it, which I was horrible at, but got through it somehow. He had me do the same thing on timpani and snare drum. He told me later on that he accepted me because I was determined to succeed, even when I was failing. He was referring to my horrible ability to sight-read in my audition. I kept trying to read the same piece of music over and over again, even when he said it was okay to move on.

I was out of my element because I wasn't playing in my barn with my rock band any more—this was worlds away. In music school, I had to follow strict and demanding orders from my teachers and conductors. They demanded precision, technique, and perfection in all areas on all my instruments. I was nowhere near the best or most talented freshman, and there was no coddling or holding hands here, no trophies just for showing up. I was on my own, and I was either 100 percent right on or 100 percent wrong. It was extremely competitive.

But this is what made me who I am today—it was exactly this kind of formal education that made it possible for me to handle high-pressure gigs, both in the studio and live, especially in super-high-pressure, high-visibility gigs like the Kennedy Center Honors, or performing at the White House, or the Grammys, or any other event where I have to read and write music and lead a group of musicians—and we are talking about some of the heaviest cats in the world—and be *perfect* all the time, without much prep or rehearsal. There it was in front of you: pass or fail. Get with it or get lost.

Here's a thing about drummers, in case you haven't already figured it out: we can be the life of the party, but we are also like soldiers that don't give up. The singer might be at the bar talking up some chick, but I'm going to be on the field fighting. I'll die for my art. It is never a choice of fight or flight. There is *only* fight, fight, fight, and I mean that in the best possible way. There is no secret: I am a relentless motherfucker—*that's* how I went from watching the Beatles on TV to playing with them fifty years later.

—◇—

As soon as high school ended and summer vacation started, I practiced eight or nine hours a day, seven days a week for ten weeks straight before going off to UMass. I practiced mallets, timpani, snare drum, and drum set all day, every day, and even kept a log on how much I practiced each day. It was an intense regimen, but it was that fear of not measuring up to the level where everybody else was that made me work long and hard.

I had announced to the universe and to everyone in my life that *this was my life*. I was going to dedicate myself to being the best drummer and musician possible. Most of my friends didn't understand why I wasn't spending the summer after graduating high school partying with them. I even had my mom screen all calls for me and tell them I was busy.

On top of all the practicing I did, I was playing in a jazz trio five nights a week, with my buddy John Sauer from the Alley Cats and an upright bass player, John Maynard. We had a regular gig in this big old grand hotel in the middle of Stockbridge called the Red Lion Inn, playing in a small tiny bar in the hotel called the Den. Maybe sixty people could fit in there.

I was really getting serious about jazz as my technique got better and better on the drums. The more vocabulary and ideas I had on the drum set, the more I wanted to express myself. In rock 'n' roll the drum parts are more defined, and everyone generally depends on you to play the same parts every time, and there is more of a spirit of fuck you and rebellion. In jazz, improvisation and self-expression are more the focus, and the cats who played it tended to be more "serious," but I loved playing both styles of music.

My parents were *huge* supporters of what I was doing, so much so that I was exempt from doing chores around the house so I could focus my time on practicing because they saw how much I was busting my ass to be great. I think my brother and sister resented me a bit for that, but I think everyone could see and feel I was extremely determined and that's all I wanted to do, or would do.

That first year at UMass was the toughest learning curve for me because I was catching up, and I always felt that I was behind in *everything*. But at the same time my fellow classmates immediately spotted me and said, "Holy shit, who's *that* guy?" because they really didn't have another student like me in their program. I would practice until they kicked me out of the building. There were talented people there, but I didn't see anyone as driven and as obsessed with their careers as I was. A lot of them were there just having fun being away from home, on their own in school, while I was there with the ambition to become the greatest fucking musician that ever walked the planet.

There were times I was freaking out, because I had so much new material to learn both in music and in my regular academics. It was like I was attending two schools. I still had plenty of fun, chased girls, got drunk with my buddies at parties, and all of that kind of college stuff, but my first priority was always my career. There were times when I literally fell asleep standing at a marimba, or woke up behind my drum set—and then I just started up again.

My practice room was right next to Peter Tanner's office, so he could hear everything I was working on. He recognized the self-competition, ambition, and hard work I did day in and out. I think he was impressed with the progress I was making, even when I felt I wasn't getting anywhere at all, because just six weeks into my first semester, he had me perform a piece on the marimba in front of the entire music school, which was terrifying. He was pushing me to see what I was capable of doing. Even though I'd been performing in front of people for years behind a drum set, he took me outside of my comfort zone and put my talent on display in front of a totally different percussion instrument.

I remember that performance very well, because as I walked onstage, took a bow, and listened to my piano accompanist, David Vincent, start the piece, I froze and couldn't remember the first note of the piece I was about to perform. I had to memorize this piece, which I did, but there was no way to anticipate how I would react to performing on a *freaking marimba* in front of an entire, super-competitive music school.

When I missed my entrance, David's head suddenly popped up and he looked at me, smiling, as if to say, "Anytime, Kenny. . . ."

I was freaking trying to figure out what the first note was. The simplest things can destroy you. I was distracted by everything at that moment, and of course missing my entrance made it worse. What felt like hours was probably seconds, and I eventually made my entrance and performed the piece perfectly. But I will never forget that feeling. I did not want to experience it ever again.

My professor became my biggest fan. He would drop in on me sometimes during my practice sessions—which lasted hours at a time—and give me pointers and constructive critiques. He really was like the equivalent of a coach pushing me as a player. People used to try and convince me to stop practicing on Friday or Saturday nights and go party, but I wouldn't leave the music building until at least 11 or 12 at night, then go party. Just like in high school, a lot of the slightly older junior and senior girls were trying to lure me away when I was practicing, seemed like everyone wanted to fuck the new freshman drummer, but I was so focused I would blow them off and take it out on the timpani and marimba.

In the second semester of my freshman year, another important door opened for me after I overheard a female cellist, who I had a huge crush on (she wasn't *rock 'n' roll hot*, but she was *classical hot*), mention that she was participating in a summer music program called the Aspen Music Festival in Colorado.

When I asked about it in an attempt to flirt with her (she definitely could have pulled me away from the kettle drums), she told me it was run by the prestigious Juilliard School of Music in NYC. Not only was I very focused on being around the best musicians and the best teachers, but if this cellist was going there, that's where I needed to go. Sex, drums, and . . . *classical music!*

During my first semester, I was already thinking I needed to transfer to a better music school, one that focused more on pure performance. Performance schools attracted the best music students and teachers in the world, and UMass focused more on music education.

The application for the Juilliard-sponsored Aspen Music Program was its own harrowing gauntlet of musicality.

I was instructed to prepare a piece in three out of four percussion categories: mallets, timpani, orchestral snare drum, and multiple percussion. Rather than picking three, I decided to prepare pieces from all four categories to help increase my chances of being accepted. Once I decided I wanted to do something, I went after it aggressively and recorded four pieces: one on marimba, one on timpani, one on orchestral snare drum, and finally multiple percussion. I sent the tape off and never heard from anyone.

When the semester ended, I planned to spend my summer back home playing in an Allman Brothers–style rock band, practicing every day, taking lessons with Arthur Press, and I finally had a beautiful, *normal* girlfriend back in Stockbridge that I was looking forward to spending time with. So the last day of school, I loaded up my dad's car with musical instruments and headed home for the summer.

I remember leaving UMass the last day of classes, getting about two miles off campus, and realized, "Oops, I've forgotten my mail." I turned around to go grab it—I think there was a paycheck in my mailbox I didn't want to wait on or something—and when I opened it, no paycheck, but instead a letter telling me I'd been accepted into Juilliard's summer program in Aspen! I *couldn't* believe it. I was excited, but realized I was about to face some of the best percussionists in the world, cats who were as crazy and driven as I was. As an added bonus, not only had I been accepted to this incredibly elite Juilliard extension program, but I got a $500 scholarship, which was a lot of money for my family in 1972. And there was the promise of the hot cellist, so there was that.

When I arrived in Aspen, I was the worst percussionist there, even though I'd eventually become one of their most famous graduates—not that fame means anything, but rock music is good for that. I mean, can you name a famous timpanist or classical percussion player?

I remember as excited as my parents were for me, they couldn't afford to cover any more than my regular school-year tuition, so my dad said I would have to cash in all the bonds my grandparents and relatives had given me when I was younger—which reminds me of an old drummer's joke (there are millions of them): What's the difference between a savings bond and a drummer? A savings bond matures.

Anyway, I used those bonds, and along with about $1,000 I had saved from gigs and the $500 scholarship, I was able to pay for the program's tuition. So I was home for a couple of weeks before I flew to Aspen for the summer, and that's where I met Professor George Gaber, the teacher who truly changed my life. Not only was I blown away with what a great teacher he was—he was ruthless but generous—but I was drawn to his amazing approach to life in general.

I took refuge in the relationship I struck up with George Gaber during my summer in Aspen. He was a heavyweight intellectual, a worldly, philosopher-type of personality, and I instantly knew that I wanted to be around him and learn as much as I could from him in the short time I had at Aspen, thinking at the time I was heading back to UMass in the fall.

But George told me about the music program at Indiana University, where he taught during the year, which was one of the top three music programs in the country.

Indiana University became one of the largest music schools in the world, because Dean Bain, head of the school, had a vision. The concept was simple: Invite the greatest musicians from the greatest orchestras from all over the world to come and teach at Indiana, and not only offer them great salaries and retirement plans, but also allow them to leave the school to perform. Let them do what they loved to do most, and in turn it would attract the most talented students from all over the world.

I made my mind up immediately that I wanted to transfer to IU and study with him. I think he initially suggested I go back to UMass for one more semester, to make sure I had given it some more thought, but I told him I had my mind made up, and didn't want to waste any more time: "I want to go from Aspen to Indiana and study with you when the fall semester starts."

"If you really, really want to do this," he told me, "to get into IU, you have to audition for professors from four different departments." As fate would have it, those four instructors were at Aspen that summer!

Rather than being fazed or intimidated by what George told me was an impossible lack of time to prepare for the audition, I was motivated and raring to go. I saw the opportunity, and I actually felt empowered by the situation. George was that good a teacher. I was not going to miss out on one second of studying with him.

So I spent the next month preparing night and day, while still doing all the required rehearsals and performances at Aspen.

I remember one highly humiliating experience in Aspen, a symphony orchestra rehearsal early on, where I had to play two crash cymbals at a critical moment in a Tchaikovsky symphony. It's where the orchestra is going nuts and suddenly stops playing and I am supposed to crash two cymbals together to fill that void.

I was so worried about making my entrance perfect that I miscounted, and came in early and left a hole where I was supposed to play. Everyone in the orchestra heard me blow it, and believe me, when you're playing in a symphony orchestra, it's not like a rock band where everything sort of covers up everything else in a live situation. This was the polar opposite, where every wrong hit stands way the fuck out. I was *counting* it, purely, and not *feeling* it, and I screwed it up.

It was a life-changing moment. I was deeply embarrassed. Painfully so. And as soon as I blew it, the conductor stopped everyone playing and went ape-shit on me and berated me in front of the entire orchestra. Everyone in the orchestra suddenly turned around and looked at me. Everyone. To make matters worse, after he finished yelling at me, he made me count out loud, so everyone could hear me, like a child, the measures leading up to my cymbal crash. When I didn't play the crash cymbals, he yelled at me again. He never told me to play, *just count*, to show him I could do it, but he wanted both, and I was mortified. There was nothing to do but stand there and deal with it. I was all alone in a room full of musicians, and no one could or would do or say anything to help me.

I know it sounds a lot like basic training in the Army or something like that, but the level of discipline really felt that serious. In retrospect, the conductor was kind of an asshole. I mean, I'm obviously all about discipline and don't need to be coddled or pampered, but this was the unnecessary humiliation and intimidation of a student. I mean, it was a cymbal crash, not the invasion of Normandy. I learned the lesson fast, long before he was done emasculating me.

Still, as upset as I was with myself, and pissed at him for wailing on me in front of everyone, my resolve was that I would never let that happen to me again. I just worked harder. I really felt like I had to develop a warrior mentality that summer. It was the furthest thing from a summer vacation I've ever had, but I learned a very important lesson: *Repetition is the preparation for success.*

I passed my audition to get into Indiana University, and a week later I drove twenty-four hours straight from Aspen, Colorado, to Bloomington, Indiana, to take the entrance exams, because the fall semester was just about to start. Freshman orientation was, in fact, already going on when I landed on campus. It was all very rushed, which was a *rush* in and of itself for me. I love that feeling. I remember my heart was racing when I flew home to Massachusetts after that, packed up all my stuff, and then drove all the way back to Indiana just in time to make the first day of classes. I never did make it with that cellist, because she never made it to Aspen, but that was okay—there would be other sexy cellists in my future.

So in one year I went from Massachusetts to Aspen, and then to Indiana, which was definitely not the easy way to go, but turned out to be the best way for me to grow and rise to the top. It was hard core.

The day I pulled into Indiana University was the day I fell in love with it. I went through something of a culture shock after growing up in such a small town on the East Coast, and even after a year away at UMass, because this town was *booming*—38,000 students strong. But people were more laid back than on the East Coast. And Bloomington was so beautiful, with rolling hills and lots of trees. Downtown was filled with tons of cool bars, great-looking girls everywhere—one year IU even won "Best Party School in America." I'm not sure if parents liked hearing that when their kids were there, but it was such an amazing town that it became my home for thirty-five years. Fucking Indiana. Not Hollywood. Not New York. Best decision I ever made.

6

Leonard Bernstein or . . . Rock 'n' Roll?

IU was one of the toughest and most competitive music schools in the country. The music school had high standards, and they were very strict about maintaining them—this was a way to weed out the people who would not be able to survive in the music business. If you didn't keep up, if you didn't have your shit together, you'd wash out. I thrived on it, though. I loved it.

Within my new music program specifically, there were one hundred percussionists, and I quickly befriended one of them, another student named Tom Miller, who was as ambitious as I was. He was a senior and the best percussionist/timpanist in the school. He was very serious, and we bonded immediately. On Friday and Saturday nights, when all our fellow percussion classmates were out partying, we were practicing till midnight. He was a badass, and we shared the same dedication and tunnel-vision focus on becoming the best.

I was dating a girl named Sheri, who kept getting annoyed with me if I hadn't asked her out by Friday afternoon for a date on the weekend (she was right, of course), but my priorities at IU were music first, then party after that. There were a lot of guys I went to school with who were more talented and had way more experience than me, and they bailed out of the program while I kept hitting things with sticks. I missed dates, I missed parties, I missed opportunities with girls, I just kept practicing.

Every year while I was at IU, I would audition in the spring to try and get into the Tanglewood music center fellowship program, which is the Boston Symphony Orchestra's (BSO) Summer Academy for Advanced

Music Study. While the BSO did their regular summer music festival series, they also mentored this student orchestra that I was trying to be a part of. It was made up of the best students in the world and considered the number-one student symphony orchestra in the United States. It happened that their summer home was in the Berkshires, just a stone's throw from my hometown in Massachusetts.

This world-famous student orchestra performed every week—with minimal rehearsals—and would also get to perform with the Boston Symphony Orchestra during certain performances. They also got to collaborate with all the world-class conductors who worked with the BSO during its summer season.

One of the most exciting prospects of getting accepted into this orchestra was the opportunity to work with Leonard Bernstein, who was among the most legendary symphony conductors in the world at that time—plus one of America's greatest living composers. He wrote the score for *West Side Story*, among other incredible accomplishments. In this world, there was no one cooler than Leonard Bernstein.

Besides working with Bernstein, we also got to learn from other master conductors like Aaron Copland, Arthur Fiedler, and Seiji Ozawa, but Bernstein was in a league of his own. He did his series of Young People's Concerts on television, but he never made classical music seem "better" than rock 'n' roll. He never ever talked down or acted condescendingly. He wasn't an elitist dick. He just loved music.

It took me four years and four auditions to finally get accepted to this program at Tanglewood, but once I did, one of the biggest highlights for me was getting to play the timpani part in Sibelius's Fifth Symphony with Bernstein conducting us on the BSO's main stage.

I almost cried during that performance. It is such a beautiful piece, such a perfectly Romantic composition, and Bernstein was such a passionate, brilliant conductor, who knew how to bring all of us to a higher level of excellence. Instead of bullying us, he would make us want to play *for* him. He brought us close to him, but still demanded a lot from us. It was an amazing combination of traits. He knew where we lived in our hearts and minds and made that the entrance point for us. He wanted to welcome musicians to the fold, not scare them away.

On the other hand, on the very first night at Tanglewood, we had an orchestra rehearsal with Seiji Ozawa, who wielded his power like some sort of evil villain. He demonstrated his genius ability to memorize incredibly involved symphonic pieces by acting like he didn't know what pieces we were going to rehearse, and then with no musical score to follow, he showed us he had everything memorized. We played a Ravel piece for sixty seconds, and then he stopped us abruptly to demonstrate his absolute power.

He scolded six different musicians in the orchestra whom he said were out of time or out of tune, and it made us all fearful of him. I understood what he was trying to do, but I preferred Bernstein's approach. On that first night when rehearsal was over, everyone scattered, and I was on the floor in the back of the orchestra where the percussion section set up, sorting out my music, instruments, mallets, and sticks, when I suddenly overheard Bernstein and Ozawa talking.

They were on the stage where the conductor's podium was, and Bernstein had seen our rehearsal and came up to say hello to Seiji. Seiji was frustrated, telling Lenny that he was disappointed in our first rehearsal, and questioned our abilities. Lenny put his hand on Seiji's shoulder and said, "No, you have it wrong! This is the best student orchestra in America, if not the world, and they will play for you. They will give you what you want and more. It's the first day. Show them some love, some respect, and they will play for you."

Another amazing experience was being conducted by the great American composer and conductor Aaron Copland, who conducted one of his famous compositions, "Rodeo." It was such an honor to have him conduct his own known composition, but at the same time, I couldn't watch him because he was getting lost in the score! There was an odd meter that he had put in there, and his baton was all over the place.

Finally, I was mentored by the brilliant teacher, stick-maker, and timpanist of the BSO, Vic Firth. Before I was accepted into Tanglewood, I spent a few summers studying with him. He was also the guy I had to audition for, but he wasn't cutting me any breaks just because I was his student.

I can't say enough about Vic: I have known him for two-thirds of my life, and I watched him when he started handcrafting orchestral mallets, snares, and timpani sticks; he started the largest and most innovative stick company in the world. I used to practice timpani for him sometimes five hours a day, not only because I wanted to have a great lesson and improve, but because I respected him and I hated to disappoint him or waste his time. If you made a mistake in a lesson, you had one chance to do it correctly before he would just move on and you'd have to do it all again at the next lesson. If you were unprepared, your lesson was over in ten minutes. He was tough, but an amazing mentor and a good friend.

At Tanglewood there was an eighteen-year-old cellist prodigy who wore the shortest miniskirts possible—she looked like a dream carrying her cello *on her head,* holding it in place with one hand as she walked confidently from one rehearsal to the next. She was a prodigy, and the most beautiful woman in our program. Vic Firth saw me gawking at her many times (everyone did), and he told me that one of my assignments for the summer was to make it with her. I laughed—there was no way that was going to happen. I had a better chance of joining the New York Philharmonic. Everyone was crazy for her, but she knew how to keep the boys at bay.

Somehow, during the last week of Tanglewood, we managed to hook up. Actually she was the one who grabbed me—I had somehow convinced her to stop by my house, because my parents were away and we had some new kittens. Girls love kittens, I figured, but I didn't figure on her telling me to "stop playing with *those* pussies and start playing with mine."

I also dated a cellist at IU for a while. I don't know, there's just *something* sexy about cello players . . . they vibrate at different frequencies than drummers. There is nothing percussive about their personalities. Somehow they manage to excite me and calm me down all at once. But the hottest girl I dated during those years was Mary Miller, who was a prima ballerina studying dance in the ballet program at IU. She was beautiful, with an incredible dancer's body, and somehow she convinced me to be an extra in a very modern production of the ballet *Ondine* at IU. This was definitely *not* rock 'n' roll, not unless you're talking about *Spinal Tap*—I had to wear tights and all the other ballet stuff, and I looked ridiculous, like a reject from Jethro Tull or Uriah Heep, but I was willing to do *anything* to be with her, such was her power.

> **Ellie Aronoff:** You cannot get into Tanglewood with anything but talent. I don't care if your last name is Rockefeller, you *cannot* pay your way in. So you audition, and if you're top of the line, they take you, so Kenny kept auditioning for four consecutive years until they accepted him! I remember Art and I were so proud, being the classical music fans we were on top of just being proud parents, and before Kenny actually came under the instruction of Leonard Bernstein, he studied under a lot of other conductors that came through Tanglewood all summer until he finally played with Leonard Bernstein. He played the Sibelius Fifth Symphony and had a beautiful timpani part, and I remember Lenny just raised his fist in the air as if to say, "Go, Kenny!" I talked to Leonard about it a couple years later and said to him, "You know what Kenny's doing now? He's playing rock with John Cougar," and Lenny did that same fist thing again and said, "Go, Kenny!"

So what did all of this orchestral training have to do with becoming a rock drummer? It taught me self-discipline and hard work. I learned *how* to practice, *what* to practice, and how to develop technique on all percussion instruments.

During the five years I was at school, I played a lot of bebop, big band, rock, funk, R & B, and fusion. But all of the lessons that I learned from Leonard Bernstein—how to play with passion, emotion, and strive for perfection (musically *and* academically), and perhaps most importantly, how to play with *feel*—fed directly into my style of playing and helped me excel at all levels. Lenny was so good because he taught me that besides the extraordinary skill set you needed to make the cut in the orchestra, it was all about feel, and not just technique. It is important to listen to everyone you are playing music with—all of our teachers pounded that into our heads, *listen, listen, listen.* You could be the most technically accomplished drummer in the world, but if you're playing without that fifth element, the band won't respond, and most importantly, the audience won't either.

What's more, all of that formal teaching taught me how to read and write music, so when I do a session or prepare for a tour, I can write out extremely detailed charts, read them cold, *and* play with feeling. This is why I can handle so many sessions and live tours, TV shows, you name it, all at the same time, because I don't have to rely on memorizing anything. I don't have enough time for that—not when I am working with so many artists at any given time and they all expect to get all of me.

Seiji Ozawa showed me what microscopic perfection was, along with a heightened sense of musical drama and dynamics, but Leonard Bernstein was hip. He had a lot of soul. He wasn't a rock 'n' roll hater. He loved jazz. He wasn't a snob. And he was nice. That goes a long way, too.

◄○►

When I finished my five years of intense classical training, I immediately started studying with two great drum-set teachers, Alan Dawson, a great jazz drummer and teacher in the Boston area, and Gary Chester a session drummer and teacher in the NYC area. I couldn't get enough; I could never be good enough. I devoted eight hours a day of practice to improve my skills on the drum set—I loved orchestral music and the entire experience I went through, but professionally, my heart was still telling me to *rock*. I realized I would rather be in a club, playing the drums for $75 a night than be playing symphonic music in an orchestra. The thing that was freaking me out a little bit was: You just invested all this time and a lot of Mom and Dad's money to become a great percussionist, and now you want to devote all your time to playing the drums in a *rock band*? What, are you a fucking idiot?

I even turned down two job offers for two orchestras, which are nearly impossible to come by. One in Israel, and the other in Quito, Ecuador. In my heart I never got over seeing the Beatles on *The Ed Sullivan Show*. The sound of screaming girls kicked Sibelius's ass every time.

I was playing with some badass jazz musicians in NYC, like pianist

Kenny Kirkland (who went on to play with Wynton and Branford Marsalis, Sting, and the Jay Leno band), but I wasn't playing enough rock 'n' roll. As cool as jazz is, let's face it, rock is where the action is. The goal was still to make records and go on tour, and somehow a bunch of my buddies from Indiana convinced me to move back and start a band. All of my buddies back east thought I was nuts—"Why are you going back to Indiana? If any place, you should go to New York, Nashville, or LA, but not Indiana. That's not where the music business is."

I moved back to Bloomington in early June 1977 and spent the next three years playing in a rock-fusion band called Streamwinner, playing everything from Weather Report to Stevie Wonder to Steely Dan to Gong and a lot of Gino Vannelli (seriously), plus some original music. Never heard of them? Well, it's because we never made it. Call it a swing and a miss—there was a lot more to being a successful rock 'n' roll band than just being super talented on your instrument. All the guys in Streamwinner thought that was enough. Boy, were we wrong.

We even had a secondhand, eighteen-foot Ryder truck, our own lights, and a P.A. system—one of the band members' dads was willing to lend us $30,000 for all of this, and we looked and sounded very professional. I got a day job for the first six months as an assistant cook and also did a lot of teaching before we started getting regular bookings, and I eventually started making enough money with Streamwinner to quit my job as a cook. It was a great experience, but Streamwinner was never going to happen.

More importantly, though, this is exactly what led me to a "Johnny Cougar" audition, and that's when my career really got off the ground. But I almost fucked that up—I hadn't figured it out yet that it wasn't about me. It was my job to make *the band sound great* and be successful on *their* terms. My responsibility was to *the song*, not to my ego and showing everyone how much technique I had. But eventually I got with the program. And then some.

7

Jazz Rock Fusion at the Roach Motel

The first year Streamwinner moved to Bloomington, Indiana, all seven of us moved into a band house that we quickly named "The Roach Motel." The house was right in the middle of the college campus, and we were known for having wild parties there all the time. I lived in a small bedroom that had once been an outdoor porch but had been converted into an indoor bedroom. It faced a huge campus lawn called Dunn Meadow where college kids hung out all the time—I picked that room to live in because I had my own entrance and my rent was super cheap, only $62 a month. My room had two doors, one that put me onto a popular campus street called Henderson, on the edge of Dunn Meadow, and the other was the original front door to the house. Having my own entrance was great when I was shuffling one girl out and another was at the front door looking for me. It was a tiny space with room for not much besides a small bed, a tiny drum set, my stereo, and some clothes.

The first year we moved into the Roach Motel, Bloomington had the biggest snowstorm of the century—one morning I woke up and my entire room was buried under snow, but I didn't care because I was living the dream—*a jazz rock fusion band in Indiana!*

We turned the small living room into a full-blown rehearsal room using part of our sound system and lights, which made it possible to rehearse there anytime we wanted. My daily routine was to roll out of bed and into my drum set and practice all day and night, unless I was playing a gig or rehearsing with the band. I was so broke that I remember I used to count my quarters to see how many beers and Space Invader games I could cover over a night at the local bars. I was truly living the starving musician lifestyle, and barely had a car that worked, but I was living *the dream*. Sex, drums, and ... *jazz rock fusion!*

For various reasons, the whole fusion thing turned out *not* to be the pot of gold at the end of the rainbow that we were dreaming of, and, at age twenty-six, I finally realized I had to move on. I remember saying to myself: "If I'm ever going to break in this music business, I've got to go to LA or New York." I was really concerned about the uncertainty of where I was going, and what I was going to do to survive on my own. It never crossed my mind to ask for help. Finally, I was on my way to move to NYC to give it a go there, when a buddy of mine who I had gone to music school with got me a last-minute audition in LA with Lou Rawls.

Lou Rawls wasn't a rock 'n' roller and wasn't like anything I had ever even considered for my musical direction, but he was a huge R & B star at the time. I think he'd sold a total of 40 million records, so I was looking at the gig, if I got it, as a foot in the door to the LA scene.

The day I was going to fly to LA, I was having lunch at my favorite health-food restaurant in Bloomington, a place called the Tao restaurant. I had only three days to prepare for the audition, so I was a bit nervous, eating a quick lunch before my evening flight. I wasn't really enjoying it—my head was racing, and my stomach was unsettled from worrying about this audition. I really had to get something going. I felt like I was starting from scratch. I was about to leave the restaurant, I was really just an anxious mess, and I said to myself, "Man, Kenny, just sit down and *chill* for five fucking minutes."

Well, had I not done that, if I had left the restaurant a couple minutes earlier, I wouldn't have wound up bumping into this local singer-songwriter I knew named Ruthie Allen, and struck up the single most serendipitous conversation of my career.

I told her I was heading to LA to audition for Lou Rawls, and she was completely surprised, since nothing I had ever done seemed to point in that direction.

She asked me, "Have you heard of this John Cougar guy? I think he fired his drummer last night, or the drummer left the band," and at first my reply wasn't any more enthusiastic than a simple "Really?"

Because in truth, I wasn't really into John's music yet. I wasn't into Top 40 radio and commercial rock. I was still into fusion and funk, progressive rock, all this stuff that is mostly popular with other musicians but never gets played on the radio. But I was familiar with him being from Indiana—he was at the very least a local star—"I Need a Lover" was a big radio hit, and I had seen some of his videos on a new music television station called MTV, which at the time was just breaking. I really had no idea the impact it would have.

As for actually playing with "Johnny Cougar," I had my doubts. It seemed even less likely than the Lou Rawls gig. As a drummer, I wasn't focused on the less-is-more approach to playing the drums yet. I was still more into technique, playing lots of notes and pushing the limit in technical ways.

Honestly, seeing the Mahavishnu Orchestra back in '72 practically ruined my career.

You have to understand the impact their drummer, Billy Cobham, had made on me. Cobham was a monster player. He looked like the linebacker of a Super Bowl championship team, and he rolled around his twelve or thirteen tom-toms faster and harder than anything I had ever seen. He had three bass drums, could play polyrhythms and rudiments beyond anything, and was completely ambidextrous, riding on cymbals with both hands. He blew my fucking mind. At the time, Mahavishnu were all the rage with their records *Inner Mounting Flame* and *Birds of Fire.* They were a group of superior musicians, and when they played you just sort of sat there and gawked at them. I had never seen any musicians like this before. I thought they came from Mars.

Ringo made me want to be in a rock band; Billy Cobham made me want to be the most intimidating technical drummer I could be. He reinvented drumming for a lot of guys, just like Ringo did, and I hated to think that it was one style vs. the other, but the truth is that what Cobham did just wasn't all that practical for me and for where I was headed. A few guys could make it work in prog-rock or fusion bands, but most bands had little use for that sort of hyper-busy drumming.

It used to be that people made fun of Ringo Starr—I used to hear that he couldn't play the drums. He was the butt of a million jokes, especially from jazzbos and super-technical musicians who thought what he did was *easy.* And let me tell you, it is not.

These days he is revered as one of the all-time greats. Everyone knows who he is, and not just because he was a Beatle—because he was a flawless drummer that moved millions of people with his feel and style, his sound, his vibe, and his impeccable simplicity and perfection. When the Beatles broke up and started making solo records, *they could have gotten any drummer they wanted, and they all called Ringo.* That should tell you right there how much he brought to the party.

Listen to Charlie Watts of the Rolling Stones. His name is always one of the first to come up when people talk about the best rock drummers of all time. He plays a small drum kit like Ringo, and he makes the Stones swing—no matter how many great songs they have written, they'd be nowhere without Charlie and Keith Richard's perfect sympathy for each other's rhythms. They are *loose but tight,* and it is all about Charlie's simple but fluid style of making the songs move. Like I said before, no one dances to the guitar solo . . . or the singer. There has never been a great band without a great drummer. Mick told me himself: No Charlie, no Stones.

I didn't know it yet, but I was about to change my approach to playing the drums. Eventually I became the kind of drummer I made fun of for years.

Billy Cobham still is my superhero drummer (he's now a friend and always an innovator on the drum set), but I was about to learn how to support the song with a less-is-more approach to playing the drums, focusing on a few core principles: play the correct beat for the song. Have perfect control of the time. Make the song groove and *feel* great. And finally, you still have to be *creative* and sometimes surprising, but without disrupting the *beat, time,* or *groove.*

Beat, time, groove, and creativity became my philosophy, ethos, *my pur-*

pose to drumming, no matter what style of music I was playing, and it remains my philosophy today, no matter with whom I am playing. Change the beat and you will change the song.

All of that aside, I needed a gig, and after talking to Ruthie and thanking her for the heads-up, I slammed a quarter into a pay phone to call Mike Wanchic, who I knew from the local Bloomington music scene, and more importantly, happened to be John's guitarist at the time. He agreed to mention me to John and make an introduction.

I found out later that John Cougar wasn't too enthusiastic about me coming down—he heard I was about to fly to LA to audition for the Lou Rawls band, and that was the furthest thing from the kind of rock John's band was making at that time. To him, it was like *how un-rock 'n' roll,* and he was right, but back then as a starving musician, you just went for everything that came your way. Actually, I still do.

But John ultimately agreed to check me out after I got back from LA. He had also asked around looking for any drummers that were worthy of auditioning, and my name kept popping up.

Luckily, as it turned out, when I flew out to LA to audition for Lou Rawls, I quickly discovered that I was not right for him *at all*—I wasn't some smooth Los Angeles R & B cat. Anyway, to me, "R & B" still meant James Brown and Wilson Pickett and early Stones, not this urban adult pop music. That was definitely not my lifestyle, and it sort of had to be if you wanted that gig. Anyway, a very good drummer who was friends with Lou's musical director ended up getting the gig, so there was no real reason to feel bad about it. I was the wrong guy.

So naturally I was excited that I had the John Cougar audition waiting for me when I landed back in Indiana, and it was now very clear in my mind and heart that this was what I should be doing. If you lived in Indiana, John Cougar was the King.

8

Johnny Cougar

At this point I was still under the spell of Billy Cobham and his magical drum kit, and in my mind I was trying to combine that sort of ultra-technical drumming and power with the aggressiveness of John Bonham and the charisma and simplicity of Ringo—but it was probably too much meat to try and stuff into one burrito, if you know what I mean.

But I was coming around. Mostly I wanted to kick ass for Johnny Cougar and rock like I always did as a kid in my barn. Never mind the frilly prog-rock and fusion, as much fun as it was to play, I was meant to rock. This is where I was supposed to land.

So when I got back to Bloomington, I immediately called Mike Wanchic about the audition with John, and plans were made to get together in two weeks at John's house. He said to be familiar with John's latest record, called *John Cougar*, which had "I Need a Lover" on it, his hit at the time.

To me, "be familiar" meant memorize every drum part played on the entire record, so that's what I did. I honestly wasn't used to playing such simple drum parts, but as I practiced (still six or seven hours a day), I started to feel how powerful that simpler approach to playing the drums really was. I loved the energy of John's music, and the determination he had as a singer. You could hear it, he was not fucking around. He was so committed. I felt it, and I wanted to be a part of that.

◄◦►

The night after the Lou Rawls audition, I'd started celebrating my twenty-seventh birthday in LA with a bunch of my friends from the IU music school, doing shots and having a few hits of pot, but the party didn't stop there. I took the red-eye back to Indiana and continued celebrating my birthday with my girlfriend. I sort of remember having sex on her living room floor at 1 a.m., my head spinning from a combination of liquor, pot, and probably other substances. Out of the corner of my eye, I saw my best friend and one of my girl's best friends having sex on the sofa. It all seemed normal enough.

Normal enough that I thought it would be cool to drive thirty miles out of town so we could wake up in my house out in the country. At that time I was living in a cool band house in Spencer, Indiana, on top of a small hill in the woods looking down at a spring-filled pond where we would sometimes fish for our dinner.

My girl and I were driving out of town down Walnut Street, the main drag with all the college bars that I drank and played at, suddenly I saw cop lights come on in my rearview mirror. I said to myself, "Oh shit. Be cool, be cool . . ."

In today's world (or anyplace other than rural Indiana), I would have been thrown in jail in a fucking hurry—it was like that drunk-driving TV commercial where there's beer pouring out of the car windows.

Of course when the cop asked if I had been drinking, I said, "Hell no," smiling at him, and he just smiled back at me. He said get out of the car. I said to myself again, "Okay, dude, be cool, be cool," as he asked me to do a few simple sobriety tests. It's a good thing they didn't have those portable Breathalyzers back then. First, he said, "Okay, touch your finger to your nose," and I remember laughing and saying, "Look at this nose. How can I miss?" He laughed, and then he had me walk in a straight line with my eyes closed, and I don't know how I got by that one—maybe because playing the drums takes so much coordination?—but it was a birthday bonus, because the next thing I knew, we were back on the road driving into the country night, feeling free and easy like nothing could stop us.

We stopped at a local grocery store in the next town, Ellettsville, to get breakfast supplies for the next morning and headed down the two-lane

Highway 46 to Spencer, where I lived. We were one mile from my house when I made the final turn out to Spencer. I was in no real condition to drive, and when someone in the other lane coming at me with their bright lights on made me blink, I shut my eyes and couldn't quite open them again until there was a loud banging noise and the car was being thrown all over the place. I woke to see that I had driven the car off the highway, blazing past trees and giant boulders, just missing telephone poles and everything else. We finally wound up in a ditch.

It was a nightmare: my girlfriend wound up smashing her head into the dashboard, and there was blood coming out of her nose and head, plus smashed eggs and groceries everywhere. It was fucked up. We weren't wearing seat belts, nobody did back then, but we were lucky—that was probably the only place off the highway where we could have survived such a dangerous and stupid event.

Once I realized we were okay, a bit messy but no serious damage, I tried to start the car, thinking I could drive out of this situation, but that wasn't going to happen. We were fortunate there were no cops around at that point, because we would have wound up in the drunk tank for sure.

We'd crashed up the road from a *serious* redneck bar called Rod's 46 Club that had a pay phone outside, and in what proved to be my final birthday gift of the night, I ran down to Rod's 46 Club and called a buddy of mine named Spanky, who happened to live nearby. He was a huge Streamwinner fan—go figure!—and as crazy as it may sound, he had a towing business.

By some miracle, he actually answered the phone and agreed to come out at 2:30 in the morning and tow us out of that ditch, but as Spanky pulled up, a county sheriff happened to drive by and spun his car around with lights flashing to check us out. I thought, "Oh no, here we go again, no way are we getting out of this twice," but Spanky knew the sheriff, and I'll never forget him talking the sheriff down in this thick rural Indiana accent, saying, "No problem, I got it covered, man, these are my friends, I'm going to pull them out, they live right up the road, and I'll make sure they get home okay." He really saved my ass.

This was no way to start a new career, but after a couple days sleeping off a vicious hangover and licking my wounds, I began preparing for the John Cougar audition. He hadn't started calling himself John Mellencamp yet. He was still going along with the record company gimmick of having this ridiculous, fake rock 'n' roll name, which he hated.

I wrote out every single drum part and memorized every song, every drum fill, everything. I would practice one song over and over, measure by measure, until I memorized the entire drum part to the song. I would take a break and come back and see if I had really memorized all the parts to the song correctly. Once I was confident I had it down, I would move on to the next song.

Once I memorized two songs, I would play both songs in a sequence over and over again, making sure I had everything memorized. Then I would tackle a third song, drill those three, playing them over and over again in a sequence, and on to the fourth song, until eventually I had the entire record memorized. Repetition is the key to learning something really well, and being able to remember what you learned under pressure on any given day, under any circumstances.

The more I played John's music, the more I loved everything about it. I felt like it was perfect for me, and that this was my true musical calling. I not only learned the drum parts, but I was rehearsing them as if I were playing a live concert in a stadium. I practiced with power and played super loud. I didn't realize it then, but I played about a hundred times harder and louder than pretty much any other drummer—it was just the way I did it.

When the big day finally arrived, I remember showing up at John's house near Lake Monroe in my old, beat-up car packing a full arsenal: two bass drums, two snare drums, six toms, three Rototoms, and ten cymbals, everything. The Billy Cobham influence was still in effect—I really thought the giant kit was the cool way to go.

John took one look at it and almost threw up. He hated big drum sets. He wanted me to play a simple, small, four-piece drum kit, like Charlie Watts. Basic, earthy, and especially not taking up more real estate than the rest of the band. This was a pretty big faux pas with a guy whose stock-in-trade was to become an earnest American songwriter, and it almost cost me the gig before I played a note.

I hopped out of the car and ran over to where John was standing in the driveway, said "Hi," and shook his hand.

He wasn't very friendly, which sucked my enthusiasm right out of the air. He kind of mumbled "Hi, Kenny, John Mellencamp" when he shook my hand, and then didn't say anything else and just turned around and walked back into his house. He really hated that big arena-size drum set, it was so completely wrong for the gig, and my old oil-leaking car definitely turned him off. To make matters worse, I didn't dress really cool either, at least not the way he wanted me to dress. And I had a beard *and* was losing my hair. The hurdles I had to leap were unbelievable.

John was not the most outwardly sociable guy, but I tried to keep a confident head, took all my drums downstairs to his basement, and set everything up, and even after I was ready to rock, he still hadn't come downstairs yet. Thankfully, the other guys in the band were great to me, and I hit it off with them right away. And then finally John came down, but not without giving my giant prog-rock drum set another dirty look. Man, he *hated* that shit.

I asked him, "Well, what do you want me to play?" And he asked me if I knew anything on the album, and I said I was familiar with the songs. He said "Okay, pick one." I called out "I Need a Lover," and I remember I played with so much confidence, power, and volume—I was way over the top. I was thinking *stadiums*. I glanced at John at the end of the first song, and it was the only time I ever saw him looking startled—he's a pretty serious character, passionate but with a poker face—and his eyes and mouth were wide open. I had no idea what he was thinking,

John Mellencamp: Kenny auditioned, and quite honestly, my guitar player, Mike Wanchic, was the guy who said, "Okay, let's use him," because we were on the fence about him. He just played too many notes. He had too many fills, too many cymbal splashes, and he was in front of the tempo, because he'd been trained to play jazz, which really confused me—he was so far in front of the beat. Kenny's a very excitable guy, which is really good for a lot of things, but not good for keeping the beat, but I could still hear he had something special about him. Also he had some kind of beat-up car, and I remember giving him shit about it after he drove away, and said, "Kenny, next time you come to my house, don't park in the driveway because you leave big oil marks."

I wasn't just auditioning that day, I was *performing*. I broke a cymbal, I broke sticks, I dented all of my two-ply drum heads. I had done all of my homework, I came prepared, and played with total conviction. I remember when I was done, John didn't say anything. He just walked upstairs and then screamed down, "Mike, get up here!" So Mike Wanchic runs upstairs, and I started packing up my drums. It was the longest ten minutes of my life, before Mike finally came back down, smiled at me, shook my hand, and said, "Welcome to hell."

◄o►

I was told that I was one of fifty drummers they were planning to audition. But all the hard work over the years had finally paid off, and ultimately landed me in the band and that launched my career. The combination of being disciplined, a hard worker and a team player, dependable, passionate when I played, and a friendly, positive person by nature would become the formula for my success over the next thirty-five years. Playing well is important. It is also important not to be a prick.

Winning the audition into John's band was the beginning of me executing the second stage of my life plan. The first was getting an education in music and then getting a job in a symphony orchestra. I achieved that goal, but somehow I ended up in a failed jazz fusion band in Indiana.

But here I was now, welcomed to hell!

I was very fortunate I found myself getting in on the ground floor of John's career, just as it was beginning to really take off. My goal had been to get the gig. Now my goal was to keep it.

I was in the right place at the right time, but I'd done an awful lot of hard work to arrive at that moment too. I remember the first person who I spilled the good news to was my girlfriend, who loved it because this meant I wasn't moving to New York City or Los Angeles. The next call I made was to my parents back east, because this was, so to speak, my first official "big break" into the music business. It was pretty funny, my mom's reaction, because the last time she'd seen me perform live was with Leonard Bernstein, and I remember her quizzing me about John's name: "Johnny Cougar? What kind of a name is that?" It wasn't her kind of music, but when they saw me two years later, in 1982, on *Saturday Night Live* and *American Bandstand*, she knew I'd made the right choice.

Ellie Aronoff: Before joining John Cougar, Kenny got two pretty prestigious job offers out of college: one was playing timpani with the Jerusalem Symphony Orchestra in Israel, and a position in the symphony orchestra in Quito, Ecuador, and when he was right on the cusp of accepting the Israeli position, I think that's when he decided that rock was what he wanted. Because if you get into a symphony, it takes forever to become the head timpanist—it's one of the highest-paid jobs in the orchestra, but he decided to roll the dice on rock 'n' roll, and my husband and I supported him 100 percent because we believed in his talent and potential.

I remember right after he'd first joined the John Cougar band, he told his sister, "I don't know how the folks feel, but I've turned in my tuxedo for a pair of torn jeans." I didn't know anything about the rock scene, it was a very strange thing, but we just went with it, having of course no idea where it was going to lead.

9

Kenny Gets Fired

Two weeks after my audition for the John Cougar band, we started rehearsing for the *Nothing Matters and What If It Did?* album from 11 a.m. to 5 p.m., with a two-hour dinner break, and then back to it from 7 to 11 p.m., five days a week.

We only had five weeks to get ready to record this record with producer Steve Cropper (the Blues Brothers, Booker T. & the M.G.'s, Otis Redding, etc.) at Cherokee Studios in Los Angeles. That was the only time Steve was available, so we had a lot of work to do in that short period of time.

Steve came to Indiana one week before we flew to LA to help us with our individual parts and the arrangements, and to make sure we were prepared. At this point in our careers, we needed to have all the arrangements and musical parts worked out well before we went into a studio, otherwise we'd be wasting our time and John's money, as John had learned the hard way on his previous records.

Right from the first rehearsal, I was blown away by how much John knew about the music business—from radio to record labels, promotions and marketing, following the charts, and touring. At this point, I didn't know much about the industry, or about creating and arranging parts for a *pop* song to get it played on the radio. There was a fine line between making a song sound unique, super cool, and radio friendly—and not sound like we were selling out.

My job was to *serve the song* by coming up with simple, cool drum parts that would help the song be immediately identifiable, feel good, get played on the radio, and ultimately be a #1 hit. This was a big learning curve for me—it was still easier for me to play with a lot of chops and technique, as opposed to simple and right to the point. What I was missing was how to make *the band* sound great without calling attention to *myself.*

John was really putting pressure on himself and us to make *all* of his songs sound like hit singles, and because we only had five weeks before we were supposed to go into the studio, it was a very intense time. He was like an ultra-demanding football coach. There was no coddling. It was more like, "If you fall down, watch out, you could get stepped on while trying to get up."

I was beginning to see why Mike Wanchic had said "Welcome to hell" after my audition. It was like being back in school. The General Mellencamp Military Academy or some damn thing, but I loved it.

John wanted ideas and parts from all of us, and he wanted ideas quickly. He told us no one owns their ideas or parts on their instruments, and he didn't care who came up with a great idea—whether it was for their instrument or someone else's. It was sometimes difficult to come up with the right drum parts when I would be getting suggestions from three different people at the same time, but that was part of the challenge, it was like being in a think tank with ideas flying all around the room, and John making the final decisions.

Honestly it was probably not the best time for John to be making a record—he was going through a divorce and it was making him miserable—but he had little choice if he wanted to keep his career going. It didn't make him very easy to be around, but he was still determined to make it and it felt like he might die trying. A lesser man would have quit.

John had taken it on the chin more times than anyone deserved. He made his first record with Tony Defries, who used to manage Iggy Pop, David Bowie, and Lou Reed. The guy was all about *image.* The way I heard the story is that Defries handed John his finished record with a cover that said "Johnny Cougar" on it. John said, "Who the fuck is Johnny Cougar?" And Defries said, "You are, if you want this record to come out." They were treating him like a hillbilly. You could see why he was pissed off, especially when the record didn't do much and he was stuck with the name. And then he got dropped from the label. It made him very motivated and aggressive.

After the Defries fiasco, he had this guy, Billy Gaff, managing him, who also managed Rod Stewart. Somehow he got from Johnny Cougar to John Cougar—which you have to admit, as silly as it is, it is still more respectable than *Johnny* Cougar, but it was an uphill battle every step of the way.

Gaff signed John to his label, RIVA Records, which was part of Mercury Records. John made his third record, *A Biography*, for RIVA.

It wasn't released in the USA, but in Australia one song, "I Need a Lover," became a big hit. John's fourth album, *John Cougar*, did get a US release, and Gaff wisely decided to put "I Need a Lover" on it. "Lover" became a hit single, getting as high as #28 on the *Billboard* charts, and I joined the band very soon after this.

Pat Benatar also had a hit with "I Need a Lover," which helped keep the door open, but John was still fighting for every scrap he got.

John came from a big family who settled things with their fists—his grandfather was like seventy years old and used to get in bar fights. His uncles would square off with anyone. They were tough motherfuckers and that's how things got settled out in the Rust Belt. His dad wasn't necessarily like that, but John had it in his blood, and you did not want to push him too hard.

Before John signed with Gaff, he was working for the phone company, installing phones, and he fucking hated it. There was no way he was going back to that job. He lived in fear of having to start climbing telephone poles again, and it gave him a very hard edge. Plus, on top of that, it was a screwy deal with Billy Gaff: John's lawyer was Billy Gaff's lawyer, and RIVA was Gaff's label, and Billy was managing John as well—everything was under the same roof. There was a conflict of interest, and when I joined the band, John trusted no one. I didn't know all of that when I met John, but this is what shaped him. He fought like a feral animal to survive in this business. I felt like I was fighting for my life in the business as well. I knew you didn't get very many chances, and I think that made us a good team.

John would write the songs on his acoustic guitar and most of the lyrics, except for those he wrote with his high school buddy George Green. John's process was to play a song for us on acoustic guitar, or play a demo he'd recorded on a cassette tape, and then after two listens, he would usually turn to me and ask me for a cool drum beat. Most of the time he didn't know what he wanted, but he was very clear about what he didn't like. Everything was very rootsy, very simple. Coming out of a fusion band, when he would play these songs, my first reaction was usually like, "What the fuck, how can I be creative with *this* song?" Everything was very stripped down.

At the same time, the guys in the band would try to come up with melodies and hook lines. That's when I realized there was so much I had to learn about this kind of music, and about songwriting itself. Being a big Beatles and Stones fan, I recognized great songs when I was growing up. I always listened to pop radio, so I could relate to songs that had intros, verses, pre-choruses, choruses, bridges, and maybe a short solo—radio-friendly songs that were two to three *minutes* long, not *two album sides*, like Yes and some of these other bands I was into back then.

In the Mellencamp band, I had to come up with the drum parts that could turn *a good song* into a *hit*. That was my job.

The challenge was I had to learn a whole new drum vocabulary that would work with John's music. That was the learning curve for me, to understand the way he thought, the way he wrote songs, and what he needed from me.

> **John Mellencamp:** We'd all played in local bands and stuff like that, and musicians being musicians often think, "Well, I got my part, I'm done," and that's not the way it works. On my records, there had been hours and hours and hours and hours of rehearsal, and everything that Kenny played—particularly in the early days—was a group decision. The drummer made suggestions, and I would say, "Kenny, don't play that, play this," *and* he had the band saying, "Try this, try that; you're overplaying here," so he would have four or five guys in the band riding herd over him, the same way that he rode herd over the guitar player, because it was a band. So he learned how to take instruction and criticism and how to work with that and how to handle that, in the confines of my band.

John had a lot of songs written, but most of them hadn't been arranged yet. If I didn't come up with the right beat for his song, his response might be, "That's a stupid idea!" or "What the hell is that?" Being the new guy, I sometimes felt like I was the scapegoat for all kinds of things, even if it had nothing to do with me. All John cared about was: "Give me what I need to make a hit single!"

The night before we left to go to LA to make *Nothing Matters*... Steve Cropper took everyone in the band out to dinner. John didn't go, and after dinner, I wound up staying behind with Steve to have a few more drinks and listen to some of his amazing stories, because this guy had written and played on some of the greatest songs in rock, like Otis Redding's "Sitting on the Dock of the Bay" and Wilson Picket's "In the Midnight Hour." Cropper was the master of the minimalist rhythm track, and he played with one of the greatest, simplest drummers of all time, Al Jackson, Jr., who was the backbone of Booker T. & the M.G.'s ("Green Onions"), not to mention he was Al Green's drummer. Just listen to any one of Al Green's hits—"Love and Happiness," "I'm So Tired of Being Alone"—there is nothing the drummer is doing that someone who had just been playing drums for a few weeks wouldn't *technically* be capable of doing, but Al Jackson's beat (and Al Green's voice) made people want to *fuck*. The groove was impenetrable. Simple as could be. No tricks, but sexy and driving as all hell. John Bonham took the same approach with "Kashmir"—*boom, crack, boom, crack*—just heavy and super fucking solid. It swung without being flashy. Not one in a million other guys could find that pocket. Cropper held the keys, he knew the formula as well as anyone who ever lived.

Well, we wound up letting time get away from us and showed up two hours late back at John's house for our evening rehearsal. When we pulled up in the driveway, even though I was with Steve, I could see that wasn't cover enough for me being late. John was fucking *furious*. His eyes were bloodshot and he had sweat rings under his arms, and he was looking at me with his head down and his eyes looking up, looking like a mad dog, and the first words out of his mouth to me were: "Aronoff, you're fired!"

Steve tried to take the rap but it didn't matter. John was livid, and said, "I don't give a fuck!" Steve persisted, "It's my fault," and Mellencamp shot back, "I don't give a fuck, Steve, he doesn't work for you, he fucking works for me!" And Steve and I were both standing there speechless. I went, "Dude! Man! I'm so sorry, my mistake, I apologize and it won't happen again." He walked back into the house without saying another thing to me, and it suddenly hit me like a bucket of cold water what I was about to lose. He was right, of course, there is no excuse for being late. I could have been discussing the spiritual future of planet Earth with the Dalai fucking Lama and it wouldn't have mattered.

It was an important lesson—I was his employee, the new guy, and he wasn't paying me to get drunk with the band's producer. He was paying me to come back and be ready to go. It was no different than if I was supposed to clock back in after a lunch break at a factory and had missed my shift's start time. John was my boss, period. That night I thought it was all over before it had even begun for me. By the next morning, he had cooled down, and I was on the plane to LA to make our record—or at least that's what I thought was going to happen.

10

Kenny Gets Fired . . . Again

Things did not get any smoother once we landed at Cherokee Studios in Los Angeles. I felt like a jackass in hindsight, because before we left, of course I told everybody I was going to California to make a record in LA, stay at the legendary Chateau Marmont—which had lots of rock 'n' roll history and was where lots of movie stars stayed when they were making movies. I saw Robert De Niro and Meryl Streep there, and this was the hotel where John Belushi had overdosed. I thought everything was going to be great walking into my first professional recording session. I had worked hard and had no reason to think that I wasn't going to kick ass in the studio.

But from day one, from the moment we started getting sounds and starting to track a bit, Steve Cropper and John were showing a lot of disappointment. They were not getting what they wanted from me, my drum sounds or my performances, and on top of that, there was still a lot of tension between John and me that probably began the day I showed up with a music showroom's worth of drums. And honestly, it was probably apparent that no matter how much I had practiced, I still wasn't relaxed or 100 percent confident in John's radio-friendly style.

To make matters worse, I had the wrong drums for the sound Steve Cropper was going for: I was using Pearl fiberglass single-headed toms with thick two-ply Evans hydraulic heads on them, which created a thuddy, dead sound that was big in the '70s and on early '80s hard-rock records, but was definitely not happening here where everyone was getting a little bit more down to earth and retro with their sound. These drums might have been okay for Gino Vannelli or Genesis. For John Cougar, at least in the studio, they sounded like death.

Living in the Midwest, I had no idea what the cool way of recording drums was in the current LA session scene.

Steve's solution was simple: *replace me.* He had two session guys on hold waiting in the wings, Rick Schlosser and Ed Green, both great LA session drummers and Steve's buddies, and they had that whole old-style drumming thing down. I got fired before I ever got to lay down a single song!

I was devastated. Of course he had his own go-to guys. Every producer does—and it's not just how good they play, it's how well they *listen,* and how well they can get the sound and feel the producer wants without too much hassle. They make the producer look good.

But I couldn't believe it. I always thought John was the one who fired me back then, but only recently John told me it wasn't him at all; it was my new buddy Steve Cropper. He had no loyalty to me. He had a job to do, and the first thing was to get the drum tracks down because of his limited time to make John's record. I was crushed and embarrassed.

> **John Mellencamp:** As we were getting ready to make the album, the guy producing the album, Steve Cropper, came to me and said, "I can't use this drummer." And I said, "Well, you gotta use him, he's in my band." And he said, "Well, I can use everyone else in the band, but I can't use this guy." And we were already in California. So the producer's suggestion was, "We just fire him." And I said, "No, if you want us to, we'll send him home, but I'm not going to fire him, because once this record's over I'm still going to need a drummer."

After the first day in the studio, I got a call from Mike Wanchic to come down to someone's room at the Chateau Marmont for a band meeting. I knew something wasn't right and thought, "Oh shit, now what?" When I got to the room, the entire band and John were there, and John basically said I wasn't going to be on the record, and that two session drummers were coming in to replace me because they had more experience making records that get played on the radio.

Then he said that Steve Cropper needed to get the record done fast before he went on tour, and we all knew that you had to get the drums recorded first in order to build that foundation of steady time and groove before adding any other instruments. You can't do any overdubs until you get the final drum tracks. I was freaking out, but there was no way I wanted to go home, so my answer to John was to yell out, "No, I'm not going home!" John and the band were speechless.

I actually surprised myself. I couldn't believe I'd just said that to John. Scrambling to save myself as my circumstances grew more desperate, the only thing I could think to ask next was, "Am I still the drummer in your band. . . . I'm still the drummer in your band, right?"

And before he could answer me, I made him the best offer I could come up with. I said, "Look, if I'm still the drummer in your band, you don't have to pay me anything. I'll go to the studio every day and watch these session drummers play my drum parts, and I'll learn from them and benefit from that. And then if I benefit from that, you're going to benefit from that also because I'm your drummer, right? And you don't have to pay me, and I'll sleep on the couch."

I can say, looking back, that was honestly one of the most humbling moments in my life. I felt like a running back in football who had just dropped the ball on a huge play. I wanted to get the ball again, but instead I got benched.

I realize now that when things aren't working out the way you want them to, you need to reevaluate the situation and figure out what you can do to improve things so that you can get back in the game and end up where you want to be. In football terms, that would be the end zone for a touchdown, but for me, at that moment, just staying on the team was a relief.

John Mellencamp: I think it was me and Mike and Larry who told him, "Hey, man, you should go ahead and go home." And Kenny just went, "I'm not gonna do it." And I said, "Well, you're not getting paid."

And he said, "I don't care." So we just paid for his room, and he just came to the sessions every day knowing he wasn't going to play, and that's really when I started to admire Kenny—his ability to suck it up and tough it out. So he said, "Okay, this is what the deal is: I want to be here and I'm going to learn. If I'm not good enough to play in these sessions, then I need to learn what I can." Because he'd never really been in a professional session before, and after that, we went out on tour, played some shows, and he started to become a better musician.

So I became a student again, and I think my passion and commitment to get better convinced John to let me stay in the band. I've always been a firm believer that you have to adapt to survive, and this was one prime example of that philosophy in practice because over the next four weeks, I became a sponge. Rick Schlosser and Ed Green were very cool with me, and they answered a lot of questions I had about recording. I felt like a fucking piece of shit loser sometimes, but I swallowed my pride, stayed there, and learned a lot. At least I ended up playing vibes and percussion on the record, and I vowed to myself, "I will be on the next record. I don't care what it takes."

I eventually went back to Indiana and started practicing eight hours a day *again*, focusing on things I thought I needed to work on to be a great drummer in *John's band*. I took all the basic tracks that the other drummers had recorded in LA and learned their parts lick for lick, plus I continued to review the songs from all the other John Cougar records for our upcoming tour. I set up a little room in a house I was renting (more like a closet with a window, muffled from floor to ceiling) and actually put myself through a little boot-camp regimen for six weeks until the band came back from LA so I could prove to them—and myself—that I was the right drummer for this band.

The stakes really couldn't have been higher for me. John had a hundred great drummers a phone call away, and his band was getting ready to go on a US tour with the Kinks. This was a big deal—along with the Beatles, the Stones, and the Who, the Kinks *were* the British Invasion. In its own way, this was about as close to being in the Beatles as I could be.

It was a dream gig for any player trying to make it. I felt like it was all or nothing. John had once said to the band, "I can find plenty of talented musicians to play in my band. I'm looking for guys I can get along with, especially the twenty-two hours a day we're not onstage." Boy, was he right about that. These are the types of things no one teaches you in music school.

We started rehearsing our forty-five-minute show over and over again, and John was very clear about what he liked or didn't like. He had a strong opinion on how we performed and how we looked onstage, and even what gear we played. The equipment you play says a lot about who you are, and John wanted me to play a four-piece drum kit with two crash cymbals, a ride and a hi-hat. That's it. He wanted that Charlie Watts/Ringo setup. And no music company logos on the gear. We had an image to project, and you had better believe our gear was part of the show. Imagine if the guitar players showed up with zebra-striped heavy-metal-looking axes and giant Marshall stacks, wearing spandex and teasing their hair up with cans of Aqua Net? That was another important lesson I learned from John: *Everything communicates.*

The cool thing about this band, though, was that our look and the way we acted was actually who we were. We were all pretty down-to-earth guys from the Midwest (well, I was from a tiny part of Massachusetts, but I had actually chosen to live in Indiana, so that counted for a lot). No one here was going to come out looking like David Lee Roth. It wasn't an act. It was real, and it was believable.

We eventually left for a six-week tour from John's house in a RV motor home and headed for Milwaukee to play our first show with the Kinks. I was so pumped. The RV was not very glamorous, but it was all John's touring budget could afford. I grew up listening to the Kinks, and now I was in a band opening up for them.

And we had the opening band budget to match: we all had roommates and had a lot of post-show dalliances with women that weren't much different than living in a dorm room, with people coming and going.

That didn't matter so much—it was all so crazy and I was having fun— but we were also being treated like an opening act by the Kinks' hard British crew, which was very common. This meant we got half of the Kinks' power and lights for our show, so there was no way we would look or sound as good as the Kinks.

They also had two ego ramps that went out into the audience, one for Ray Davies and the other for his brother, Dave Davies. These two brothers never looked at or talked to each other on tour. That blew my mind, because as crazy as any of us were, as nuts as all musicians were, this was some deep-rooted pathological shit. It was so bad, Ray and Dave each had bodyguards that made sure they didn't even pass each other in the backstage areas, per each of their requests. The only time they saw each other was onstage. This was just a whole new kind of weirdness for me.

We set up our gear in front of theirs, and were told to kindly stay in our places. John was specifically told not to go down those ego ramps. That was the Kinks' set, and also, no smoking cigarettes onstage, which kind of sucked because John smoked four packs a day. Sometimes we wouldn't even be allowed to sound-check, so our sound check was performing our first song onstage during our show. It wasn't uncommon, but it was a shitty way to be treated.

I would come onstage first and play the beat to "30 Days in the Hole" by Humble Pie. I would hit every drum and cymbal for our front-of-house sound man, and when he was satisfied, he would flash a light at us, and then our bass player, Ferd, would come out and start playing. Once the sound man got the bass sound happening, he would flash his light again, and one by one, the guitar players would come out and play, then the singers, and when the band was really sounding great and in a deep rock 'n' roll groove, John would come out. That was our sound check, live in front of the entire audience. We only turned it into part of the show because we had no choice.

John didn't give a fuck about the Kink's rules. Once the band had sound checked and we were in a heavy rock 'n' roll groove, he made his entrance smoking a cigarette running down one ego ramp all cocky like a rooster, the full Mick Jagger attitude. He'd flick his cigarette into the audience and run down the other ego ramp and do the same pose. It was so badass and cool. Of course the the Kinks' crew were furious with John for smoking and running around the stage, and after a few warnings and threatening to throw us off the tour, one night they just turned the power off on us while we were performing. It was so rock 'n' roll to us—we were the new young punks on the circuit, and the English crew were having this pissing contest with us.

I loved it, but it was so stupid. We just wanted to put on a great show. We were turning professional, and this was our chance to put it over on a big audience. Anyway, *why be mean to the opening act*? Or anyone? It made no sense. I thought musicians were supposed to be a big family that watched out for each other. It wasn't like the John Cougar band was going to be a threat to the Kinks for chrissakes, no matter how loud we played.

We were building the John Cougar brand—it was a business, and it took money, hard work, and many years to develop an artist or a band that could find and maintain a large, loyal fan base. We were fortunate to be living in a time where record labels had lots of funds to invest in bands over a long period of time.

That's not the case these days—if your first single or record isn't a smash hit right out of the gate, expect to be cast to the Fortress of Solitude, or wherever it is musicians go to die. But the bottom line was those funds and the record deal could be terminated if we didn't show growth—by getting music played on the radio, selling records, and putting butts in the seats. We needed to make money for the label that was investing in us. That was all that mattered. During that tour, I made my mark and established myself as a touring drummer in John's band. I was focused like the fucking Terminator, looking ahead and wanting to get back into the studio and prove to myself and everyone else that after the tour I could make John Cougar records. I could tell John appreciated my hard work and my dedication, but he would never tell me or show me. That wasn't his style, but that's okay, just one more thing I had to learn.

11

"Jack and Diane"

We survived our tour with the Kinks and had everything on the line heading into the recording of John's fifth record, *American Fool*. It was the last album on John's deal with RIVA/Mercury Records, and John knew if we didn't have a huge hit, the record company was planning on dropping him. Sorry if that makes me laugh—*five records into a great career, the guy's a star on the radio and MTV, and some fucking suit is still fretting?* What were these people thinking? And they all had ideas on how we were supposed to look and act. What idiots. John was clearly the real deal. We just had two *Billboard* Top 40 hits on the Hot 100 Singles chart from the *Nothing Matters . . .* record with "Sometimes" (#27) and "Ain't Even Done with the Night" (#17), but the record label obviously didn't think that was good enough. No wonder John was constantly freaked out. And those were the days when labels allegedly took their time and developed artists.

The week before we headed down to Miami to record at Criteria Studios (by now I had the gear figured out, at least!), the band drove into Bloomington for some fun after our last rehearsal. The sun had just set, and even though there was a little light in the sky, we had to put our car headlights on to see where we were going. It was springtime and I could smell the Indiana farmland, which is amazing. I got into Ferd's car at John's house and we took off. After about ten minutes, we hit the first straightaway on a windy two-lane country road, and that's where John passed us on his Harley, wearing no helmet at seventy-five miles an hour. Suddenly, we saw the headlight from his bike violently jerking all over the place and then *Bam!* Sparks were flying, with John's chopper spinning down the road into a tree.

Ferd slammed on his breaks and we were screaming, "Oh no, Oh fuck, Oh no. Where is John? Shit . . ." Ferd put his bright lights on, and there was John frantically hobbling back and forth across the road on one leg while trying to use the other one. He was in shock. An enormous dog had cut across the road and had run right into John's bike, knocking it down and forcing him and his bike to spin down the pavement into a tree. The dog didn't make it.

John somehow managed to not only jump on top of the bike while it was spinning, but he knew just when to push himself off the bike before it hit the tree. It definitely would have killed him if he had stayed on the bike. This all happened so fast, and John was so lucky he only damaged his leg and knee, which a doctor put into a twelve-week cast. The nine lives of John Cougar! A week later, we were headed to Miami as planned, with one of John's other Harleys, of course, to make the record that would finally break John in a big enough way so that the suits at the record companies would shut the fuck up and leave us alone.

◄o►

In Miami, they brought in Don Gehman to produce. Don had worked for years as a soundman, doing monster tours with Crosby, Stills, Nash & Young, among others, but he wanted to get off the road, and eventually he made his bones in the studio producing our band. We had a lot of hits with Don, but that first time with him was seriously one of the most stressful times I've ever had in my thirty-five years of making records.

John was not an easygoing guy in the studio. Our days were long and very structured. John, who was co-producing with Don, ran things very much like an NFL team, demanding immediate results and becoming frustrated when things didn't progress the way he had hoped they would. I felt John's frustration and I felt a lot of pressure because I didn't want to be benched or sent home this time. All of those stupid reindeer games were still always at the back of my mind.

But the way I saw it, we were a team, a band, and if John made it, we all made it, and if he didn't, we didn't. We were in it together. While we were working, we lived in a luxurious rental house in Key Biscayne on the water, where we ate together, practiced together, partied together, played together—it was a 24/7 commitment. But it seemed like every day was a struggle—and John wasn't happy most of the time. Halfway through the nine weeks, John and Ferd got into an argument, and Ferd slammed his bass down on the studio floor and said, "Fuck it, I quit." I was shocked because that was the furthest thing from what I would have done. Doc, the keyboard player who was Ferd's best friend, defended him, and John told Doc basically that if he didn't like what was going down, he could fucking leave, too. So Doc reflected for a moment and then he got up and left. Holy shit, he had a mutiny on his hands! Two band members just quit, so now the band was John, me, and the two guitarists, Mike and Larry. What just happened? I was in shock, asking myself, "Now what?"

> **Album Producer Don Gehman:** *American Fool* was immense. We made albums later that were extremely organized, where we knew what we were doing, and did things quickly. But our method was developed during the *American Fool* album, and it was developed very much out of the fact that nothing was working. We were trying to do things all at once and finish it, and it didn't work—we didn't like anything we did, and the record company *hated* everything that we were doing. The relationship between John and everyone was always very confrontational—with everybody, all the time.

The thing I'd come to learn about John's personality as a bandleader years later was that it wasn't personal when he got into our faces, even though it sure felt that way when it was happening. He barked at everybody! It only became personal when I took it personally, which was easy to do because he would go way over the top back then, especially when we were making the *American Fool* record. John obviously did not want to be dropped by the label and go back to working for the telephone company, like he had done before earlier in his career when he was dropped by a label.

A lot of the songs didn't sound as good as we thought they would when we recorded them, and some of the arrangements weren't as cool as we thought they were when we were rehearsing them. But this record *had* to be a success.

Near the end of the nine weeks, John and I almost got into a fistfight. He kept fucking with me in the lounge, hitting me on the head with a pool stick while he hobbled around the pool table (he was still pretty fucked up from his motorcycle accident), talking shit to me. I moved to a table across the room to avoid his insanity, and he came over and brushed some sugar that was on the table into my face. I just snapped. I picked up a metal garbage can and threw it across the room, and when he saw I was coming after him, he took off hobbling down the hall. I picked up a beer bottle and threw it at him as hard and as fast as I could, but luckily for the both of us, I just missed him. He hobbled back into the room and we stood face-to-face with our fists clenched, and the only thing that stopped me from decking him was that I knew if I had, I would have been looking for a new band to play in. It was better to smile and walk away.

> **John Mellencamp:** The first thing you have to understand is, *Kenny Aronoff never sounded better in his career as when he played for me.* His records never sounded better, his performances were never better. What made Kenny work so well inside that band we had throughout the 1980s and early 1990s was his ability to get along with everybody and his ability to be helpful. He was never late, he never argued with me about the music, he only tried to help and participate. We'd make records and Kenny'd be done and he'd still be in the studio, participating and being part of the group, which most guys wouldn't do. Most musicians would go, "I'm done, I'm going home," but Kenny never was like that.

Somehow all this tension only made me play better, made me play with a lot of conviction and intensity, and you can hear that intensity and energy on the recordings. Personally, from the first album onward, I was always under a gun to come up with drum parts for John's songs that suited his style of playing. He needed that from me. That's what he was paying me to do: that was my job.

One of the greatest challenges on this record was what to do with the song "Jack and Diane." John knew it was a great song, we all knew it was a great song, but we didn't know how to arrange it. The truth is, that song wasn't going to be on the record, because we couldn't figure out what to do with it until our producer, Don Gehman, walked in one day with a Linn 1 drum machine. I remember the first time I saw that machine I was disgusted. I couldn't believe we were going to use *a fucking drum machine* instead of a live drummer, i.e., *me*, on the song. I was sick to my stomach when I saw that thing.

These days, programmed drums are so common it's no big deal, and I use them all the time to set tempos, but back then, it was sacrilege for a live rock drummer to be replaced by a drum machine on a single. So I grabbed the Linn 1 and programmed the beat I was playing on my acoustic drums by replacing my real kick drum with a Linn 1 floor tom, and replacing my real hi-hat with the Linn 1 tambourine, and instead of my real snare drum we used hand claps.

Every sound on the Linn 1 had a separate output that went to an individual track on our tape machine, which gave us more options when building the song later. But eventually, the song needed something more after the second chorus, and it wasn't going to happen on the Linn 1.

I was in the lounge playing pool and I heard John scream, "Aronoff, get your ass in here. We need a drum solo!" I remember at the time thinking, "Drum solo? Are you nuts? On a ballad?" I'm thinking Buddy Rich, or Billy Cobham, and how am I going to do a *drum solo* on a slow pop song?

The first thing we did was spend most of a day getting a huge drum sound in the big room. Except for John Bonham with Zeppelin, and then Phil Collins,—whose massive, gated, and compressed drum sound on "In the Air Tonight" was as much part of the song's hook as the actual melody (and how cool is that?)—this approach had not been used very much, especially for music being played on commercial rock radio stations. Most people were recording drums in the small padded rooms used for vocals.

Today, everyone knows how to get a big drum sound, but in 1982, it wasn't the thing.

Zeppelin was a beast of its own, a tower of blues and bombast, but Collins's "In the Air Tonight" was a *pop* radio hit and had its own impact on the industry. John wanted our drum sound to kick everyone's ass on the radio, and he was not afraid to explore and try things that no one else was doing. He was relentless, pushing everyone, including himself, to make things better. We experimented with placing the room mics at different distances and at different heights. All these mics went through lots of processing gear in the control room, and then eventually blended together to make this new sound. Now they teach this sort of thing in music schools, or you use a sample, but back then it wasn't like there was a formula you could just dial up.

Now it was up to me to create a drum solo, and I felt like it was do or die. If I didn't hit a home run, they might bring another drummer into the session and replace me, just like they had done on the last record. It was a ruthless business.

It had to be simple and powerful. I had to make a statement, but not about myself. It was all about *the song*. But I had to make a big entrance, a statement that would grab the listener's attention immediately. It was a fine line to walk.

I played what I like to call "boom bam" or "and four" on the kick and snare. It was pretty foolproof—classic stuff. I thought John would like that, and he did. I looked into the control room, and sure enough all seven people had their thumbs up. Phew!

But now that I made my entrance I had to create something that had a genuine hook, a musical statement that people could sing and repeat, which is not so easy on the drums. I had two thoughts: play the floor tom rhythm that I had programmed on the Linn 1 on my acoustic toms, but instead of going *down* the toms on the kit like everyone else usually does, why not go *up* the toms?

When I finished, I looked up and John had his thumb down. He didn't like it.

It felt like that scene in the movie *Gladiator* when the Emperor shows

78

his thumb to the crowd, and they decide whether the gladiator lives or dies. I tried a few other things, and I ended up in the control room with all kinds of comments and suggestions coming from everyone. Nothing was resolved. Eventually I headed back to my kit, thinking, You have twenty-five feet to save your career, you have twenty feet now . . . fifteen feet, oh shit, ten, five . . . *what are you going to play, Kenny?* This could be it. You could get replaced again. *WHAT ARE YOU GOING TO PLAY, KENNY?*

Before I turned around and sat down on the drum kit, the thought popped into my head at the very last second to play the *same tom-tom rhythmic pattern I had just played*, but this time start that rhythmic pattern *one eighth note later*, which would add an element of anticipation to the whole thing. It was simple but unexpected. I was definitely taking a chance.

I did that, and before I could look up, John was already screaming at me in my headphones, "Hit a fucking crash cymbal!"—which meant he liked what I had played. I hit a cymbal crash and I knew I had to go down the toms now, since I had just gone up the toms, so I made an accurate reference to a Phil Collins fill, finished the phrase with an Aronoff triplet fill, and bingo: I had my short, two measure composition, which has somehow stood up as part of the hook of the song.

John was very happy, *more* than happy. For the first time in our working relationship he was yelling for me, not at me. "Kenny, don't stop playing! Groove, motherfucker! Play a beat!" So I started to play the beat of the song that I had always played, but playing sixteenth notes on the hi-hat, opening them on beats "three e and ah" leading into beat four, which I played on the floor tom and snare together to create a really huge, very powerful accent. But that was too much. John barked, "Too much hi-hat." We went back and forth, and eventually I ended up playing the hi-hats only on beats "three e and ah," and that completed my beat.

It was Mick Ronson—who used to play guitar with David Bowie and Mott the Hoople—who suggested that we overdub a lot of vocals a cappella on top of my beat.

Mick was like a great rock god, one of the original Spiders from Mars. I think Mellencamp knew him from his days with Tony Defries, and he asked Mick to come down and maybe help out with some arrangements and inspiration.

Mick was the coolest—he always had a cigarette in his mouth and a drink in his hand. Super happy, very positive guy, the type of guy everyone likes being around.

One morning, after a big night of partying in the house we were renting, I came downstairs to the kitchen, and there was Mick, asleep, *standing* in the doorway to the living room, with an empty bottle of beer and a cigarette in his hand. I woke him up gently, and he said, "Hi, mate," and shuffled around the kitchen and living room, pouring unfinished drinks from the night before into a glass, lit a fresh cigarette, and started drinking again. And somehow he made it all seem normal. He was incredibly charming.

His idea was like a thunder clap. Very grandiose and . . . well, perfect: "Gonna let it rock, let it roll / Let the Bible Belt come and save your soul. . . ."

What else can I say? Mick fucking Ronson! YESSSS!

"Jack and Diane" eventually went to # 1 on the *Billboard* Hot 100 Singles chart and is still played in regular rotation on the radio today all over the world. This was the song that put me on the map as a drummer and helped *American Fool* become the #1 Album of the Year and win a Grammy Award.

> **John Mellencamp:** "Jack and Diane" really was Frankenstein's monster; it was cut up, and I bet if you look at the master of that song, there's 50,000 edits on it. Down the hall from us at Criteria, the Bee Gees were recording an album, and they had a prototype of the Linn drum machine, and back then nobody'd ever heard that sound before, and the Bee Gees were using it on their record. So I kept walking by their session hearing that sound, and thought, What is that sound? So we asked the engineer if we could borrow that machine. The only live drums on that song is Kenny's breakdown.

John also had Waddy Wachtell come down to work with us on a song. Waddy is also a total rock star. Great musician, and he has the attitude.

When he got there, he made himself a drink and lit up a joint and said, "Whatta ya got? Play me something." He sounded like a New York gangster.

I was wondering if Mellencamp was going to explode, but Waddy was like mafia, you couldn't really fuck with him. I had to laugh because if one of Mellencamp's regular guys tried that shit, we'd be out looking for a new job.

Don Gehman also brought in Albhy Galuten, the Bee Gees' producer, to help us with the arrangement of "Hand to Hold On To," and he spent an hour dissecting my drum parts with the whole band there watching.

He examined every beat I played, every stick stroke, every hit on the bass drum. He would make suggestions, like, "Add an extra kick drum every four measures, but on the fifteenth measure, do something different like a floor-tom thing, and in the second verse, do it different than the first verse . . . ," on and on and on. So it was those little surgical, subtle things that most people wouldn't hear that made the song flow more and influenced everyone else in the band. That was the first time I had ever worked with a producer who was so deeply involved with every note I played, but that kind of detail was similar to the experiences I had performing in orchestras and my studies in classical music, and I was absolutely ready for it.

At the end of the nine weeks of recording, we all thought the album was finished. We had all been through a lot and wanted the record to be done. I felt great, because I had turned everything around with John. I thought all was good, I was solid in the studio, all the bad shit was behind us. But a few weeks later, I got a phone call from John: "Kenny, the record's not done, and the label doesn't like it. We only got four songs!" They felt there were no singles and didn't understand what our direction was. Astonishingly enough, our label had actually dropped us for a hot second—they thought John should be like the next Neil Diamond. Seriously?

Man, that was so hard to hear. I couldn't believe it, and John was also bummed. But back to the work we went with our tails between our legs, and when John, me, Mike, and Larry got together a few weeks later, we didn't know what to do. We just sat around and talked, but slowly we got back into it. John started writing again and we started experimenting and arranging songs, then one day, John came in with a chorus to a song he called "Hurts So Good," and we all quickly knew he was on to something.

> **John Mellencamp**: There were probably 100 arrangements on "Hurts So Good," because we just never could get it right. We knew it was a good song, and we knew it was going to be a hit record, but we knew we hadn't recorded it properly and knew we didn't have the right arrangement, and we didn't have the bass player either. So Kenny, myself, Mike Wanchic, and Larry Crane sat down and messed with that song for probably two months every day for eight hours a day trying to figure out: How do we make it so simple that anybody can play it? How do we have a drum feel that's different from what everybody else is playing, but still the same? That's the only success of "Hurts So Good," that it's *familiar*, but it's *not* the same as what everybody else was doing at the time.

We stripped all our parts down and went for this simple yet powerful approach to John's music, kind of like AC/DC. Sounds easy, but we found out that was one of the hardest things to do authentically: play simply, but with that indescribable feel that was magic to everyone's ears. This is what Steve Cropper was trying to explain to me that night we were out getting drunk.

John told us he'd written this cool chorus in the shower, and when he started playing it for us on acoustic guitar, I quietly started playing a simple beat, leading with my left hand instead of my right. I got this left-hand lead idea from Gary Chester, a teacher I was studying with in New York four years before I moved back to Bloomington. He was one of the heaviest New York City studio drummers ever. He was to New York what Hal Blaine was to LA.

Practicing left-handed helped simplify my drumming style. It was as if I went back to being twelve-years-old again, just keeping the beat, and it ended up giving me a whole new sound and feel to work with.

When I did the simple eighth-note tom fills with my right hand in that song, I was able to keep the hi-hat going with my left hand, playing constant eighth notes—it kinda felt like my left hand was playing an eighth-note shaker part through the entire song while I played beats and drum fills with my right hand and kick drum. I kept the swishy shaker sound on my hi-hat chugging along and the drums with the rest of the band together, but everything sounded a bit greasier and looser. I remember John's head popping up real fast when I started playing—"What beat is that you're playing and why haven't you played that beat before?" All I had done was switch from a right-hand lead to a left-hand lead, and that was enough to give it a completely different feel. Crazy easy, and another lesson learned.

I will never forget that moment when I sat down in the control room to listen to that final take of "Hurt So Good," and while I was listening to the playback through these huge speakers, I *finally* got it! I mean, *really* got it. I realized how perfect and powerful a *simple* drumbeat with feel was. It had relentless conviction and *felt* amazing. I thought, Holy shit, I can hear the spirit and vibe of Kenny Aronoff when I was playing—and without a zillion notes, without flams and paradiddles and drummers' tricks, or any showing off of my jazz chops.

Everything I did was so *exposed.* I was musically naked, just me and my sticks, and it was a bit surreal to think you could feel emotion coming from me, through my sticks, to my drums, to the mics, through the cables, into the mixing board, onto the tape, through the speakers, and finally to our ears. I finally learned and understood how to be super creative in a super-simple way. "Hurts So Good" was the breakthrough in developing that formula.

—◦—

I remember distinctively where I was the first time I heard "Hurts So Good" on the radio. I was driving down 6th Street on the West Side in Bloomington, and I pulled over to the side of the road to really listen to the song, opened both doors to my car so the song was blasting out of the door speakers, and I started dancing right there *on the side of the road!* A few cars honked their horns at me. I think they were listening to the same radio station as me. Bloomington only had one major rock station, and John was a hometown hero, being from Indiana, so it was really like everybody from our hometown was on the radio that day, at the same time, grooving to that song. It was like that scene from the movie *That Thing You Do* when Liv Tyler and the band are just yelling, "Holy shit! I'm on the radio!" And it sounded just like John had wanted it to sound, coming out of a dashboard radio: loud drums, loud guitars, loud everything. Because all the parts were so simple, the value of every part came through the car speakers with power, volume, and a ton of attitude. John wanted "Hurt So Good" to sound louder and more powerful than the song that came on the radio before us and the one that came after us. It definitely worked.

"Hurts So Good" stayed at #2 forever; you couldn't get away from that song. It was always on the radio and played on MTV all day long. Then, as it started to slightly come back down the charts, Mercury Records decided to release "Jack and Diane" to keep the momentum of John's album going.

"Jack and Diane" started climbing the charts fast, and "Hurts So Good" wouldn't go away, it was hanging in there, and all of a sudden, we had *two* hits in the Top 10 at once! I remember at one point, it finally hit me for the first time when I was looking at a *Billboard* magazine one week: Holy shit, I think we made it!

I was staying in the same hotel, the Chateau Marmont, where I got fired from the *Nothing Matters . . .* record when "Jack and Diane" went to #1. I was so excited—for about one second—and then I got real concerned. The next reality that immediately entered my mind was: Can I do this again?

GRAND-UNCLE
HARRY CANNON
GREAT GRANDMA
ARONOFF

GRAND AUNT IDA
FLORENCE
BETTY

GREAT
GRANDPA
ARONOFF

GRAND
UNCLE
JAKE
ARONOFF

GRAND PA
MEYER

My great-grandfather, grandfather, and relatives, from Russia, on my dad's side of the family around 1908.
My grandfather had to escape to America right before the Russian Revolution. (Author's collection)

My twin brother, Jonathan, and me, age thirteen, and my
sister, Nina, age nine, 1966. (Author's collection, photo
by Clem Kalischer)

Practicing drums in my parents' family room at
age thirteen in 1966. (Author's collection, photo
by Clem Kalischer)

My son, Nik, and me, enjoying the same French fry. (Author's collection)

My son, Nikolai Aronoff—all grown up. (Janell Lenfert Photography)

My father, Art, and
my mother, Eleanore,
celebrating their sixtieth
wedding anniversary.
(Author's collection)

My sister, Nina, my wife,
Gina, and my mom at
Christmas in Stockbridge,
Massachusetts,
where I grew up.
(Author's collection)

My brother, Jon, came to see me play drums with the Goo Goo Dolls at the University of Massachusetts, where I went to college my freshman year before transferring to Indiana University School of Music to study another four years. (Author's collection)

Gina and me, trying to capture the vibe of Marilyn Monroe and Arthur Miller. (Photo by James Lomenzo)

Talking with Leonard Bernstein and the Tanglewood Fellowship Orchestra percussion section after a concert we did with Bernstein conducting. (Author's collection)

I performed a violin concerto on marimba with a sixty-piece orchestra at Indiana University in 1975. Introduction and Rondo Capriccioso, Op. 28, by Camille Saint-Saëns. (Author's collection)

Streamwinner publicity still, shot in Indianapolis, Indiana, 1979. (Author's collection)

John Cougar Mellencamp publicity still (*Uh-Huh* era), shot in a pigpen on a farm in Southern Indiana. (Author's collection)

Publicity still for Mellencamp's album *Big Daddy*, 1989. (Author's collection)

My first recording studio in the basement of my first house on Bluebird Lane in Bloomington, Indiana, 1983. (Author's collection)

Filming the John Mellencamp video "Hard Times for an Honest Man" in Savannah, Georgia, 1987. (Author's collection)

Filming the John Mellencamp video "Paper in Fire" in Savannah, Georgia, 1987. (Author's collection)

12

Bona Fide

We started making videos to play on MTV for every single we released for radio. "Hand to Hold On To" was my *very* first music video shoot and we shot it out at the limestone quarries outside of Bloomington. It was like making a mini-movie, and we were very fortunate that MTV liked us so much, embraced our band, and played our videos all the time. We truly were one of the first rock bands of the MTV generation.

The second video we shot was "Hurts So Good" in a little Main Street pub in Medora, Indiana. Medora was another small town in Southern Indiana, which was like twenty miles away from Seymour, where John grew up. If you were driving through and you sneezed, you would miss it. It was a real one-stoplight town.

All the patrons you saw in the video were the real deal, mostly local bikers. I always thought it was really cool of John to include them—he was embracing his Midwestern roots, and people in America were really digging that, because no rock star had ever really done that before. It was the first video that really put small-town Midwest on the map in music videos, and that established what would be the band's official backdrop for years of video shoots to come. Bruce Springsteen owned New Jersey, and the John Mellencamp band was about to claim the Midwestern rock sound and scene.

After *American Fool* won Album of the Year at the Grammys, we hit the road in the summer of 1982, flying in two six-seater planes—a King Air and a Cessna 310—opening up for Heart on 120 shows for nine months in the USA and Canada.

We went through so many obstacles making this record, and we were finally seeing some amazing results. We still didn't know how fans were going to react when we played it live, but John compelled people to get out of their seats and dance and sing along—he actually yelled at them to get out of their seats and start moving, and they loved it. He was becoming a great front man. He was signed in the first place because someone thought he was a bona fide star, and he was starting to prove that they were right. It had just been a matter of time.

A few years later, on the *Scarecrow* and *Jubilee* tours, when we were head-lining arenas, sometimes the first three rows of the venue would be seats reserved for season-ticket holders, people who had year-long ticket sub-scriptions for sports, whatever, and who usually weren't our fans. I remember they'd always be coming in late, dressed up fancy, and you could see that they couldn't really tell us apart from the next band, but they had the best seats. John would get right in their faces and they'd be sitting down with their cocktails, and he would say—right into the mic—"Get your fucking asses up off your seats, you're ruining the show for everybody behind you! Get up, get up!" He'd be screaming at them, and they'd be looking at him laughing, saying, "Who is this guy?" Meanwhile, the true fans were behind them going nuts singing and dancing to our music.

John eventually worked out a deal that gave him control of the first two or three front rows. Harry Sandler, our tour manager, would go up into the nosebleed seats, where many of the true fans were, and would randomly give them seats in those first two or three rows. So now, the front rows would have rabid fans, and that would set the pace of energy for everyone behind them. He always had the pulse of the people in his live performances and in his songwriting. You could instantly relate to the people he was singing about, *and* he cared about who he was singing for.

We started getting hard core fans that would be waiting outside the venues after our shows each night on the road. They were old-school rock 'n' roll nuts—chicks sitting on guys' shoulders ripping off their shirts, throw-ing their bras at us and flashing us during the concerts. We weren't Mötley Crüe or Van Halen—we were from Indiana, not the Sunset Strip—but we were definitely creating a wild rock 'n' roll scene everywhere we went.

I would tell my tech, "Dude, see that chick three rows back with the big tits and the striped shirt? Go down there and give her a backstage pass." So he would stumble down there in a crowd of 20,000 crazy fans, stand behind her, and I'd nod my head and he would slap that after show pass on her. Okay, that part was kind of like Mötley Crüe, and it definitely isn't happening now, but that's what you did when you were in a headlining arena band, and your audience were just as young and wild as you were. Sex, drums, and . . . rock 'n' roll!

While we were out opening for Heart, even though they were way more successful than us, had sold more records than us, had more hits than us, and had been around longer than us, they also had a record that was not happening on the charts while *American Fool* was becoming one of the hottest records on the radio and MTV. We started selling more and more tickets, which helped fill seats on this tour.

I think it was a bittersweet thing for Heart. They loved us because we were selling tickets, but I also think they resented us a little bit because we were happening and they were starting to fade. That was the business. But unlike the Kinks and their road crew, Heart and their team were super cool and treated us really well. They were *nice*. And the Wilson sisters were sane. Heart made us feel like family.

◄○►

Sometimes we flew after the show to our next destination, and a scary fly-the-*unfriendly*-skies moment came when we were flying from Miami to Biloxi, Mississippi. We were up there in the air partying our asses off, living it up when suddenly I heard this loud "ding" from the cockpit. That meant the autopilot had been turned off and now the pilot was flying the plane manually—Toby had convinced the pilot to make us go weightless by raising the nose of the plane way up into the sky, and then dropping the plane downward toward the ground real fast. It's also known as "the vomit comet."

When the pilot did the nosedive, we all had our seat belts on, except our bodyguard Tracy, which caused him to start floating above his seat like he was in space! All our drinks started floating out of the cans and glasses like there was no gravity, and the flight plans started floating from the cockpit to the back of the plane. It was crazy, and the g-force was so intense I thought I was going to puke. I remember I could see the lights of the city rushing up at us because the plane at that point was heading down nose-first, right into them. Then the pilot quickly, but steadily, brought the nose of the plane back up and leveled the plane off. Ahhh, sweet relief, anything for a gag, but then we heard a rapid *"Ding ding ding ding"* from the cockpit and saw *a lot* of lights flashing red on his dashboard. The pilot was going nuts, moving fast trying all kinds of stuff while we were all screaming and freaking out. The plane had stalled, I mean *stopped dead* in the sky!

I remember someone telling me that you can't start a plane in the sky once it stalls, and my life flashed before my eyes. Seriously, I know it is a cliché, but that actually happens, I mean there I was getting yelled at by asshole conductors, playing the "Alley Cat" at a high school party, screwing a million girls, getting fired by Mellencamp—as the plane was now gliding down, down, down toward the earth, with everyone in the band discovering religion and praying to God to save us—*HOLY FUCK ARE YOU FUCK-ING SERIOUS?*

Well, he must have heard us, because a miracle happened when the pilot finally got the plane started again. It felt like an eternity, though. One minute we are having a wild party and the next minute we might have been crashing. What we later learned was when we went up and then down, the gravity pulled the fuel out of the fuel lines—causing the plane to suddenly run out of gas. When we landed, I remember we all kissed the ground. We never went weightless again, at least not like that.

—◦—

When Heart took breaks from their tour, we would stay on the road and do our own shows, or open up for other bands when it made sense financially or because it was a high-profile gig. On one of the breaks, we opened up for the Who at three stadium shows in Boulder, Colorado, Scottsdale,

Arizona, and San Diego, California. John didn't want to play these shows because he thought the audiences weren't there to see him and so it was a bad idea.

John was right. Most of the 60,000 to 80,000 people didn't give a shit about us, so at the first show in Boulder, we opened up for Stevie Nicks, who was second on the bill, and all our rental gear was right in front of her gear onstage and everything sounded like crap because we had no sound check. Sure enough, the audience hated us and started throwing shit at us: clothes, shoes, food, beer bottles, soap, and whatever else they had! The funny thing was, most of it missed us and went flying into Stevie Nicks' equipment. John finally ended our show after three or four songs and made us leave the stage. We were bummed, but John was crazy mad, and we could hear him screaming and yelling at the promoter in his dressing room while he threw furniture into the walls. John tried to cancel the other two shows, but we had to honor our contract and play them.

The next show was in Scottsdale, Arizona, and this time it was us, Loverboy, and the Who. The audience threw stuff at us again, but this time someone knocked John out with a wine bottle as he sang and danced on top of a tall stack of speakers! I couldn't believe it. I saw the whole thing go down in slow motion. I tried to yell at John and warn him as I saw the bottle fly way up in the air from the audience and come down to smash perfectly against his head. Bam! He fell off the speakers and hit the stage and was unconscious for about ten seconds.

We obviously had to stop and leave the stage. I thought we were finished, but John wanted to go back out and play once he got his head stitched up. He came back out wearing a yellow construction worker's hard hat and yelled into the mic, "Who was the fucking coward that threw that bottle at me? Fuck you!" And we went into "Hurt So Good." The crazy thing was, when the Who played, the audience threw twenty times *more shit at them.* I had never seen so much crap come out of the audience: clothes, food, drinks, bottles, even bottle rockets were flying past the band, and I saw John Entwistle bat one off his bass while he kept playing. Roger Daltrey would stand in front of the audience whipping his mic around, singing and dodging all this crap coming at him super cool and relaxed like a confident ninja warrior. None of this fazed the Who at all, they were way too cool.

On another break we had on the Heart tour, we opened up for the Beach Boys in an outdoor festival in London, Ontario. We had horrible rental gear, and I told John after sound check that I had to have my drum tech nail and duct-tape all the cheap low-budget cymbal stands and drums down on the stage so I could play the show, but I said jokingly that I was going to do a Keith Moon and destroy the kit during the show. John was already furious because his name was not on the concert tickets and he had sold most of the tickets for this concert once his name was added to the bill. The Beach Boys weren't really selling well at this point.

During the first song Mike's rental amp broke, then Larry's amp broke in the second song. My gear was falling apart, and John finally turned to us and screamed "Play 'I Need a Lover,'" which was our last song.

He had had enough and went that quickly from the second to the last song, and then made a gesture for us to bring it way down in volume to he could talk to the audience. He told the audience that they had been ripped off and screwed by the promoter, and then he proceeded to point the promoter out to the audience because he was on the side of the stage and very visible. The promoter freaked out, as you could imagine. John continued, telling the audience we would come back to give them a free concert.

Next thing I know, he was walking up to my drum kit and pulling the mics off the drums. He took my drums one by one and threw them into the audience. I watched as my drums disappeared into a crowd of 15,000 people. It looked like ants trying to carry food on their backs. It was amazing—a photo of John tearing down my drums actually made it into *Rolling Stone*. We left the stage and got into our vans and headed back to the hotel, all hyper and laughing at what had just happened.

Back at the hotel, we were told the Beach Boys were pretty pissed off and basically wanted to kick our asses, which, oddly, they were known to do. We decided we better leave for Detroit immediately because the Beach Boys were staying in our hotel, so we went looking for our pilots and found them eating dinner in the hotel restaurant.

Even though they had just finished drinking a bottle of wine, we convinced them that they had to fly us out immediately. I am not sure how they pulled that off because there are so many logistics.

Well, we got out of there okay, but had a lot of explaining to do at customs in Detroit. They weren't expecting us until the next day, and they wanted to know why we suddenly flew across the border in the middle of the night in our small planes because it sure looked like a drug-smuggling deal. And how the hell are you supposed to explain to someone that you are scared of Mike Love?

Besides touring and selling records, we started getting booked on a lot of TV shows. We played on Dick Clark's *American Bandstand* a few times, *Solid Gold*, *Don Kirshner's Rock Concert*, *Second City TV* with John Candy and Martin Short, the first-ever *American Music Awards* hosted by Dick Clark, and even the *Late Late Show* with Tom Snyder, where we were booked with guests James Brown and Muhammad Ali! I have to say James Brown acted and looked like a prizefighter and Ali was just as mellow and cool as can be.

But the highlight and most exciting show was doing *Saturday Night Live* with the Original Not Ready for Prime Time Players, who were still there and still crazy: John Belushi, Dan Aykroyd, Chevy Chase, Gilda Radner, and Jane Curtin were like the Rolling Stones of comedy. They were rock stars in their own right and the show had an insane amount of energy. We performed on that show four times, which may be a record for most appearances by a musical guest on that show. I performed there two other times later on—once with Smashing Pumpkins, and also Willie Nelson and Paul Simon together. What made *SNL* intimidating was it was literally live with only a seven-second delay. If you fucked up, everyone would see it. I don't get nervous at all about doing a show like that now, but the first time we did it I was shitting in my pants. Sixty seconds before we had to perform, a makeup artist came racing up to the stage to pat down my head with powder to get rid of the glare. The band and the audience burst out laughing. I was nervous enough without having to be humiliated.

The *American Fool* tour and album really established us as a touring and recording band. We were like rebels and John was trying to do things more and more on his terms and this was just the beginning. He was already sick of making records in LA or Miami, was fed up with being an opening act, and sick of being called "John Cougar." I didn't know it yet, but John was about to make some big changes.

13

The Bunker

I remember the exact moment when John played "Pink Houses" for me the first time. It was a rare moment when it was just John and I hanging out.

You know how it is, how music has that magic of locking events into our minds. I can even remember the *weather* that day: it was a beautiful fall day in October with the sun shining on the acres of trees surrounding John's house. The foliage was actually *glowing*, with bright yellow and orange leaves.

The *American Fool* tour had just ended and I was dropping something off at his house, and it wasn't like he invited me in. He pretty much just grabbed me and dragged me into the house and picked up a guitar. He told me, "I played this for my dad, and he thinks it's the best song I have ever written," which obviously meant a lot to him. Like I said, John's people were incapable of bullshit. And then he sang the first verse for me, "There's a black man, with a black cat, living in a black neighborhood, he's got an interstate running through his front yard. . . ." It was all very real. When he sang the chorus, even I knew it was going to be a huge hit. I could feel it. It was a perfect song.

Eventually, he showed me where the guy's actual house was in Indianapolis, and John even had the guy sitting on his porch next to the interstate in the "Pink Houses" video. But more than the poetry and the imagery, this was the signal that John had his head back in the game and that we were going to start our next record. The urgency was back.

In the first eight years I was in John's band, we never took much time off. From 1980 until 1988, we would only take one month off between records and tours. Our two-year cycle was always the same: John would write the music, we would arrange and rehearse the music for a record, then record the album, do promotion for the record, rehearse for tour, hit the road to promote the record—which could be a year on the road touring—and then take one month off before starting that whole process all over again.

A lot of bands at that level work like that. Once you're on the wheel, you can't get off, and with a guy like John, who lived in constant fear of losing whatever advantage he had gained, whatever audience he had or accolades he had earned, it was very intense. There was no slacking.

It was constant work, and not the best thing for my personal relationships, but I was living the dream. And most importantly, because John was so driven, we never had a chance to feel complacent or totally comfortable with the success of any of our records or tours because he drilled it into us that we had to deliver another great record to sustain a long career. It was an old-school work ethic.

We saw so many bands come and go around us, on the charts and road, and sometimes it seemed like the bigger they were, the harder they fell. There were lots of one-hit wonders, flash-in-the-pan bands, or dinosaurs who had their day playing arenas and were now playing theaters or clubs just to hang on. Riding high in April, shot down in May. It was a very unforgiving business. John was like a fighter who didn't wait a year and a day to defend his title; he wanted to get back in the ring and prove that he had earned it. He was no paper champ—after we'd had a Grammy-winning, multi-platinum-selling album with two Top 10 hits that had reached #1 and #2, and a third in the Top 20, we just pushed harder.

As soon as John wrote "Pink Houses," we were all in, all over again, and started the process of writing and arranging songs for the next record. We did all of our pre-production for our albums in a small, concrete room with two small windows that used to be a dog kennel before we took it over as our rehearsal space. It was built right above his house on a steep, sloping ravine, and we nicknamed it "the Bunker." It was about twenty feet long by ten feet wide with a very low ceiling, and the only natural light the room got was from those two small windows, which never even got direct sun. It was all pretty dark. We squeezed all of our instruments and a small PA into this musty, damp, dungeon-like room. We were about five miles outside of downtown Bloomington in the woods, and about a million miles from Hollywood or New York.

But living in the Midwest kept us humble and focused. John really understood how the music business worked—he was cynical, but successful because he had figured out the formula of how to be himself *and* be radio friendly.

Let's be honest, the record labels and the industry don't care about art, they care about hits. It is a brutal business. You have to sound fresh, but never full of shit. You can never trick your fans, because they won't forgive you, but you have to aim wide. It's a sick combination of raw talent filtered through an industry driven by numbers, and it takes a lot of guts to come out the other side sounding like yourself.

A lot of bullshit gets promoted. It's not a meritocracy. A lot of talented people never figure it out. John didn't get to where he is because he is "the best," because he won *American Idol* singing someone else's song. He got there because he was good *and* honest, he worked his ass off 24/7 for many years, and he knew how to sound honest even in the face of people who wanted to change his name and screw with his sound. This was the first record that he was even allowed to use his real name.

Well, sort of: he didn't lose the "Cougar" entirely, but he was on his way. This record went out under the name John Cougar Mellencamp, but just imagine the war this guy had to rage to get from being called *Johnny Cougar* to *John Cougar* to *John Cougar Mellencamp*. It wasn't as easy as John telling the label my name is now John Cougar *Mellencamp*. They were concerned about any possible confusion when it came to promoting and marketing John's new record. Would record stores place it under "C" for *Cougar*, as they had been, or now under "M" for *Mellencamp*?

But most importantly he knew a few hits on the radio didn't mean we would *stay* successful, and if we didn't hit again, and hard, he could be back climbing telephone poles for a living.

There wasn't a shred of entitlement in John. It didn't necessarily make him easy to work with, but in those first eight years, I went from playing in local clubs in the Midwest to selling out multiple nights in 18,000-seat arenas with no opening act. *American Fool* alone put thirty-four gold and platinum records in my house and eventually 150 from all the other records I made with John. We won Grammy Awards, and were nominated for many more. We did all the big TV shows and festivals around the world, flew in our own jet, and got involved with every level of weirdness you could possibly imagine, sex, drugs, whatever, but in this band, work always came first.

John wasn't afraid to stand up to anyone. He truly marched to his own beat. He did things his way and wasn't afraid to tell someone what he thought or get in someone's face to make his point. Sometimes he shot himself in the foot, but most of the time he got what he wanted. When we were in Cherokee Studios recording the song "Hurts So Good," the vice president of our label came to the studio to listen to what we were doing. He basically said he hated the song and hated what we were doing, he didn't get it at all. John walked him to the back door and *literally* kicked him in the ass out the door and onto the sidewalk. It was like something straight out of a movie, but it was *real*. Probably not the smartest thing to do to the VP of our label, especially when they were thinking of dropping us.

But John's intense attitude worked in his favor, probably because at the heart of it all the guy could not only write songs that were hits for a few weeks or months, but because he wrote songs that lasted for years. They became *classics*. People connected to them in a very real way. "Hurts So Good" eventually became a #2 hit, and the album won a Grammy for Best Male Rock Vocal Performance. This is one of those rock 'n' roll stories where the record company was completely wrong, but you can bet that when the record was successful, they were right there taking credit for their own great genius.

◄○►

John was fed up with making records in LA or Miami. He wanted to record in Indiana, which sounds insane considering how far it was from the industry, but being John, he figured out a way to do this with Don Gehman while the band was down in the Bunker arranging and rehearsing songs for the *Uh-Huh* record. In the end, John was smart to stay in Indiana. It wasn't a gimmick; he is from there and he believed in it. He was making enough money. He could have moved to Malibu—but he didn't. People talk about keeping it real. John walked the walk.

He made a deal with his sister, who lived with her boyfriend in a small, five-room house in Southern Indiana that needed a lot of work done to it. John offered to make a bunch of improvements to her house if we could take it over, convert it into a recording studio, and use it for about a year. He did a bunch of work inside the house and laid gravel down the long dirt driveway so a big vehicle with a mobile studio in it could drive in and park next to the house. Gehman organized bringing the equipment up from Miami, and a bunch of technicians constructed a studio in that house, which we eventually dubbed "the Shack."

The Shack was deep in the wooded part of Southern Indiana. Outside it smelled like a pig farm because there were pigs, goats, chickens, and horses running freely all over the property. It took me fifty minutes to get there from my house in Bloomington, but on the way home at night, we could drive super fast because there was no traffic, though we had to keep a lookout for deer crossing the road. That could be a serious life-ending experience if you hit one, as I found out firsthand years later driving back from Columbus, Ohio, on Interstate 70 after a Joe Cocker show I had just played.

I hit a deer head-on going 75 miles an hour. I came up over a hill and there were some deer right in my lane, so I did the obvious, which was try and avoid the deer by swerving to the left, and instead of moving, the deer followed my headlights and *WHAM*. I killed the poor thing, totally messed up my SUV and was lucky I didn't end up in the hospital or dead. What I learned from that experience was you don't swerve away from the deer, you just *slow down and head right into them*. They will move. You actually have a better chance of missing them that way. Now that I think about it, I probably could have used that knowledge in the studio with a lot of the artists and producers I have worked with.

14

The American Dream

Before we recorded *Uh-Huh*, the record that eventually featured "Pink Houses," we tested the Shack by recording a Mitch Ryder album there that John produced and I played drums on called *Never Kick a Sleeping Dog*.

Mitch Ryder presents the perfect lesson that it doesn't matter how hard you rocked or how many hits you've had—in 1983 the industry didn't have much use for him. One song on the record, the Prince cover "When You Were Mine," actually charted, but by then he was a legacy act—a term that a guy like John lived in fear of: if it could happen to Mitch Ryder, it could happen to him. I mean, Mitch had lost some of his swagger, but this guy was a killer, a hero of Detroit rock 'n' roll. Don't forget that Bruce Springsteen broke out and became a legendary live act at least in part based on his medley of Mitch Ryder hits, including "Devil with the Blue Dress On," which was one of my favorite songs to play the drums along with when I was a kid. It was rock and soul and R & B all at once, and I was very excited to work with Mitch. It was a very heavy experience for me.

Working with Mitch, we were able to work out all the kinks in the studio, but we also trashed the house over the course of that record and ours, so maybe it wasn't the best idea to let a bunch of rock 'n' rollers record their records in your house.

◄○►

After the *American Fool* record and tour, John gave everyone in the band a check for $10,000. It was a bonus and a gift of appreciation for all our hard work—or maybe it was a tax write-off?—but who cares, right? The bottom line was John handed me a check for $10,000. I couldn't believe it! I didn't expect it. I didn't see it coming, and back then, to me, $10,000 was like getting $100,000.

My immediate thoughts were, Down payment on a house. I was so excited with that idea, I couldn't wait to tell my girlfriend, but when I did, she said, "Are you fucking crazy? We should travel. Let's go to Paris, let's have fun, let's drink!" And I thought, Are you fucking nuts? Here's a chance to put a down payment on a house, stop renting, and build some equity.

To me, this was living the American Dream my father had raised me to believe in—ply your trade, work hard, and own your own home. In 1983 you could get a lot for your money in Bloomington, so I ended up buying a new two-story, three bedroom, three bathroom house out in the country on Blubebird Lane, with a cool front porch and deck in the back. It had a large living room with a fireplace, dining area, kitchen, and a finished basement that I turned into an office and recording studio. The basement had an efficient fireplace with a fan that helped heat the entire house in the cold-ass Indiana winters. I had a few acres of lawn with scattered trees that went right up against the biggest, most beautiful state forest in the state. I tilled a piece of my property and made a 45-foot-by-35-foot garden and grew all my own vegetables that year. It was amazing. I bought that house for $87,000, and the $10,000 plus a bit I had saved was enough for my down payment. Of course, now I had a mortgage, and who knew how long this whole rock 'n' roll thing was going to last. It certainly wasn't a career built on security—but as someone once told me, "The best investment in life is to invest in yourself."

◄◦►

Lisa and I got married on July 3, 1983, and of course I had a wild bachelor party in the back room of a super-cool steak house called Jankos. You name it, we were doing it. Everyone was getting hammered on booze and whatever else was available. At one point, a limo pulled up in front of the restaurant and in walked seven strippers strutting along with a ghetto blaster blasting. My twin brother, Jon, and I ended up dancing on one of the dining tables in our underwear with one of the strippers in between us. I remember looking down and saw my dad—he was shaking his head as if to say, "What the fuck are you doing?" I think that was right after I had disappeared with one of the strippers into the bathroom for an hour.

When Jankos finally closed, we continued partying at one of the waitress's houses, and I didn't get home until 6:30 a.m. There were a lot of questions asked that morning, but somehow I got past all of that. Make of it what you will, but being in a popular rock band seems to be a pretty good Get Out of Jail card for outrageous behavior. For now. Later I learned that card had an expiration date on it.

Two days later, we had a beautiful outdoor wedding, and we continued our crazy partying with a lot of the same people from the bachelor party, minus the strippers of course. Everyone was instructed not to take pictures until after the ceremony, but as I was about to say "I do," I noticed one of my oldest friend's sister was on one knee in a dress facing all of us taking pictures. I was cool with that part, but she wasn't wearing any panties and I could see a white cotton string hanging out from between her legs. I couldn't believe it. It was just too much. I looked at my bride, back at the girl, back at the seven ushers and seven bridesmaids, back at the girl, and then at my bride one more time, who also had that look of "Are you serious? Is this really happening *now?*"—and sure enough, everyone was seeing what I was seeing. At that exact moment, an elderly couple related to my wife's side of the family got up and stormed out, mumbling like mental patients, in genuine shock. It was just way too much for your basic Midwest mind-set, unfettered by rock 'n' roll. After that, things calmed down long enough for me to get married before the party started and everyone got crazy again. The evening ended with me trying to pop wheelies on a sit-down lawn mower while everyone chased me around the lawn convinced that this was a bad idea for someone who needed his arms to make a living.

—◄○►—

Two days after I got married, we were back in the Shack rehearsing and starting work on the record that would become *Uh-Huh*.

I remember the day we were tracking "Pink Houses (Ain't That America)." We tracked—as we always did—live off the floor with the entire band, and every little nuance you hear, say, for instance, my tambourine shaking along with the guitar during the opening verse of that song, was recorded live all at once. After the first chorus, I dropped the tambourine onto a towel so you wouldn't hear it and quickly grabbed my drum sticks so I could do a drum fill into the second intro of the song, pushing the tempo a little to create more excitement and give the song a lift. I really give John a lot of credit with encouraging that sort of experimentation. It definitely heightened the level of creativity in the studio.

On the *Uh-Huh* record, I started to establish my signature snare sound and drumming style for John's music. I experimented with a 5" x 14" 1962 brass Ludwig Superphonic 400 snare that I had used on the Mitch Ryder record, but I also used Don Gehman's 5" x 14" Ludwig Acrolite snare that he brought to the session, and somehow it was perfect for our music.

> **Don Gehman:** Starting on *Uh-Huh*, we got into the Rolling Stones type of snare-drum tuning. I had an old Ludwig Acrolite, a student snare drum that I had found somewhere. It was aluminum and had an unusual kind of ring, a *boink* thing to it whenever you'd hit it. So I brought it out to the studio, and we liked that ring—it was really obnoxious, and that became our snare sound. That is what the John Mellencamp–Kenny Aronoff sound is—the sound of a highly cranked-up, almost Jamaican-style snare drum that is tuned to ring too loud, and when you put that in a rock 'n' roll track, it just sounds unbelievable.

We finally started to find our groove and method to making records. But even after the album was finished and mastered, John still felt we didn't have a kick-ass song to be the lead single for radio. Back then, radio was still the most important vehicle to get your music heard and therefore sell records.

John called me up one day and said he wanted to come by my house immediately with Larry to play this new song he had just written called "Crumblin' Down." Within five minutes after hanging up, he was in front of my house on Jackson and 7th (where Lisa and I were still living) in his little black Ford truck. He had a couple of cool cars and some Harleys, but he was definitely not over the top with fancy rock star cars yet. The cool thing about living in Bloomington was there was no pressure to look or act like a rock star, but at least I had finally managed to get rid of the oil-leaking old clunker I had bought from my dad for $500, the one that almost cost me my gig with John.

Anyway, John and Larry came by, and John started playing "Crumblin' Down." He was very excited—right before he was about to start, he said, "I've got this great song I just wrote, *so don't fuck it up, Kenny,*" which didn't help me relax when I was already concerned about coming up with the perfect beat for a song I hadn't even heard yet, but I came up with a simple beat that I had never played before and have never used anywhere else. While John played the song on acoustic guitar, I was playing softly with my fingers because I didn't want to fuck up, but it became a pulsating steady eighth-note beat on the my kick drum, which doubled the acoustic guitar rhythm, while I played beats two and four on my snare drum. But I only hit the hi-hat once every two measures, on the "and" of beat three. It landed in the perfect spot after a guitar or vocal phrase. Simple and musical. I didn't fuck it up.

15

The John Mellencamp Football League

John bred fear of failure like a football coach. Fortunately, everyone in the band was into sports and super competitive. We always played football and basketball, but sometimes when we were home we rode John's dirt bikes and his ATV four-wheelers on a crazy figure-8 track he built in the woods and fields near his parents' house in Seymour, Indiana. When we raced his ATVs, we created teams and it was full-on mayhem. There were some serious crashes with ATVs colliding into each other at that figure 8, or sometimes we'd fly off the track into a tree. Someone almost drowned one time when they flipped over into a water-filled creek and they were pinned under their ATV. It was horrible. They couldn't get their seat belt off and couldn't lift themselves from underneath it. A bunch of people rescued the driver just in time.

In the winter, we played ice hockey on John's pond below his new house. Toby and I built hockey goals with chicken wire and wood at my house. John built a big bonfire on the side of the frozen pond, and everyone brought tons of booze.

I remember back when I was first in the band, we would play contact basketball, and when I'd go to make a jump shot, John would run up behind me and pull my shorts down. Or he would fake punch me in the nuts, or *actually punch me in the nuts* to *distract* me while I was shooting. We played by our own rules—ninja ball!—which had a lot to do with why we became so successful.

The football thing started as a fun get-together on weekends in the fall every so often. We all loved football and we all played it in high school or with our friends and dads growing up as kids. It started casual but then became mandatory with uniforms, and we started playing other teams. We were the MFL (Mellencamp Football League) or as the band called it, the *Mandatory* Football League. It was supposed to be flag football, but you know how that goes: it quickly became tackle without pads. It seemed like every week someone got injured, be it arms, wrists, fingers, ankles, or knees getting blown out.

One game, I broke my little finger and had to record "Rooty Toot Toot" for *The Lonesome Jubilee* album that same night.

John had his own studio and kept his band on a retainer so he could call us at any time and ask us to come down to record a song he had just written. It was the same basic thing Prince was doing with his musicians in Minneapolis. We were always on call, like firemen.

That game was the one where John's manager, Tommy Mattola, and John had made a $1,000 bet. Tommy flew to Indiana with some ringers from Penn State and they beat us. John was so pissed off . . . our team had a shit day getting beaten by these college guys, and our quarterback totally panicked. He froze and couldn't throw. John was so angry and frustrated, after one play he slugged someone on Tommy's team in the head. I found out years later when I was having drinks with that guy that he had faked being knocked out so he wouldn't get hit again.

> **John Mellencamp:** We had the MFL (Mellencamp Football League), and it was like the rule: if you're in the band, you're doing it, and everybody else just accepted it. I've always played football, and I was—and still am—kind of a benevolent dictator. When I make suggestions, they're not really suggestions: they're directions. There's a difference. I'm open to suggestions—but me personally, I'm not open to direction—but I expect everybody around me to be open to direction, so it was like, "Okay, let's go play football," and sometimes people would go, "Uhhh, I don't want to play," and I'd say, "Guess what, you're in the band, you've got to play."

We played MFL on tour also, no matter what country we were in. I remember playing one time while we were on tour in Cincinnati, and during the game, Big Ed—who was our monitor engineer—was acting as the referee for that game. He made a call against John, and John fired him immediately as they argued over the call! John had to win and he would do whatever it took to win. Ed made a bad call, and . . . you're fired!

Another time, the band was in Germany on the *Scarecrow* tour, and John decided that we were going to play football while it was snowing. For some reason, I was on John's shit list that week, and he put everybody in the band on his team, but stuck me on the opposing team with a bunch of German crew guys who didn't know how to play American football. This made me want to beat John's team big time. I was taking the game seriously, but no one on my team was. Still, somehow, during that game, I remember we managed to score, and I could see that pissed John off. I watched him scream and yell at Mike Wanchic while he threw the football at his head over and over again.

After we scored, I kicked the ball off right to John, and I ran down the field as fast as possible to stop him by pushing him out of bounds. The rest of my teammates were taking their time because they were just trying to have fun, but not John or me. We both were trying to win—we are both super competitive.

John—who is *super* fast, probably the fastest white guy I've ever met—caught the ball and took off running as I came at him, faster and faster, closer and closer until he saw I was going to push him out of bounds with a full-on tackle. Just at the last minute, he clocked me in my face with his forearm, and I went flying on my ass and spilled into the snowy field. He'd blindsided me! I was so pissed, as soon as I got to my feet, I went ape shit and came flying back at him ready to kill him. Thank God Warren Kaye, our 300-pound, 6' 8" bodyguard, stopped me. He was on my team, and he saw what was about to happen and leaped in between us and held me back with one hand and John back with the other. I was seeing red and a bit out of my mind, so I was yelling things at him you should never say to your boss, like, "You fucking cocksucker, fuck you!" My feet were spinning on the snowy, wet field like Fred Flintstone. When the game was over we moved on, of course, but that's how seriously competitive it got sometimes, but it created this great energy onstage with the band. We matched each other with energy and aggressiveness, and if we were not putting out onstage, John would start screaming at us during the show to keep moving and kick some ass. He certainly was.

◄○►

John's intuition was right about "Crumblin' Down"—it was successful on radio, cracking the Top 10 at #9 on the *Billboard* Hot 100 Singles chart, and the record peaked at #2 on the *Billboard* Top 200 Albums chart. MTV was rotating the video twenty-four hours a day. It was a great first single to launch the *Uh-Huh* album and show the world we were a force to be reckoned with.

Lots of people have hits. Some have two or three. By now we were fucking mighty. Four of the five singles that were recorded at the Shack ended up on the Top 40 Singles chart in *Billboard*, and the fact that we were recording our style of heartland rock back home in the Midwest made it all that much more real.

When it was time to shoot videos for this record, John decided to bring the film crew to Indiana and film us in the Shack and a few other locations around Southern Indiana. The videos, including "Pink Houses," really showed what rural Midwestern farmland looked like, and no one else was showing that in their videos at the time for sure. It was summer, and at least 100 degrees out with 100 percent humidity the day we shot. To be cost-effective, John made two videos in twenty-four hours with no breaks, so we were up all day and night. All the local farmers would drive by and stare at us or pull over to watch us making these videos because they'd never seen anything like that before. It certainly wasn't a routine occurrence around there. John was obviously trying to do everything in Indiana now. He felt confident about making his records, filming videos, and doing all his business out of Bloomington. He bought a small house just outside of town and put in his own studio with two offices and made that his home base for everything. The studio was called Belmont Mall, and John has been recording all his records there ever since.

When it was time to tour again, John decided that he didn't want to be an opening act anymore. He wanted to be the headliner, so he figured out how he could afford to do this by playing for his hard core fans in smaller venues across America.

John was definitely starting to come into his own fully as a star, which also meant he was in the process of shedding his John Cougar identity that had been on the cover of *American Fool* and becoming John Cougar Mellencamp. That lasted two more albums before he finally was able to use his own name, John Mellencamp, on *The Lonesome Jubilee* album.

We toured for six weeks with an opening act from Bloomington, Indiana (John's loyalty to Bloomington was very real), playing in venues with 2,000–5,000 seats, and finished the tour in LA at the Universal Amphitheater. I remember seeing a lot of bands, artists, and people in the movie business backstage after our shows. It was getting wilder and wilder all the time. But the cool thing about going back to Bloomington was, people treated us like we were *not* famous at all. We ate in the local diner and had beer in the local bar. It was all very normal, and I loved it. There was plenty of craziness on the road, but having a place to come back to, that really made things much simpler and kept us grounded. John had achieved his goal—we were now making records at home and touring as a headliner. And as long as I kept working, I was happy. It's probably why I've lasted so long in this business.

When we had a few weeks off from the tour, Lisa found out she was pregnant, and we finally moved into the new house on Bluebird Lane. And then, right on time, after the tour finally ended, my son, David Nikolai Aronoff, was born on May 10, 1984.

I missed a lot of things by choosing this career, but I wasn't going to miss the birth of my son. Then again, if Mellencamp still had dates, I'm not sure what I would have said. The tours and gigs always came first, and that would eventually create some problems in my personal life.

16

Scarecrow

When Nik (we always called him Nik) was being delivered, the doctor looked at me and started singing "Jack and Diane." Changing the lyrics around a bit, he sang, "A little ditty about Lisa and Kenny, two Bloomington kids having a baby in the heartland." Could my life get any weirder? I couldn't believe the doctor was singing that song to me while he was delivering our baby. But it did make me smile, even though I was definitely nervous about becoming a father and totally freaked out watching my wife's surgery. From her belly button up she looked normal, but below it looked like a war zone.

My wife had a C-section after many hours of trying to deliver Nik naturally, and when he came out, the nurse gave him to his mom immediately and then to me so they could stitch her up. With no thought, I started singing softly to Nik this beautiful melody that I had learned while I was studying classical music at the IU school of music. For some reason that melody just popped into my head and I started singing. I forget what it was—Mozart, maybe? Definitely not a rock or pop song, something simple and pretty, perfect for a newborn. Nik just stared right into my eyes, gripping my finger with his tiny little hand.

After Nik was born, it worked out perfectly, and for a change, I was home for most of the rest of that year. We still did TV appearances, like *Saturday Night Live*, and some one-off shows, but we weren't on tour or recording yet because John was already busy writing music. He had moved into a new house just outside of downtown Bloomington and had started building his own studio eight miles east of his house. Once that studio was built, we never left Indiana to make a John Mellencamp record.

◄○►

Ten miles east of the studio was a 2,000-seat venue called the Little Nashville Opry, just outside of Nashville, Indiana. Nashville is a tourist town that attracts visitors all year round, but especially in the fall because of the colorful fall leaves. The Little Nashville Opry tried to emulate the vibe and format of the Grand Old Opry in Nashville, Tennessee.

A lot of big-name country acts would play at the Opry because it was located perfectly between Nashville and Indianapolis. These big acts would sell out the venue every weekend, and there was a local country house band that would open up for all these big acts. The house band had great musicians, and they played country music authentically with some regular singers that the local audiences loved.

The house band had a local following that was committed, loyal, and dedicated. I got a call one week to sub for the regular drummer in the house band, and after that weekend the musical director asked me to join the band as their full-time drummer. I thought, Hell, why not, I'm in town, off the road, and it will be cool to learn how to play country music the right way, which eventually paid off in a huge way. I would see the same church-going Cracker Barrel regulars sitting in the same seats every weekend, watching every move we made. The Opry was their life. At first they didn't know what to think about me, but because I was always respectful and friendly to them, they liked me. They also liked the fact that I was a local rock star they could see on TV.

Playing at the Little Opry groomed me to be a session drummer in Nashville, where I ended up recording with some of the biggest names on Music Row for the next twenty years.

Everything in Nashville moves very quickly—the first time you hear a demo, someone is busy writing the chart, and then they get it printed and you get one more listen, and then you push "record." And the demos are great—exquisite, really. I am always impressed. They sound finished and are very precise, so when it comes to do the real thing, you have to nail it or get lost, and honestly, I sometimes wondered how the actual record could be better than the demo. There isn't a lot of time to experiment in the studio when you are cutting basic tracks. The song and the feel are most important, all the creative ideas, arrangements, and parts have been worked out when the demos are made.

A normal Nashville tracking day is based on three separate sessions. We work from 10 a.m. to 1 p.m., break for lunch , work from 2 to 5 p.m., break for dinner, and then work from 6 to 9 p.m. I've done as many as nine or ten songs in a day, and then went back the next day and did it again, five days a week. Sometimes I would have three drum kits set up in three different studios, or my cartage company would take the No. 1 kit I was using in the 10 a.m. session and set it up for the 6 p.m. session, while I was using kit No. 2 in the 2 p.m. session.

When I recorded with Hank Williams Jr., we recorded all day—10 a.m., 2 p.m., and 6 p.m. sessions for three or four days straight, which I dug a lot. It would start to feel like we were a real *band.* He did things the way Nashville likes to do 'em , but he had a lot of rock 'n' roll in his attitude and behavior.

Hank is like a force. He is a rock star in the country world. He's got the balls to go toe-to-toe with any motherfucker. He was a hard partier, notoriously wild at the highest level. He took no shit from anyone, his sponsors, his producers, label heads, no one, and I loved him for that. It was also scary as shit, you did not want to cross this dude. He had the best players, always. I was a rock 'n' roll guy, not a Nashville cat, but in John's band I was always very visible. People knew who I was and knew what I did. All of that Americana turned into a lot of good gigs with people who wanted a powerful but earthy drummer, no frills but lots of horsepower. That was at the heart of what Hank did.

So I was eating dinner and hanging out on Hank's bus, which was his home away from home, and he said to me, "So, Kenny, where did *your* family come from?"

I was stunned that he would ask me, let alone think about it. I'm just the drummer and who cares, but of course now I'm thinking, All right, I've got this *big nose* and I'm an *East Coast college boy,* and this guy is the standard bearer of the South, stars and bars, whisky and brawls, and all that, and I really don't know what to think, except I felt like Woody Allen in that scene in *Annie Hall* when Diane Keaton's evil Waspy relatives look at him and all they see is this little Hassidic Jew, basically a punching bag for all of their fears and prejudices.

I looked at Hank and said, "Well, ya know, a lot of people think I'm *Italian* because of my nose." And he says, "With that name?"

"Well, actually," I told him, "my grandfather was pre-Revolution Russian, and they escaped. It was like Dr. Zhivago, seriously deep *shtetl* shit—they came and they beat up my great-grandma, and my grandfather shot that motherfucker. Now he was a marked man, and they got him out of there fast and put him on a boat to Ellis Island." I kind of exaggerated. I don't think my grandfather ever shot anyone; he just threatened to do that. Either way he had to leave Russia because he was a marked man. . . . I wanted Hank to know I come from some tough people. *Don't fuck with the Aronoffs, because we will shoot you.*

When I started doing sessions in Nashville, I worked with the legendary producer Jimmy Bowen, a real badass who had worked for Frank Sinatra, Dean Martin, and Sammy Davis, Jr., in Los Angeles before going to Nashville to work with a run of superstars from Glen Campbell and Kenny Rogers to Hank and Garth Brooks, and he told me—he saw I was an aggressive rock drummer, and I was starting to work in Nashville and he could relate to me. He had come in as an outsider, too—his Rat Pack connections meant nothing in Nashville. People are friendly, he told me, and after making a record they will take you out to dinner, and then to the airport, and say have a nice day, and wave bye-bye, which means *bye-bye*. They do not fuck around there. You can be totally badass, but that is not what it is about. You can't just walk into Nashville and take over the scene—it's never going to be just about how good you play. There are plenty of people down there who can play. It's about playing *and* how you fit in on the team. If they want you on the bus, you've got the gig. You can be a badass on your own fucking time.

Hank listened to my story and laughed. He probably knew I was exaggerating just a little bit, but he loved it. "Fucking Jew from Massachusetts turns out to be from a family of outlaws, too," he said. "Well, alright!"

—◦—

Meanwhile, back in Indiana, while working at the Little Opry, I met a great fiddle player, Lisa Germano, who played in that house band, and eventually invited her to record with us when John needed a fiddle player on the *Scarecrow* album. She eventually toured and recorded with us on a regular basis before leaving to concentrate on her solo career.

John's songs were beginning to take on a more serious tone. Gone were the days of "I need a lover who won't drive me crazy . . ." John's lyrics in songs like "Small Town," "Rain on the Scarecrow," and "Minutes to Memories" were about people growing up in small towns and about the family farmers who were being squeezed out by the bigger government-run farms. These small family-run farms were all around us and we knew these people. This is why John, Willie Nelson, and Neil Young started Farm Aid. They wanted to help raise money for these folks.

As John matured as a songwriter, we also were growing as musicians. I was always trying to get better, and looking back I realize there are no short cuts to becoming great at anything in life. It takes self-discipline, hard work, lots of passion, and lots of repetition (over and over again). Being on a number-one hit doesn't mean you can stop working. It's just the beginning.

During the process of making *Uh-Huh*, I was getting better and faster at coming up with what John needed for his radio-friendly songs, because after John played a song once or twice, I had to immediately come up with a cool beat for that song. John was impatient and he'd say, "Alright, Aronoff, what do you got?" He had a great instinct for what was cool or good, even if he couldn't tell us what to play. Many times when we were working on a song and we thought the song was sounding great, John would say, "Nope, not good enough, we've got to do better or start over."

John Mellencamp: I want to hear drums, tambourine, and my voice.

Everything else has to fit in and around those items. Those were the things we focused on, and the two guitar players had to work around Kenny—"Kenny's doing a roll there. You can't play that. We can't have it that sloppy." So you can't just imagine the amount of hours and hours and hours we spent in the rehearsal room.

John knew it was the little things that made good songs hits. It's being super-critical, over-analyzing every beat and every sound, but when you figure it out and suddenly it's got that thing that the industry feels like it can accept, that radio wants to blast all night and day, *that's* when you get to be yourself. Otherwise you can wind up just being a tree that falls in the forest—what's the point of making a record if no one hears it? Art is nice, but someone's got to pay for it.

By this point in his career, John was fast becoming a superstar and was very much the master of his own destiny. He was on the phone all the time talking to his manager, Billy Gaff, his lawyer, his record label, "Why aren't there enough records in the stores? They're not getting the records in the front of the stores? I don't believe you. We've sold more records than that . . ." John had people check out all the local stores to see if they had records on display when you walked in. It made sense for everyone to go the extra mile to promote and sell John Cougar Mellencamp records while we were in that city. Of course he was right. He was getting screwed, but it just made him more determined to make more and better records. John could be difficult, but no one worked harder.

He was relentless. One day while we were arranging new songs for the *Scarecrow* record, John walked into the Bunker with a box of hit records from the '60s, '70s, and '80s and said, "I want you to listen to these records and learn all these great songs note for note. Kenny, I want you to know the drum parts, Mike and Larry the guitar parts, Toby the bass parts, and I want you guys to learn these songs and figure out what made these songs so great."

That's when I came up with what I called the "Book of Beats," where I transcribed the drum and percussion parts from these great records we listened to. We did that for about two months, and whenever John played us a new song he'd written, I could look through my Book of Beats to see if there was something I could use.

Sometimes ideas or inspiration came from unexpected places. For example, with "Rain on the Scarecrow," I was influenced by a David Bowie's hit "Let's Dance." I took the one-measure beat from that song and created a two-measure beat, which worked great for "Scarecrow."

We had just moved into John's new studio, which was a complete relief after being in that bunker for five years and the Shack for a year. Finally, no dark, hot, humid, low-light, low-ceiling dog kennel. No pigs, goats, horses, chickens, and the smell of a farm. We were now in a brand-new studio. It was like being moved from a work camp to summer camp, and as soon as John started playing that song on acoustic guitar, I started playing that groove, and "Scarecrow" was completed in fifteen minutes.

This was years of work paying off: we were really working together now. He would play the song on his acoustic guitar a few times, then I'd come up with a beat, and it was like "That's it!" Once you had the beat, the groove, and the feel from the drums, that would dictate or heavily influence what everyone else in the band would play. I knew what John didn't want more than what he wanted, and that helped me find a cool beat that he would like

On *Scarecrow*, John wanted sounds that made you feel the vibe of the hardworking farmer. For instance, there's a sound on "Rain on the Scarecrow" that sounds like me hitting an anvil on beats two and four with the snare drum, metal on metal. We wanted to have a sound almost like a chain gang, a guy working, or a blacksmith hitting that big metal horseshoe with the hammer. Our producer, Don Gehman, said, "Hey, why don't you hit this fire extinguisher?," which is what I did. I hit it with a metal rod. Eventually, live, I took a brake drum off a car and used that. That sound was crucial to the vibe of the song.

I remember the first time I heard him play "Small Town," another of the Top 10 hits from that album that I still hear on the radio almost thirty years later. He played it for the band as an acoustic ballad, but John definitely wanted this song to rock, so I opened by playing a super-simple beat, which made it possible for me to build throughout the song. I started a basic rock beat, but I didn't play hi-hat or ride, just a minimal kick and snare-drum beat—until the entire band came in, and then *POW!* It was very much in the spirit of the farmers we were singing about. It gained strength as it went along; it felt like a rural uprising. It was very American in the way it sounded, was basic, but therein lied its power. And once again, this was me learning my lesson that more often than not on the drums, less is more.

◄○►

We spent nine months rehearsing and recording the *Scarecrow* album, which became one of the bestselling albums of 1985. I think in many ways, it was the equivalent of John's *Born to Run* because its themes hit so close to home with the Midwest and the farm culture he'd grown up around, the same way Bruce Springsteen could translate his experience of growing up on the Jersey shore. "Small Town" went to #6 on the *Billboard* Hot 100 Singles chart and became a huge hit on MTV.

On the other end of the spectrum musically, John really wanted to celebrate his rock 'n' roll roots on that album, which is why we were learning entire catalogs from the '60s, '70s, and '80s—everyone from the Stones to the Who and the Beatles, the Beach Boys, and even further back to Mitch Ryder and James Brown and the Young Rascals, everyone he calls out in "R.O.C.K. in the U.S.A." We started experimenting with a sound that really came through shining on the songs we put together for *Scarecrow.*

Don Gehman's Ludwig Acrolite student snare was the snare we ended up using on the entire record, except for the first song we recorded called "Rumble Seat." On that song, I ended up recording with two snares duct-taped together! Crazy idea, but it worked. This was before I had my enormous collection of snare drums, but I had a small four-inch deep-wood snare that had lots of attack but not great tone, and I had another six-inch carbon-fiber snare that had great tone but not great attack. John said out of frustration, "Can't you just fucking duct-tape the two snare drums together?" I thought about it and said to myself, "Hell yes, why not." So I did.

I took the bottom hoop, the snares, and head off of the 4-inch wood drum and then took the hoop and top head off of the carbon-fiber drum, lined up the bearing edges, and duct-taped the two snare drums together, and bam, we had a cool sound with crack, lots of tone, and out of the way of the guitar tones. That worked on "Rumble Seat," but we decided we still hadn't found that magic snare sound yet.

Don Gehman: We had a routine from album to album that allowed us to repeat what we did, where we all took a lot of notes, and were all very scientific about what we evaluated, in addition to using our gut. Kenny became a professional drummer during that process. When we found him, he was a fusion-jazz drummer and couldn't play a rock beat if he tried.

John was difficult to get along with—always has been. He pushes people to their limit and sometimes didn't back off. So consequently, here was a group of really talented people with a leader that was just *maniacal.* He would be focused to the point where he'd have something of "This is what we're trying to beat." It was crazy-making, because you really can't compare records that much. Having said that, John is a very good taste master and an excellent entertainer as well, but he just has this gift of design where he understands how things fit together artistically.

John Mellencamp: In the studio, when we were making the *Scarecrow* LP, I knew when the sound we were getting was wrong and I knew when it was right. . . . I was always a risk-taker, I'm still a risk-taker, and when it sounded right to everybody else, I knew that it wasn't right for me—it wasn't loud enough, or the reverb or echo was off—and I'd say, "Does that sound right to you? Okay, well, add 2K to it, would you?" And they'd look at me and say, "That sounds fucked up," and I'd go, "Naw, that's not fucked up, because when you hear it on those little tiny speakers, it's gonna sound great."

I really loved the drum sound on the *Scarecrow* album. I met Brendan

O'Brien a few years ago at the Record Plant in LA. Brendan is one of my favorite producer-engineers ever—he's produced everyone from Pearl Jam to Bruce Springsteen, Audioslave to Neil Young, AC/DC to Bob Dylan, Korn, and Limp Bizkit. I was working in the next room and bumped into him in the hallway. He was very nice and came over to me and said, "Kenny Aronoff? I've been using a sample of your snare drum for the past fifteen years when I mix on a lot of my records. Stone Temple Pilots records, Pearl Jam . . . It's got a frequency that really, really works—it's great for mixing." I thought, "Wow, how cool!" Then wondered to myself if that was something I should be getting a royalty for. Then I woke up and realized that will never happen. I told Brendan, "Thanks . . . I would love to record some music with you."

I've heard this a lot over the years—people sampling my sound, or using it to replace the sounds of other drummers, edited, put on a grid, quantized to sound like a drum machine. More times than not, this business makes no sense.

17

"R.O.C.K. in the U.S.A."

R.O.C.K. in the U.S.A." was one of the last songs we recorded for the album. John hated it—but ironically it became the biggest hit, reaching #2 on *Billboard*'s Hot 100 Singles chart. Originally he just wanted to add it as a "party song bonus" on the cassette and CD. He didn't think it fit well with the rest of the record.

> **Don Gehman:** *Scarecrow* as an album was definitely more highly produced than the first two albums John and I had made together, and seemed the next logical place to go, because we'd figured out how to capture our sound. I was always into more highly produced product. John had a pop side to him that I liked that he didn't, and I'd say *"R.O.C.K. in the U.S.A."* was a good example—we almost threw it away. I thought it was amazing and everyone in the band hated it. Eventually, we all agreed to put it on in the very end. There were others like that that were pop songs he didn't really want on his records. That's what gave him his credibility—the fact that he didn't do too much of that.

So he knew it was a hit, but the truth is: he *wasn't there in the studio* when we recorded it. You can actually hear me goofing around with a cowbell at the beginning of the song, and as the song built, I was again trying to start it off very simply and get the same kind of vibe as those old '60s hits John had had us study so hard before we'd begun recording the *Scarecrow* album.

This was—as the title spells out—a tribute to '60s rock, and the video we shot for the song demonstrated that louder than anything else, because we went for the total black-and-white 1960s *American Bandstand* TV show concept. When we shot the video, they put me up front and I dressed up with a beret, looking like a New York City early 1960s Beatnik drummer, and shook my head like my first drumming hero, Ringo Starr, when I was playing.

-◄o►-

Ahead of hitting the road in support of the *Scarecrow* album in '85, John told the band we would be acting as the backing band for the first Farm Aid benefit concert, which John had co-founded along with Willie Nelson and Neil Young. John had first come up with the concept for the concert in response to what he saw going on around his hometown in Indiana, where the family farm was being destroyed economically, and it really was a direct reflection of his extreme passion and attachment to the American farmer. Those were his real family members, so it wasn't just like some rock star jumping on the bandwagon. He really was the voice of that generation of people, and we were proud to be saluting them and working for them from the stage.

John sometimes liked to do surprise performances at a local cool club in Bloomington called the Bluebird with our band. In this case, after rehearsing at his studio for Farm Aid, we all drove into town and took over the stage at the Bluebird and surprised everyone with a killer performance. It worked great, and this was preceding the cell phone generation, so kids would be flipping out, running to the pay phones to call their friends to come down to the show. It was a different time—if you weren't there, you missed it. No camera phones, no YouTube. You had to be in on it, or else it was gone.

At that very first Farm Aid concert, in '85, we played in front of 80,000 people. Bob Dylan, Roy Orbison, and B. B. King played—genuine royalty—and John had us be the band supporting artists like Bonnie Raitt, John Fogerty, and Lou Reed.

The concert featured sets from Billy Joel, Tom Petty and the Heartbreakers, Bon Jovi, Foreigner, Sammy Hagar, Huey Lewis, and heroes of ours, including Johnny Cash, Lou Reed, Neil Young, and country music superstars like Willie Nelson, Loretta Lynn, Kris Kristofferson, Merle Haggard, Waylon Jennings, George Jones, Glen Campbell, Alabama—just on and on. It was a huge day for me—I have recorded and or performed with twenty-eight of the artists that played at Farm Aid that day. That was the show where Eddie Van Halen went onstage and announced to the crowd that Sammy Hagar was the new singer for Van Halen, and then the whole show's broadcast got knocked temporarily off television because Sammy said "shit" or something like that on live TV. Years later, when I was playing Farm Aid in Indianapolis with Iggy Pop, just as Dick Clark announced us, Iggy "accidently" kicked Dick in the ass and started swearing so much, the TV network took us off the air.

That concert was the first time I ever played with John Fogerty—who knew that it would lead to an entire chapter of my career? I ended up playing with Fogerty for twenty years (and still going strong)—the same John Fogerty whose face I used to roll joints on back in Massachusetts. Talk about surreal—and yet, it gets even weirder. That night we played "Fortunate Son," and a very pointed song called "Vanz Kant Dance," which you probably never heard of, but was a song about Fantasy Records head Saul Zaentz.

Saul and John had a long history of lawsuits and animosity, and John *hated* him and even wrote a *couple* songs about him—"Mr. Greed" and "Vanz Can't Dance."

During our set, when we played "Vanz Kant Dance," John actually had someone dancing across the stage with a humungous pig's head on. It was a total surprise to me, and I died laughing watching a pig head spin across the stage.

The song was originally called "Zanz Can't Dance" (*"Zanz can't dance but he'll steal your money"*), but Zaentz sued John (not the first time), and so John had to change the name—but he still wasn't pulling any punches. As I would find out, he is a very focused and driven guy.

◄○►

The momentum of releasing three consecutive hit albums with John (Mellencamp, that is) over a four-year period took us out of small venues and pushed us right into selling out large arenas across the USA, Canada, and Australia, and with *no opening act.*

American Fool, Uh-Huh, and now *Scarecrow,* not to mention songs from previous records, gave us enough material to do a three-hour show all by ourselves. Sometimes we sold tickets 360 degrees all around the arena, which meant there were as many as 2,000 people sitting behind us.

Our audiences never sat still when we played. John wouldn't let them! But by now, they didn't need his prodding. They were up dancing, rocking, and singing all our songs, spilling their drinks on each other, girls on guys' shoulders throwing bras and panties at us, flashing their tits and sometimes more. Up close, I was always engaging with the hot girls, but I also loved trying to connect with people standing way, way in the back. That's an old show-biz secret, playing to the back of the room. If you can reach the nose-bleed seats and the last row in the house, then you are doing it right.

We had an extra-long stage on this tour with all our smaller monitors hidden under the stage and our bigger monitors flown above, blasting down on us. The guitar amps were hidden behind a screen, which helped make the stage look super clean and large, and the stage was on a slight slant toward the audience, which gave it a cool visual effect.

What made everything even more exciting was that our songs were being played on the big hit radio stations everywhere in the USA and Canada at the same time. We were also all over TV, performing on all the important music shows, and our music videos were on heavy rotation on MTV all day and night. We weren't an oldies act, we were happening *right now,* and we had created all of it from scratch, from the Bunker and John's studio and this was our time. It was our music and we were the new, cool American band.

We played places like Madison Square Garden and the Forum in Los Angeles, and our peers and friends in the entertainment business would come to our shows. We used to see Sean Penn, Tom Cruise, Madonna, Martin Scorsese, Tom Petty, and on and on. . . . I remember one time, when we played Madison Square Garden, just as I was about to go onstage with a full house sold out 360 degrees, I saw four chairs on the side of the stage, which was basically on the stage. I asked my drum tech, Larry, who those chairs were for, and he said Phil Collins and family.

I couldn't help but think about Phil Collins being right there behind me the entire show. I never looked once at him. It was a bit intimidating. But after the show, my tech said Phil kept staring at John and then at me, back and forth, all night long. That made sense since Phil was both the drummer and the singer in Genesis. Well, a couple days afterward, the wardrobe girl, Spanky, came up to me and said, "Kenny, I'm going to tell you something that John probably won't tell you: I was in the dressing room when Phil was talking to John, and Phil said, 'You've got the best rock 'n' roll drummer in the business in your band right now.'"

I said, "Are you shitting me, he said that?" And she smiled and replied, "Yeah, that's what he said to John."

Obviously I loved that Phil said that, but honestly, I didn't feel that way at all. I always think I can play better. I am never satisfied. I always tell myself, "I will never be as great as I want to be, but I am willing to spend the rest of my life trying to be as great as I can be." I call that the human condition.

◄o►

We all traveled together on the same tour bus, with a lounge in the front and one in the back with stereos, TVs, and DVD players. Nowadays, most buses have Sony PlayStations, huge selections of movies, satellite cable TV, and Wi-Fi. We each had our own bunk bed with a TV, DVD player, light, air vent, and sometimes a small window. There was a bathroom, and the rule was you could only pee on the bus, which has always been the rule on any tour I've ever been on. We had a kitchen with a large fridge and microwave oven, so it was like our home away from home. John hated the bunks and hated being in the back lounge, so he always slept in the front lounge on the long bench-sofa so he could smoke and see where we were going. He was smoking three to four packs a day back then. Sometimes we flew in our own private jet, which was way cool. No airports, no terminals, no security lines, no waiting to board or waiting at baggage claim. We would drive right up to the plane, climb in, and be flying in ten minutes. I love that.

In the drum world, I had become one of the new guys on the scene. A band guy, in a famous rock 'n' and roll band. I was also starting to do sessions and a lot of drum clinics. I had already been featured as an up-and-coming drummer in *Modern Drummer* magazine back in 1982, and in 1986, I got my first of three covers in *Modern Drummer* magazine. I started winning or placing in the Top 5 in drum magazine polls, and that's been going on nonstop for twenty-eight years. In 1987, *Rolling Stone* magazine named me Drummer of the Year and, in 2016, named me one of the 100 Greatest Drummers of All Time. At one point I had won Best Pop Rock Drummer five years in a row in *Modern Drummer* magazine, and after that they decided to not let me be in that category anymore.

◄◇►

When the John Cougar tour ended in Japan, my wife, Lisa, and I spent a week in a temple, living with the Buddhist monks at the base of Mount Fuji. While there, we meditated and chanted every day with the monks. It was so peaceful and quite the opposite to the rock 'n' roll lifestyle I had been living. I was into practicing a form of Japanese Buddhism called Nichiren that focused on a daily ritual of chanting in the morning and the evening. It was a form of meditation that I found to be both very peaceful and exhilarating. It helped me focus my mind, and it gave me mental and physical energy. Eventually I fell out of practice—my life was still too rock 'n' roll crazy for me to be able to find the inner focus I really needed to stay balanced. But Lisa continued, and our son, Nik, eventually decided to practice also. Lisa is not only still practicing, but years later she helped bring eight Tibetan monks to Bloomington, Indiana, where they built a small temple in a house to practice their faith, give lectures and classes, sharing their knowledge with the community. Recently the monks completed building a brand-new, much larger structure that sits on top of a small mountain range overlooking thousands of acres, just outside of downtown Bloomington. Nik is very involved with studying and practicing Mahayana Buddhism with these monks. He has told me some amazing things he has learned practicing Buddhism, and it's obvious that I can learn a lot from him.

> **Nik Aronoff:** Around sixteen, I started studying Buddhism very seriously, and that was the impetus of changing not just my relationship with my dad, but how I related to everything, because how I viewed all that stuff changed. It started out as "I don't care about this. You don't care about me, why should I care about your schedule?" And it lost all of its flair and importance, and there was something very liberating about that because I started to strip down everything about me, about my dad, about the way I perceived reality and my relationship with him, and it became more about like, "Who are you, and who are we as father and son?" Because of that transition, today my relationship with him is probably the best it's ever been in our entire lives.

◄○►

After the *Scarecrow* tour and before we started working on our next record, *The Lonesome Jubilee*, I did drum clinics all over the USA and played in a cool local Bloomington band called the Raging Texans. I always had a local Bloomington band to play in. Around the *Uh-Huh* period, I played in a band called Kix, with music-school musicians that have since been very successful in NYC and LA, like trumpet virtuoso Chris Botti, and musicians who wound up playing in bands like Steely Dan, and with Branford Marsalis and the Leno show band. There are a lot of great musicians from Indiana.

The Raging Texans was a wild Texas swing and rockabilly band. We drank onstage, and sometimes I would jump onto the guitarist's back and ride him around as he soloed, which is no little feat. People loved it. Playing with the home team was such a blast that once when I was in London doing some live promo TV shows with Mellencamp, I took the first flight back to Indiana, just so I could play a set at the Bluebird.

This was a great time for doing drum clinics, too, because there were budgets to support these events—kids still wanted to be in *rock* bands. Computers had not yet taken over.

Things were going so well in 1986, I bought a bigger house on a private cul-de-sac that was closer to downtown Bloomington than where we had been living. My neighbors were doctors, successful businessmen, and Indiana University professors. I was the weirdo in the neighborhood, the rock star who woke up late, went to bed real late, and always had people visiting and partying at my house. They loved having me there, though. I could see the neighbors point my house out to their friends when they drove or walked by. "Do you know who lives there?" I'd like to think they said. "Kenny fucking Aronoff!" But more likely they said, "John Cougar Mellencamp's drummer!" But that was fine by me. I built a soundproof room and recording studio in part of the garage, where I could practice twenty-four hours a day.

> **Nik Aronoff:** With Dad, he was 100 percent immersed, living and breathing music, so as a young kid, I was around drums and music immediately, and in fact, can't remember a time when they weren't. He used to go to bed at four or five in the morning, and he'd be up at nine in the morning. He never really slept when I was a kid. I think that has something to do with the competitive nature of his business, but he's always been like that, and it certainly is one of his most admirable qualities. I mean, who can touch him?
>
> His studio really wasn't that big back then. He had one drum kit set up in there all the time, with some electronics and a bunch of spare gear and drums stacked up in cases, and had a hallway devoted to all his snares, and he had, like, a workshop where he'd do all his drum repairs, and to a little kid, whenever he'd get a new drum set in, he'd bring everything out into the living room and set stuff up there and try different things, and I wanted to be around him more than anything, so I was always around that.

John started writing songs for our next record as soon as the *Scarecrow* tour was over. We didn't know it yet, but *The Lonesome Jubilee* was going to be a very successful record. It would be our fourth consecutive hit record that would elevate us even higher in our popularity, with more hits and a new sound that would change John Mellencamp's sound forever.

> **John Mellencamp:** Once I heard the violin and the accordion playing a line together, I knew that was a sound that nobody'd really heard, and it was still in the vein of what we wanted to do. Guys had been doing it for years, but we were the first band that was able to bring it to the general public. Rod Stewart had used that combination of instruments, the Rolling Stones, a lot of people had used that combination of instruments, but they were almost novelty on their records, if you know what I mean. The record didn't consist of those sounds, and they never really used the sounds in the way that we used them.
>
> When we made the *Lonesome Jubilee*, I spent half the record arguing with Don, because Don kept saying, "What are you doing? Why do you want to put this stuff on here, John? You got a good thing going. Why are you changing it?" And if you notice, that's the last record Don and I did together. We were just so far away from where we thought we should be going musically that we made up other excuses to fight about it. With "Paper in Fire" specifically, at the time everybody was looking at me like I was crazy. I remember my road manager. I played him "Paper in Fire" when we were in a rough-mix stage, and he said, "What are you doing? That's terrible," and I still tease him about it today!

We reinvented ourselves again, but at the same time, we still sounded like us. Loud vocals, loud drums, simple guitar and bass parts, energy, power, dynamics, hook lines, memorable choruses, smarter lyrics, and radio-friendly songs.

John came up with a cool idea to prepare us for this new record. "I want you guys to all learn new instruments. Instruments you have never played before." John was searching for something new. He didn't know exactly what that was yet, but he knew he wanted something new and cool to add to what we already were doing. I had already played vibes, marimba, and glockenspiel on previous records, so I had to look for another instrument. I eventually picked the hammer dulcimer, and not the small one, but the big one with two bridges. It had fifteen groups of strings crossing the treble bridge and fourteen groups crossing the bass bridge, and the strings spanned three octaves. Each note had three strings tuned in unison.

I even had to take lessons—it was like learning a new language. I played the hammer dulcimer by hitting the strings with two delicate, light, thin sticks with a hammer on the end of them. The hammer kind of looked like half of the paddle part of a rowing oar. The hammer that hit the strings on the dulcimer either had hard felt on it, or no felt at all. I ended up playing the dulcimer on three songs when we recorded *The Lonesome Jubilee* album, including one of our hit singles called "Check It Out." I doubled the hook lines with the violin and accordion and played two-note chords during the verses.

John was experimenting with various combinations of our new instruments, and one day he had the idea to hear the hook line in "Check It Out" played with the accordion and violin together, and we all flipped out. John loved it so much, he started putting the accordion-and-violin combination on every song, until we figured out where and how to use those instruments in the most effective way on the record.

John had created a new sound for his music—it was an old sound, rooted in zydecco, cajun, and Appalachian music, but new for us—and we were very fortunate that we now had time to experiment in John's studio without record label people breathing down our backs telling us what to do. Finally, they knew well enough to back the fuck off and stay away from us because our success had made it very clear to them: Just let us do our thing—stay away and we will make you money.

18

Americana

*T*he *Lonesome Jubilee* was an even more mature effort for John as a song-writer than *Scarecrow*, from "Paper in Fire" to "Cherry Bomb" to "Check It Out" and on and on. For me as a drummer, that meant I had to keep coming up with new ideas, new beats, and new grooves for John's songs. John would always say, "It's up to you guys to come up with something new and unique."

"Paper in Fire" was a challenge for me at first, because the song started dynamically way down. At the same time, it still had to have some drive and momentum to it. So I played a simple 1-2-3-4 marching-type beat on my kick drum, creating a driving pulse, while I also played an accented eighth-note pattern on my hi-hat, making the entire beat percolate. This—along with cool stabs on the fiddle—created a great sense of suspense. I added this cool Stewart Copeland–ish three-against-four cross-stick pattern on my snare that added even more tension against the steady hi-hat and kick-drum patterns. This set up the first chorus perfectly.

That's where I came in with that exploding beat that drove the chorus hard, until I brought it back down again for the second intro and second verse. When we started recording that song, John told me not to play that cross-stick pattern at the top of the song, because he thought it was too busy. He said to save it for the end, and I thought, Why wait? That cross-stick part was unique—we had never used it on our records before. It grabbed your attention immediately, and at the same time, it was subtle. There was almost a jazz flavor to it. I strongly felt it had to be there right at the beginning. So when we went back out to record that song again, I stuck to my instincts and played that cross-stick pattern like I had been doing. I remember while I was playing, I had a feeling John was going to stop me at any moment, but he never did.

Don Was: You can hear Kenny in any Americana record. Listen to an album like *Lonesome Jubilee*. This kind of Americana music—with fiddles and acoustic guitars—Kenny fused it with rock 'n' roll. You can look at the Band and Levon Helm, who played some of the most amazing stuff of all time—he played almost like a jazz drummer—he kind of skipped through the songs with the kind of swing that he had. Kenny brought a different kind of rock 'n' roll energy to that sound.

Stephen Perkins (Drummer for Jane's Addiction): I think it was a perfect marriage: the songwriting of Mellencamp back in the day, which was historic because it did grab you by heart and had some of that bluegrass at heart, real country-western bluegrass, where the story matters and the music is just the pillow. The story is what you're thinking about, so there you had a storyteller as a songwriter, who had to have a storyteller as a drummer—and Kenny tells a story with his parts.

"Paper in Fire" was a good representation of the deeper level of songwriting and arranging we were getting into. It was a lot different than "I Need a Lover" or "Hurts So Good."

John had always respected songwriters like Woody Guthrie, Hank Williams Sr., and Bob Dylan. He had his sights set on trying to be a rock star, but also wanted the credibility these artists had as songwriters. John related to the hardworking underdog that was portrayed in the movies that he was always watching, classics like *The Grapes of Wrath* with Henry Fonda, or *Hud* with Paul Newman, or *On the Waterfront* with Marlon Brando, and he especially related to what the American family farmer was going through across the US. This was a deep part of who John was, and I think these new instruments had the sounds of what he was feeling in his soul as the voice for those small, struggling family farmers. We were experimenting with a kind of fusion of rural Americana and with a rock sound that hadn't been heard on Top 40 radio stations up to that point.

It was an exciting time for us creatively in the studio—we knew we were on to something new and cool—but not everyone understood what we were doing, at least not at first. We still rocked as hard as ever, but we sprinkled all these new sounds on top of what we already did. It was all getting very rootsy, but without changing the foundation of our sound too much, knowing that we could risk losing our fans. I have seen that happen many times with bands or artists—it's a challenge because to stay successful and hopefully become more successful, you want to keep your existing fans while grabbing new fans with each new record. But it's a delicate situation. Fans can be stubborn and fickle and unforgiving, and the industry is even worse. One misstep trying to grow creatively, and you can grow yourself right out of a career.

◄○►

To prep for our upcoming tour and the release of *The Lonesome Jubilee* in 1987, we shot three videos in Savannah, Georgia. John was into using film when we made our videos, which made everything look warmer and more real. In the "Cherry Bomb" video, John sang and danced next to a jukebox in a bar, while a black man and a white woman danced real close together in front of him. While we were on tour and the video was in heavy rotation on MTV, we actually got a threatening letter from the KKK demanding we stop playing that video! That didn't stop John or MTV from playing the video, and in the end no one bothered us. We knew we were pushing boundaries with that video, but we loved that the public was embracing a bold statement of unity.

The Lonesome Jubilee quickly went double-platinum. The new formula worked so well that we added four more singles—"Paper in Fire," "Check It Out," "Rooty Toot Toot," and "Cherry Bomb"—to our existing arsenal of hits packed into our three-hour show. Highlights from that set list included staples like "Hurts So Good," "Jack and Diane," "Hand to Hold On

To," "Pink Houses (Ain't That America)," "Crumblin' Down," "Authority Song," "I Need a Lover," "Ain't Even Done with the Night," "Rain on the Scarecrow," "Small Town," "Lonely Ol' Night," and of course, "R.O.C.K. in the U.S.A."

◄○►

I was loving life. I could not have been happier. My childhood dream to be a drummer in a famous rock 'n' roll band had come true—and it was just the beginning. But I was paying a hefty price for it, namely my marriage.

There was no sense of balance in my life. It was all career, all rock 'n' roll all the time, and it was very obvious to my wife, Lisa, what came first. That had to be frustrating—it wasn't a great situation for her at all, but that's who I was, and back then there was no way I was going to compromise, or slow down, for anyone or anything. It just wasn't in me.

I was never home. At one point on the *Scarecrow* tour, we were on the road for eight weeks straight, took one week off, and then went back on the road again for another seven consecutive weeks. It was nonstop. In the meanwhile, Lisa was raising our new baby, Nik, working as a full-time lawyer, and running the entire house all by herself, which was crazy. In her eyes, I was having the time of my life while she was back home trying to hold everything together.

You've heard the story a million times, I don't have to bore you, but when you try to live both lifestyles at the same time, like I was doing it, there's a good chance both those worlds will collide, and they eventually did for me. I was acting like a teenager living in a rock 'n' roll dream world: private jets, cool tour buses, the biggest venues sold out in all the big cities, staying at the Four Seasons and Ritz Carlton hotels . . . there was too much fun to be had. You can imagine the details—and then throw on more sex, more partying, and more wanton idiocy, because it was all there for the taking. It was every man's dream.

I didn't want to mention any of this stuff because I don't want to be a cliché, and because I am not living my life like that anymore. When it came to my marriage, I wasn't an honorable guy. But if I said I wasn't having the time of my life, I'd be lying. That's where I was, and I am where I am today because of what I learned from all of those experiences, and maybe just a little bit in spite of it all. It also means I don't get to be judgmental. All I can do is try to be a better person.

I realize now that if you have your shit together, mentally, physically, emotionally, and are truthful and honest to all the people in your life, it will make *everything* in your life better. It's living your life at a higher and better place. Once I figured that out, I never went back to where I was.

For all the good times I was having, this was all very painful, the worst emotional experience of my life. It sucked for everyone involved. Nik was only three years old. I remember my lawyer trying to reassure me at the time, "Trust me, it will get better." He was eventually right, but when he initially said that to me, those were just words coming out of his mouth. They didn't help me, Nik, or Lisa with our emotional pain.

Nik Aronoff: When he was home off tour, he would take me places and we would do things together, and he was trying to make an effort to set aside some time, and we always played sports outside together.

When it came time for Christmas and stuff, he was always there and I loved it. It was my favorite time of year because he'd be there, and I didn't have to be in school for two weeks, and he'd spoil me. It got to a point where I remember every year he'd give me pretty much whatever I asked for within reason, and more.

But his schedule was so weird. More often than not, if he said he was going to come home on this day, everything would change, so I'd be like, "Oh, Dad's coming home this weekend," and no, he couldn't come home. Anybody that meets my dad knows there's something very magnetic about him, and he's very charismatic, and he draws you in, and you want to be around him, and as a kid, you want to hug him and hang out with him and push him and wrestle him and laugh and do all this stuff, and so there was nothing I wanted to do more than be around him. Even when I'd see him every day, there's a lot of that, but then when I wouldn't see

him and he'd suddenly be home, it was ten times more extreme. I wanted
to be around him all the time, but that's just not how it went.

It broke my heart, but of course the show must go on. And I still had to
provide for Lisa and Nik. At least I still had a job, and a good one.

The John Cougar Mellencamp band (it would be another four years
before he finally was able to drop that stupid Cougar business) was huge
around the world. We toured for the next six months solid from October 1987 through July 3, 1988, and our shows were sold out everywhere
throughout the USA and Canada. In some cities, we would play two sold-
out arena shows in a row, and in Indianapolis, we were able to play four
sold-out shows in a row! In Sydney, Australia, demand was just as wild that
we did five shows in a row, and in Melbourne, four shows in a row performing in 15,000–20,000-seat arenas. The whole thing was like *A Hard Day's
Night*. There were rabid fans waiting for autographs wherever we went. In
Japan, the fans somehow knew our travel schedules and were at every train
station we arrived at, waiting to meet us. Life was truly amazing, and it
made me feel like I was finally in the Beatles.

19

The Best John Mellencamp Band Drummer in the World

When our tour finally ended, John completely surprised us with some very generous bonus checks. But they came with some bad news.

The Mellencamp band performed our last *Lonesome Jubilee* concert in Milwaukee, on July 3, 1988. It was immediately after that show that John announced he was taking three years off and threw the end-of-tour bonus check at me.

I couldn't believe he said that. I was just about to celebrate the end of another great tour and, *bam,* now I was trying to digest the concept of being unemployed.

John made the lion's share of the money because he had the record deal and was also the songwriter, while all of us in the band were on salary and worked for him. So despite the millions of albums we'd sold as a band and the countless sold-out arena tours we'd played over the past eight years, I was far from financially set, and I had just gotten a divorce.

I was in a tailspin: That very night back at my hotel, I quickly began calculating that I had enough money saved to cover my expenses for the next five months, which told me I had to get my wheels spinning fast. For starters, now that I was a bachelor, I immediately rented two rooms in my house to two drummers attending Indiana University to help cover my monthly mortgage.

◄○►

Most drummers are only as successful as the bands they play in.

If you're a drummer, you can't really go out as a solo act. You can't set up your kit in a night club and expect people to want to see you play a forty-five-minute set of just drums, no matter how good you are. Drummers need context. Somehow the best ones found it—Bonham got his Zeppelin, Elvin Jones hooked up with Coltrane, Keith Moon landed in the Who . . . what would any of them have been able to accomplish without each other? You could say that John, Paul, and George had enough talent, that they could have done it with another drummer, but I don't believe it. And even Mick Jagger has said that Charlie Watts is the only guy in the band they can't replace.

I don't care how good a drummer you are. If you want to have a career, you need the right collaborators. Without Neil Peart, where would Rush be? And he writes the lyrics, too! But that sword cuts both ways—where would Neil have landed without Rush? And that's why my goal for the last eight years wasn't to be *the best drummer in the world*, it was to be *the best John Mellencamp band drummer in the world*.

I wasn't there to impress other drummers. I was there to make the artist or band sound great. To make hits: being on the radio with a big beat was a lot more important than proving I could play triple-flam-a-diddles and a one-hand press roll like Buddy Rich. Which is not a bad thing, but that's not what gets anyone gigs. Beat, time, and groove are what counts. The beat, *and the song*. There are a few prog-rock bands fortunate enough to have survived—Rush and Yes, but Yes had to go pop to do it.

A great thing about playing with John is that I was very visible with him—all that TV exposure, the videos, plus stuff in the music press—I was getting a lot of attention, which opened lots of other opportunities. I didn't become the Billy Cobham–style drummer I had dreamed of and had made my mark playing simpler, a less-is-more style, and suddenly I was very much in demand as a session drummer.

My first non-Mellencamp #1 single was with former Go-Go's singer Belinda Carlisle's "Heaven Is a Place on Earth," from her *Heaven on Earth* album, which I played on shortly after we had finished *The Lonesome Jubilee*.

I didn't realize it then, but this was the beginning of the third phase of my life. When John said, "I'm going to quit the music business for three years," at first, it felt like my glass was suddenly half empty, but I was *wrong.* Years later, I realized my glass is *never* half empty. It's always full. *Always.*

I had no choice but to create a new source of income outside the Mellencamp band, and after the hit with Belinda, figured I could probably get more sessions booked once people knew that I was available.

I was starting a John Eddie record in Mellencamp's studio two days after our tour ended, but I had nothing else booked beyond that.

What a lot of people don't realize is how many talented people there are who never make it, or almost make it, or come really close and still don't make it—making it, meaning having radio hits, selling out venues, establishing some sort of sustainable career.

Of course it can't all be like John Mellencamp or Bruce Springsteen, but take a guy like John Eddie: great songwriter, was signed to Columbia Records, and then Elektra, actually had the guys from Bruce Springsteen's band play on his first record, did tours with Bob Seger and the Kinks, has had three of his songs covered by Kid Rock, and has had a few hits of his own. People would die for a career like that, but he still felt like he had to put out a record called *Who the Hell Is John Eddie?* He never became a household name. Great talent, but always fighting to break through. It is such a tough racket; you see a guy like that and you can understand why Mellencamp was so fucking *driven.*

We rehearsed and recorded John Eddie's record for three weeks straight, which was amazing because with today's recording budgets, we would never be in the studio for anywhere near that amount of time. It would have cost way too much money. Today, it's not unusual for me to record ten or twelve drum tracks in *two days*—when you get to the studio you are expected to start recording, not to start working stuff out. It seems like every year the artist and the bottom line become more and more inseparable.

Throughout the making of John Eddie's album, every minute I wasn't sitting behind the drum kit, I was on my phone, letting producers and managers know I was available and ready to work, trying to book more sessions and live gigs.

I didn't mind taking red-eyes between LA, NYC, and Indiana working seven days and seven nights a week. I hated saying no to any job and did everything I could to make everything fit into my busy schedule. No one was handing me anything. I was going after all of this work very aggressively.

A vision was quickly developing for expanding my Kenny Aronoff brand outside of the John Mellencamp band. Eventually this created a lot of tension between me and John, because he thought I was going off the reservation, but for now it was working fine, and I was enjoying every minute of it. What it comes down to is I love playing the drums, and if you can get a gig doing what you love, that is what I call "making it."

I'd actually started doing session work outside of the John Mellencamp band in 1986 when I worked on Brian Setzer's record *The Knife Feels Like Justice.*

Making Brian's record was so much fun because it felt like we were creating something new—it was his first solo record after he left the Stray Cats, and I'm laughing now, because could you imagine Brian's reaction if I showed up to make a *rockabilly* record with that crazy double-bass-drum prog-rock kit I brought to the Mellencamp audition?

Brian and I were both working outside of the bands that we were known for, so we were extra-pumped to make this record sound amazing and be successful. You know, anytime you get out of the box, you are taking a risk. It seems counterintuitive, but like I've said before, this isn't a business that necessarily rewards creativity.

Two days after I finished John Eddie's record, I flew to LA and started working on a Greg Alexander record with producer and songwriter Rick Nowels, two more guys who aren't as famous as John Mellencamp but have written tons of hit songs, have Grammy Awards, have had their stuff in films, you name it. You would know their work if you heard it, even if their names by themselves don't conjure images of sold-out arenas. There are a lot of folks like that—men and women who aren't known by the casual music fan but are stars within the industry.

I met a lot of people in the studios I was working in. I was recording at studios like A&M, the Record Plant, Capitol, the Music Grinder, Ocean Way, Cello, Sunset Sound, NRG, the Village, One on One, O'Henry's,

Rumbo, or Conway (to name a few), and I would always run into other musicians, artists, producers, engineers, managers, or record company people in the hallways because they were there working in one of the other rooms. We would all hang out, and many times, they would ask me to play on the record they were working on right there on the spot, or hire me to play on some other future project. I could be recording in Studio B at A&M, and in Studio A U2 was recording, while Don Henley was off-tracking in Studio D, with Mötley Crüe back in the mixing room. That was very common back then. Seemed like everyone was working. (Amazingly, I recorded a song with Korn that almost ended up on their record. They were in the same studio I was recording in with Joe Cocker. I stopped by to say hi, and producer Steve Thompson immediately asked me to play drums. Everyone in Korn switched instruments for a jam, and bam!)

I found myself moving from a panicked place to a great one. Everyone had their own unique style and sound, and now the challenge for me was to somehow fit into their style of music. Today, I look at sessions as if I am an actor in a movie. I figure out what my character is, or what my musical role is in the song, and then everything I play comes from the personality of that character in that song. I can't stop being Kenny Aronoff, but I can definitely be *the best Kenny Aronoff for whatever the job is.* My job is to serve the song and the vision of the artist and the producer who is hiring me. That's the secret of being a good session guy. I get hired because they want *me*, but it is always their song, their record, their vision. It's important for a session drummer to remember: Listen, learn, lead, but understand that you are not the boss.

Out in LA, the club and bar scene was just as great for meeting people. Everyone was checking out new artists and bands that were hustling to get signed. There was no Internet, so people had to get out and be seen. There were many more live clubs and places to go to make connections in the music business than there are now, and everywhere I went I was hooking up with people, and this led to more and more work. The LA music scene in the studios and around town was like a beehive with everyone buzzing around hustling, talking, and making deals. It was an exciting time in the music business.

I knew I had to act on the success of the Mellencamp band and my current reputation *immediately*, because we were still relevant, and more importantly, I was relevant, and I knew that could change real fast. In the music business you can be popular one day and invisible the next. You're only as good as your last success.

◄○►

After an improbable romance, my new girlfriend, Liz, had moved in with me at my place in Bloomington.

I met her for the first time, literally, onstage at Madison Square Garden, when we were there for the *Scarecrow* tour.

She was a huge Mellencamp fan. She and her girlfriend Tracy had seats way in the back of the arena, but by the end of the show they had managed to move up front, and got there just about the time John would pick a girl out of the audience to come onstage and dance with him while we played "Under the Boardwalk." She just wanted a picture with John, dancing. That was her ultimate souvenir.

I didn't see her after the show, but she was there two shows later in New Jersey—she was an accountant and very methodical, and she was determined to get that picture.

Someone on our crew saw her during the show and slapped a backstage pass on her, and when I got backstage, that's when I met her. She was very cool, very sexy, and we had a late dinner at a greasy spoon diner near the arena. Nothing happened that night, but I really liked her. Two weeks later, I called her from a hotel in Peoria, Illinois, just to talk.

Ten months later, I had a gig in New York and wanted to see her, but like an idiot I had lost her number. I called the hotel in Peoria where I had made the call from, and they found the phone records from my room for me—on microfilm! It was a good thing the woman on the phone was a Mellencamp fan. She was definitely breaking some rules doing that kind of NSA investigation.

I ended up talking to Liz's sister, who put us in touch, and then it all happened. Eventually Liz moved to Indiana, and we lived together for a long time before we made it official. She also took over running my office and was a great business manager, really helping me hold all of this chaos together. From the Mellencamp stage at Madison Square Garden to being married to the drummer fifteen years after I met her. Crazy.

—◦—

While I was recording with Gregg Alexander at A&M Studios, I got a call out of the blue from John Mellencamp—I sure as hell wasn't expecting to hear from him for a while, like three more years, but he had written a bunch of new songs and wanted to start a new record.

It had been only six weeks since he had told us he was quitting for three years. I think when *The Lonesome Jubilee* tour ended, he needed to say to everyone, including himself, "I am done, I'm quitting the music business," because he was fried. He needed a break, and emotionally I think he wanted to feel that he could quit for a while.

Maybe just thinking he could walk away was enough? John's life was way more stressful and complex than mine was: he wasn't just performing while we were on tour; he was involved with all the day-to-day, moment-to-moment business aspects of his career. This meant he was working non-stop around the clock, twenty-four hours a day. Back then, we were all strong-minded, emotional, and intense guys, but especially John, so when he said, "I quit," I believed him. He was deadly serious. But I should have known there was no way he was going to quit the music business for three years, not being as prolific a songwriter as he was. He was like an addict with his music. The best ones always are.

This new batch of songs became the *Big Daddy* record, which was a huge departure from anything we had ever recorded before. It was way more serious, darker, quieter, and intimate, except for one song that was a radio-friendly rock song called "Pop Singer," which was about John not wanting to be a pop singer or a rock star.

Go figure.

I think he wanted to be taken more seriously as an artist and as a legitimate songwriter and didn't want to be just a pop star anymore. Technically, I played much more quietly on this record to help complement the intimate quality of John's songs. I played a lot of unique and musical percussion parts on this record. Sometimes, I considered the percussion to be the lead part, and the drums to be the background—I reversed the roll of the drums and the percussion on some of the songs and enjoyed the challenge, was genuinely excited with the new approach.

After a week recording *Big Daddy*, I was right back in LA again for two weeks with Greg Alexander, then took a red-eye to the Midwest for a two-week drum-clinic tour, and then flew back to Indiana to record for two more weeks with John Mellencamp. I had one week off, and *bam!* I got a call from Gary Stamler, the manager of British singer-songwriter and virtuoso guitarist Richard Thompson. His drummer, Dave Mattocks, had fallen and broke a few ribs, so Gary called me and wanted to know if I could fill in for the last three weeks of Richard's tour. The crazy thing was the Mellencamp band had been playing Richard's song "Shoot Out the Lights" on a previous tour, so I was already a huge fan and familiar with Richard's music.

My first show with Richard was in a 600-seat club in Bloomington that I had been playing at for many years. I had less than a week to scramble and write out charts, which really helps me in situations like this—our first sound check was my only rehearsal.

Super-detailed charts have been a huge factor in making it possible for me to take on tons of work, far more than I would have been able to do if I could not read or write music. When I am working on three records more or less at the same time, or gigging all over the place, there is no way I can memorize it all. I have to write it down. And I do it in far greater detail than you could imagine. My charts show every cymbal crash, tom fill, kick, snare, hi-hat, and ride cymbal part all written out. They show dynamics, open or closed hi-hats, who to look at for cues, who to cue for endings, who to count off to when we start the song, tempos, and whatever else I feel is necessary to make me play consistently and sound as perfect as possible. I also have cues on my charts as I am reading them, telling me what song is coming next, the beat, the feel, the tempo, and who to count off to. In some situations—like the Kennedy Center Honors concerts—we only have three rehearsals, and I am constantly rewriting my charts, making changes that I have to remember. There is no way anyone can do a show like that if they can't read or write music. This has always been a huge key to my ability to work so much and probably a secret weapon of my success—there are so many times when I am on an airplane writing out very detailed charts for a recording session or a live show that I have to perform immediately after I land. Being able to write charts definitely helped me with Richard's music because it has lots of twists and clever odd-measure phrases in it.

We toured the Midwest and East Coast in a big white van doing clubs and theaters, which was a big change from what I was used to, touring in private jets, traveling in fancy tour buses, and performing in sold-out arenas. But it didn't matter, because Richard's music and the quality and vibe of his band was so positive and fun. Two days after that tour ended, I flew back to LA and recorded a Seth Marsh record at A&M Studios for eight days before taking a red-eye back to Indiana to continue recording with John Mellencamp. Seth might be another guy who doesn't immediately ring any bells, but back then someone was paying for him to record at A&M, and I was making more money recording for two days than what I was getting each month from the retainer John Mellencamp was paying me.

◄○►

I remember the date was December 2: I was home taking a shower, thinking how fortunate I was to have worked so much that year, feeling very much that in spite of everything, my glass was very fucking full. I had made the leap from being a guy in a band to being a solid session drummer. John calling it a day had actually created possibilities. Life was good.

I was thinking, hey, it's Christmas, and I was probably not going to get any more work for the rest of the year since the music business slows down two weeks before the holidays, but while I was in the shower, the phone rang. It was Sammy Llanas from the BoDeans on the other end. He said in his rough James Brown kind of voice, "Heeeey, Kenny, it's Sammy from the BoDeans, what are you doing *right now?*" He then proceeded to ask me if I was available to record some songs up in Milwaukee in a few days. I love getting calls like that.

That was the beginning of an amazing relationship that is still going on after twenty-five years, making records and playing live shows with the BoDeans. Sammy left the band years later, but songwriter-singer-lead guitarist Kurt Neumann is still rocking and leading the band, and I still love working with him.

The record we recorded was called *Home*, with super-badass engineer-producer Jim Scott (who has worked with Tom Petty, Rolling Stones, Red Hot Chili Peppers, Sting, and the Dixie Chicks). We recorded in an old eight-story brewery that had been vacated, a real corpse of a building. The BoDeans rented a big room on the eighth floor with exposed wood and brick everywhere. Jim ran cables out the window down to a Ryder truck that was parked on the street with a mobile recording studio in the back. We had cameras on us so Jim and Mark, the BoDeans' manager, could see us from the truck, and they had a mic in the truck to communicate with us.

That makeshift studio had a great vibe, totally on the edge of civilization. Very industrial. And it was freezing fucking cold—like nine degrees below zero. Serious Wisconsin cold. One very late night, as we were leaving the studio, we heard dogs running down the hall and they were heading our way. Someone's guard dogs had gotten loose—a mean-looking Doberman and a German shepherd—and were now biting at our heels as we took off back to our room. We barely made it back. It was like out of a movie. The only way out was opening up a window and somehow making our way down eight stories to the street and trying not to freeze to death. We felt like criminals at our own session. It was a great way to end the year.

But all of this—the sessions, the BoDeans, the clinics—were just the beginning of my new plan. The year 1989 was about to explode, and a lot of that had to do with meeting one of the coolest guys in the whole damn business, Mr. Don Was.

20

Welcome to Sessionland!

The New Year of 1989 started out strong for me, with recording sessions in January with John Eddie in New York City, and then in Los Angeles with Marshall Crenshaw, a fantastic session with producer-engineer Ed Stasium (Living Colour, Talking Heads, the Ramones, Motörhead, and the Smithereens). While I was out in California, I wound up playing on two songs from *March,* the debut album from Michael Penn.

It was a unique session because the album's producer, Tony Berg, also had the legendary session drummer Jim Keltner playing drums on one of the songs I was on ("Evenfall"), because basically he couldn't decide which one of us should play. I wasn't sure what Tony was going to do with both drum tracks, but when they mixed the record, he just put me in the left speaker and Jim in the right. It was a really cool effect. I remember Jim and I really listened to each other when we were recording that song, and the end result sounded like one big drum section with different fills and accents popping out of each speaker at different times.

I stayed busy that spring, recording both with John Mellencamp (so much for retirement) and James McMurtry in Bloomington, and out in LA with Belinda Carlisle, the Jefferson Airplane, Bruce Henderson, Corey Hart, and Sue Medley, to name a few. In April, we did *Saturday Night Live* for the fourth and final time with Mellencamp. (Years later, I got to do *Saturday Night Live* with the Smashing Pumpkins, and another time with Willie Nelson and Paul Simon performing together.)

I remember Executive Producer Lorne Michaels and the cast were furious with the Mellencamp band because John refused to come out onstage with the cast at the end of the show, when the credits rolled while the host said thanks to the audience, which was the tradition for all musical guests. I have no idea what went wrong, but John was pissed about something. He was yelling at our tour manager, Harry Sandler, that he wasn't going out, and Harry asked John what about the band. John said, "No one goes out. Fuck them," meaning the *SNL* people.

The next day at the airport, I ran into some of the guys from the *SNL* band, and they said everyone at the show was offended when John didn't come out at the end of the show. They couldn't understand it. Things like this happened often in John's band.

I got a call to record with the original Jefferson Airplane (Grace Slick, Marty Balin, Paul Kantner, Jorma Kaukonen, and Jack Casady), and I was very excited because I was a super fan of the original Airplane when I was fourteen. I used to listen to their first album, *Surrealistic Pillow*, all the time, and radio played their hit songs "Somebody to Love," "White Rabbit," "She Has Funny Cars," and "Today" all the time. I eventually saw them play all those cool hits with the famous Joshua Light Show at an outdoor venue near my house at Tanglewood. They represented the hippie movement coming out of San Francisco: peace and love, acid and freedom, and they were at Woodstock, which was just a couple hours away from Stockbridge. I still regret I didn't go—I was planning on it, but my mom wouldn't let me because the girl who was going to drive was pretty reckless. Everyone was back then. Of course we had no idea that it was going to be the most historic rock 'n' roll event of the era.

We rehearsed and recorded the album in LA at the Record Plant. I remember Paul Kantner's weed was so good and strong that whenever he left, people fought over the roaches in the ashtray.

The engineer-producer was Ron Nevison (Led Zeppelin, the Who, Bad Company, Meat Loaf, Ozzy Osbourne, KISS, and Heart, to name a few). He is a very focused, intelligent, and intense man, and I learned the hard way to stay away from Ron when he was working. I pulled up a chair and slid next to him when he was doing something at the mixing board, just like I always did in Mellencamp's studio. He slapped my hand real hard when I touched the edge of the mixing board, and I slid back and never got near him again. After we made the record, the Airplane asked me to tour with them.

There was so much pot smoking at their concerts that it always rolled up onto the stage like a thick fog, and you couldn't avoid getting some contact high, which I hated. I can't play drums stoned—it makes my muscles weak, and I get spaced out. Pot always turned me into a vegetable. When I'm stoned, I can't get anything done except eat food and watch TV.

Playing with the Airplane was like some teenage fantasy, and thankfully there was no conflict with the Mellencamp schedule, so I was able to tour with the Airplane across America. We performed our last show at the famous Fillmore West in San Francisco with the Joshua Light Show, and it was like I was reliving the '60s—honestly, I pretended we were at Woodstock. It wasn't that big a leap if you saw their audience.

We did one final performance in Washington, DC, with one of the most famous promoters in the music business, Bill Graham. It was a concert for the homeless, and was a classic American '60s-type march to DC, and the kind of protest that the Jefferson Airplane loved to be part of. We were supposed to continue touring at some point after that, but it never happened because the managers and lawyers representing each member of the band could never decide on anything unanimously. So much for the hippie dream.

◄○►

Heading into my first meeting with Don Was, let me say I am very fortunate that he is beyond any fucking doubt the mellowest and the coolest dude in the entire music business.

Don had called me one day unexpectedly and said in his low, FM DJ voice, "Hey, Kenny, it's Don Was. So I'm doing this Iggy Pop record and I'd love for you to play on it." Don told me they probably wouldn't begin recording until February, but to come down to the Record Plant to meet and talk more about the record.

When I walked into the Record Plant, someone at the front desk said Don was in the kitchen lounge area. At that point, I had never met Don in person and didn't know what he looked like.

> **Don Was:** Kenny happened to be in LA, and we arranged to meet, and he came over to the Record Plant, where I was working on something, and at that time, there happened to be this kitchen-cafeteria I was sitting in when he first walked in. I was all excited to meet him, and we were talking for ten, fifteen minutes, and finally he says, "When is Don Was getting here?" He had seen all those videos with my band Was (Not Was), and thought I was *the singer*.

I felt so fucking stupid. I just assumed Don was the suave black guy singing in the videos—that's who I was looking for. This guy was barefoot, had sunglasses on, and wore a headband with his Jewfro popping out of it like a psychedelic mushroom. It couldn't possibly have been *him*. So much for research. But Don just laughed it off. Don is one of the kindest people I have ever met or worked with: he's truly musical, an incredible musician and badass producer, a great leader, very bright, and very wise about people and life in general.

Once we got past the introductions, he explained that Iggy wanted to meet with me to make sure I had the right energy and personality for him before we started recording. So I went to Don's house in Laurel Canyon a few weeks later and met Iggy. We talked about playing percussion and timpani when we were younger—he had started off as a drummer—and we got along great. He liked me, so I was now going to play on his *Brick by Brick* album in the spring. Sessions would start in a few weeks.

Word started to get around town that I could play anything stylistically, from heavy rock to Top 40 to B. B. King rhythm and blues, to Johnny Cash and country, to Alice Cooper and Elton John. And because of the budgets in those days, record labels could afford to fly me all over the world to make records.

No matter how many sessions I did, though, I always knew I was going to return to Bloomington, Indiana, to make records and tour with John Mellencamp. I liked being part of a band, a gang of musicians that everyone knew. John definitely ran that band with a Machiavellian approach. At times, he ruled with fear, but because our popularity kept getting bigger and bigger, from album sales to concert crowds, it seemed impossible to walk away from. Plus, for me personally, my signature on his sound was getting stronger and stronger with each album. I also felt like I'd invested so much of my blood, sweat, and tears creatively into those records that I was a part of them, and I wanted to keep performing those songs live. Most of all, I loved being in a *band*. We were a gang of guys, and everyone had a face and personality fans could recognize. We were not invisible sidemen.

I was offered to tour or join other bands, but I wouldn't accept the offers if it meant leaving the John Mellencamp band on a permanent basis. I was asked in the early 1990s to go on tour with Elton John, and I turned it down because it conflicted too much with the Mellencamp schedule. I remember Bernie Taupin came to the LA Forum where we were performing to a sold-out crowd, and he took me aside before our show and said, "I can't believe you turned down *Elton John*."

My stomach turns even as I write this, at the thought that I actually said no to Elton John. It was like saying no to Don Corleone. I remember telling Bernie at that time, "Man . . . I am so sorry, I would love to tour with Elton, but I would have to leave this band to do it. Just look at where we are: at the LA Forum. Two nights, totally sold out, with no opening act, just us. This is the band I've been working with for thirteen years. These songs, my beats, mean so much to me, because I was involved with creating them from the ground up. Whenever I play the drum solo in 'Jack and Diane,' the entire crowd air-drums with me!"

I wish I could have toured with him and stayed in Mellencamp's band, but I couldn't be in two places at the same time. I still remember the pay phone in the Four Seasons Hotel in Toronto, Canada, that I used when I called Elton John's management. I fumbled putting the coins in. I couldn't believe I was going to say no to Elton fucking John to stay with John fucking Mellencamp. I actually stuttered when I made the call: "N-n-n-no, I won't be able to tour with," heavy sigh, "Elton John . . . at this time." Gulp.

Even Mellencamp looked surprised when I told him what I had done.

21

Bob Dylan, Iggy Pop, and Me

When Don Was called me, I thought he was going to talk about the Iggy Pop album, which we were going to start recording in February, but instead, he asked me if I was available to start working on a Bob Dylan record, what would become *Under the Red Sky*.

This was a real "holy shit" moment. Not that Iggy Pop wasn't impressive, but I had been listening to Bob Dylan since I was twelve years old.

Because of Dylan's busy touring schedule, I did the basic tracks on four separate days over four months. Don used a different band for every session, except he had me play on all four sessions, which I thought was super cool.

The first session included Stevie Ray Vaughan, Jimmie Vaughan, David Lindley (Warren Zevon, Jackson Browne), and me, plus Jamie Muhoberac (Fleetwood Mac, the Rolling Stones, Rod Stewart) on keys and Don Was on bass. I had an especially great time hanging out with Stevie Ray Vaughan. We talked about him being totally sober, and how much he loved music and how great his life was going. He was a real happy man at that time.

When Bob Dylan introduced himself to me for the first time, he surprised me by tapping on my shoulder. I didn't know it was him until I turned around. He shook my hand and spoke the only words he'd say to me for the entire project: "Hey, Kenny, Bob Dylan, nice to meet you." Then he went into the studio and started playing the piano. That was it.

As soon as Bob started playing, I immediately jumped onto my kit and started playing along with him. The rest of the musicians came running in from the lounge after they heard us jamming. Somebody in the control room was smart enough to roll the tape and hit record. In many cases, those jams became the final take for the record. I had this intuition from the very start: "This guy is not going to go for a lot of takes, and I have to keep him inspired or he's going to bail!" So I kept my eye on him, and any time he went out into the live room and picked up an instrument, I'd start playing along with him. One session, Bob was in a small vocal booth they had constructed in the big room, right in front of me, facing my drums. He wore a baseball hat with a hooded sweatshirt over his hat and head, dark sunglasses covered his face, and he had huge motorcycle gloves on. He looked *dangerous.*

Bob had a total vibe going—he can be a very ominous presence—and I never saw him talk to anyone but Don. I felt like he was in his own world and I didn't want to bother him in any way, so I just played the drums. I always say that communication skills are a big part of your business, right up there with how well you play your instrument. And that also means knowing when not to talk. Later, though, when I'd run into him, at Farm Aid, for instance, he was like a different guy, very friendly.

On the second session, the band was Waddy Wachtel on guitar, Al Kooper on organ, Don Was on bass, and me on drums, and rock royalty just kept on coming: the third session was Bruce Hornsby on piano, Robben Ford on guitar, Randy Jackson on bass, and me on drums. Elton John, George Harrison, and David Crosby played on the album as well.

The Dylan record probably wasn't remembered as one of his best—I think Bob was having a hard time finding himself in the studio during the 1980s, but I was thrilled to read the review in the *Village Voice,* which concluded that "*Under the Red Sky* is Dylan's best album in 15 years, a record that may even signal a return to form. . . . The tempos are post-punk, like it oughta be, with (Kenny) Aronoff's sprints and shuffles grooving ahead like '60s folk-rock never did."

Don Was: *Under the Red Sky* was an interesting record to make, because my co-producer, David Was, and I didn't really know what the songs were when we started recording. So what we tried to do was just have a different band backing him up every day with really good musicians, a great example being the first day of tracking Kenny mentioned where the lineup was Stevie Ray and Jimmie Vaughan and David Lindley playing together. That was pretty incredible, and I think even Bob was blown away, because he didn't know who was going to be there from day to day backing him up. It was kind of a deal we made with him going in, so it was like, "Alright, we don't know the songs, you're surprising us, we'll surprise you with the musicians."

So the songs seemed like jams at the time because Bob wasn't necessarily singing with us. He was playing with the band live out on the floor. So he'd start playing some chords and we'd pick up on it, and then he'd say, "Alright, the bridge is C sharp minor, A/B, play that." So we'd play that, and then he'd say, "Alright, so it's verse-verse-bridge, verse-verse-bridge-verse," and we didn't really know what we were playing to, but I think he had an idea of it in his head as the song would get going. So everyone working on those sessions had to be really on their toes, and had to listen to what Bob was doing, to try and play the right thing within our own performances. And again, because he wasn't really singing, you could only go on the subtleties of his playing, which brings up another great thing about Kenny: he's a great listener and reacts to what the other musicians and what the singer's doing, and just leans back into it. That's an important quality to have as a player.

In February, we started recording Iggy Pop's album at Ocean Way Studios with Waddy Wachtel on guitars sitting to my left and drummer Charlie Drayton playing bass sitting to my right. Slash and Duff from Guns N' Roses came in one day to record a few songs with Iggy. The whole time I was playing so hard, with no shirt on, and I had to secure my headphones by wrapping tons of duct tape around my head like a hospital bandage. At one point, Waddy turned around and screamed at me, "Do you have to play the drums so fucking loud?!" On an Iggy Pop record? Hell yes!

"Candy," a duet with Kate Pierson from the B-52's, ended up being a single on Iggy's record. Some of the other songs on Iggy's album were "Butt Town" and "Pussy Power."

Iggy Pop, of course, is known as the "Godfather of Punk," and this is exactly what I am talking about when I said I took to my gigs like an actor might a role in a film. Basically, Iggy needed a hard-slamming beat, a great primal energy to match his—and there is no one more energetic than Iggy Pop. It was a lot different than playing with Mellencamp—or was it? It was still just rock 'n' roll, pure and simple, but a highly distilled version. John didn't come up trying to intimidate audiences the way Iggy had, but they both started with the Beatles and the Stones. Iggy had a little more fuck you in his music—it was rock 'n' roll, just a highly distilled version. Don was smart like that. He knew how to put it all together. He could see past labels and boxes and got right into the people.

Don wasn't in the studio one day—he had to attend the Grammys—and honestly, I didn't think much of it at the time because I was so focused on making Iggy's record. I wasn't even aware that Don was nominated for Producer of the Year, but that evening we watched Don win three Grammy Awards! There he was on TV giving a speech, holding three trophies with his white-man Afro, headband, glasses, probably barefoot, and smiling just like when I met him. He won Producer of the Year for Bonnie Raitt's *Nick of Time* record (which also won Best Female Pop Vocal and Best Female Rock Performance), another Grammy for Album of the Year for the same record, and finally one for the B-52's hit single "Love Shack." Don was now the hottest producer in America and his life was about to change, which meant my life was about to change, because Don started hiring me to play on a lot of the records he was producing.

Don Was: I certainly first became aware of Kenny—like everybody else— from his work with Mellencamp, and I don't know if those records really get the credit for the pioneering spirit they had, but they're brilliantly produced records. As a record maker, I did then—and still do—listen very closely to other people's records to see how they deal with issues of like dynamics and just getting under other people's skin. What I noticed about the Mellencamp records, particularly *Scarecrow* and *Lonesome Jubilee*, was Kenny doing all kinds of stuff, which I now understand was probably tied into his classical training and understanding of orchestral percussion, because within his playing on those records, he would leave a lot of space. And he would let the thing build, and build very dynamically, and then bring it way back down, or maybe just play a figure on a hi-hat. I just loved where he chose to play in a song, and musically, as importantly, where he chose not to play, and when I heard he was available, I wanted to make records with him. He does things that no other rock 'n' roll drummers do, and I thought it was pretty revolutionary.

Brick by Brick was the second record we did together, and I remember I was trying to think of who to cast with Iggy, who he could play with that would give him the proper energy but also the nuance, because even though everyone just thinks of Iggy as just being all energy, he's finely nuanced, and the thing that makes him different from everybody else is that he's got a power with all kinds of subtlty going on, on many different levels, and I thought Kenny could match that.

One of the first things we cut on Iggy was a song called "Something Wild," written by John Hiatt, who it just so happened was also working at Ocean Way, and we asked him to come play on the song, and he said, "Yeah, sure, as soon as I'm done with my session, I'll come over." When he did, it was around 6 p.m., after everyone had been there for a while working and we were eating dinner. John was done with his day, and you could tell he was tired and didn't want to hang while we ate and then learn this song. So he kind of said, "Oh man, look, if you're wiped out, don't worry, we'll do this another time," and he split.

Iggy was really bummed out because he thought he'd insulted John Hiatt by not putting dinner down and going in the other room to work. He thought we were being disrespectful to John. So we finished dinner and went in the live room, and you could see that Iggy was dispirited and was kind of going through the motions with the song, and Kenny was not gonna have it. He was determined that we were going to get this song right and do it well, and on the first take of the song, Kenny came out driving 170 miles an hour! He put so much energy into it—not just because the song called for it, but because he wanted to change the vibe in the room, and he did: in about twenty seconds. In those twenty seconds, everybody's mood did a 180, and it was a killer take. It was the clearest example that I had up to that point—maybe ever—about how the attitude that people bring into the studio impacts the records.

After working with Don on Iggy's and Dylan's records, I began to see how unique Don was as a producer. He was great at casting people for a session and letting them be great at what they do best. This is what great team leaders do. They hire the right people and let them do their job. Don is very smart about understanding the big picture when he's making a record. By making broad suggestions to me, I was able to do what was right for the song, but still be creative in every possible way. I took a lot of knowledge from what I had learned making records with John Mellencamp into my sessions, and I took a lot of ideas from making records with so many other artists and bands back to John Mellencamp's sessions. This was a perfect situation for me.

Don Was: I was inspired by guys like Brian Wilson and Phil Spector, who were not guys that wrote out charts for their musicians but rather worked kind of one-on-one with them and would sit down with the guitar player and say, "Hey, let's do this here and that there," and just verbally tried to talk things through. I like having everyone in the room together when we tracked, so I would have ideas about dynamics and how to build the record and how to give them signature hooks and musical and instrumental hooks. And just let them build over three and a half and four minutes, so I would just set everybody up on the floor, and we'd never do a whole take. We'd just talk through a section, and say just play the first verse, and with Kenny, I don't think I would say things like, "Don't go to quarter notes on the hi-hat until the chorus." I would just tell him what we were trying to do and rely on his creativity to come up with something far cooler than anything I would have come up with. There didn't seem to be any point in making the same record that someone else had made the day before or a week before or ten years before. So we had some amazing musicians, and with Kenny, I wanted him to take as much license as possible. During those years we worked together in the late '80s and early '90s, I used Kenny on every record, and that only changed when Mellencamp went out on tour, but I'd book him whenever I could.

John Mellencamp: I never really was angry with Kenny because of his ambition to go other places and do other things. But what makes Kenny great is what also makes Kenny not so great: ambition is a great thing, as long as you can keep it in check. He wanted to bust out on his own, but he still wanted to be in the band. I always loved Kenny's ambition on one level, but after so many years of being in the band, Kenny—in my mind—couldn't decide what was right and what wasn't right.

22

Blaze of Glory

I t was only May, and the rest of the year was about to explode with new sessions with Elton John, Bob Seger, the Indigo Girls, Hall & Oates, Bonnie Raitt, B. B. King, Neil Diamond, James McMurtry and . . . John Mellencamp! Amid all of those sessions, I also managed to produce two small projects, traveled through the USA and Canada doing drum clinics, flew to Japan for a show, and ended the year sitting in with Paul Shaffer's band for three nights live on *Late Night with David Letterman*, subbing for house drummer Anton Fig.

It seems like everything starts with a phone call, and one of the best was when the voice on the other end of the line said, "Hey, Kenny, it's Jon Bon Jovi . . ." I live for calls like that.

Jon got right down to the point and said, "Listen, I want to record two songs for a movie I'm writing music for called *Blaze of Glory*. It's a Western and I'm co-producing the songs with Danny Kortchmar."

Jon Bon Jovi: I had this opportunity that was a great experiment, because unlike my own records, where you're trying to pull from life experience to write a song, this was handed to me in a hundred-page script. So when I went to that movie set, I wrote "Blaze of Glory," played it for the director, Geoff Murphy, and he said, "That's fantastic, thank you, you're done," and I remember saying, "Yeah, but this is so inspiring and so easy, why don't we have a little fun and write some more songs," and he said, "Sure, it only benefits us if you're involved." I was very prolific at that time and wrote ten songs pretty quickly, but then I didn't really know what to do with them—because you're writing a sound track for a movie, and not all the songs are going to appear in the film, so it was "songs inspired by," and it just became this huge experiment. It freed you to just go in the studio with whoever, however, to cut the tracks.

He kept calling me every two weeks, and every time we talked more songs were added to the project until there were finally ten songs—"It's also going to be a Jon Bon Jovi solo record."

He told me we'd be recording at A&M Studios in LA, and that either he or his co-producer, Danny Kortchmar, would be calling shortly with the final details as far as dates, etc. Well, it goes without saying that I was really pumped now, and, in fact, I remember my heart was literally racing with excitement after that call because I *love* doing entire albums as opposed to just a few songs or a single. I'd rather be the supporting actor in a *movie* as opposed to having a small part in one *scene*. Anyway, Jon called me back a few days later and said, "Kenny, Jon Bon Jovi. I've got good news and bad news, which do you want to hear first?" I thought about it for a moment and said, "What's the good news?," to which Jon replied, "Well, the good news is Jeff Beck is playing on the record," and I said, "Holy shit, that's fantastic! I love Jeff Beck and have always wanted to play with him. What's the bad news?"

"Well, the bad news is that Jeff wants to use Terry Bozzio, because that's who he's been playing with lately."

In that moment, I remember my head dropped because that might have been good news for Jon, getting Jeff Beck on the record, but it sucked for Kenny Aronoff. I totally understood why Jeff wanted Terry there. He's one of the most creative badass drummers alive, and respecting Terry and Jeff as I do, I told Jon I understood, and that was that.

But after I hung up the phone, it started to really sink in, and I was really bummed out—I remember pacing the floor in my living room and literally saying out loud to myself (and anyone within shouting distance), "This sucks!"

Now, remember what I said about how I know now that the glass is always full? Five hours later, Danny Kortchmar called, all chipper-sounding, and said, "Hey, what's up, Kenny? Listen, have your tech bring your drums to A&M Studio D at 9:30 a.m. on Tuesday." I thought I was in the *Twilight Zone*. I was thinking to myself, What the fuck is going on? Did that call with Jon not just happen?

I asked Danny, "Have you spoken to Jon Bon Jovi?" And, completely clueless, he said, "Yeah, why?" So I proceeded to fill him in on my earlier conversation with Jon that day, about how I wasn't going to be playing drums on the album anymore because Jeff Beck wanted Terry Bozzio. And after hearing that, Danny said, "Bullshit! You're the right guy for this record. Besides, there's no way in hell Jeff Beck's going in the studio for twelve hours a day while we do take after take after take. We'll bring Jeff in when the record's done and have him overdub his solos later. He's not going to sit there and track with the band, *no way*."—and that's exactly what happened.

◄◦►

When I heard "Blaze of Glory" for the first time, I knew instantly this was going to be a huge hit. It sounded like a complete story or movie all in itself. It was a signature Bon Jovi–type song, but rendered in a sort of cinematic style. A rock 'n' roll Western! It reminded me of actually going to the movies when I was a kid and seeing these old Technicolor, spectacular Westerns that really brought you to another time and place.

After every take I would dry off, and then *action!* Do another take, dry off . . . *action!*

I had a gut feeling that this song was going to be a huge radio hit, and ultimately it went to #1 on the *Billboard* Hot 100 Singles chart; the album peaked at #3 on *Billboard*'s Top 200 Albums chart, selling 2 million copies.

Through the process of making the record, Jon and I were also becoming good friends, and I remember him asking me one night after a session, how was Mellencamp doing, and how were things going with me and the band? That conversation led me to confess, "I wish John would appreciate the band more. I mean, sometimes it just feels like he's the boss and we're *just* the band. It used to feel more like we were in it together. It's hard sometimes because Mellencamp doesn't seem happy. He's angry most of the time, and I hate it when he gives me shit when I'm trying to do the best I can for his band and his music. The bottom line is I'm always going to play my ass off, and be the best I can be, whether John's in a good mood or a bad mood, because I always want to be the best I can be no matter what, and I want the band to continue to be successful."

> **Jon Bon Jovi:** All Kenny wanted to do was be in a band, and what I mean is he wanted to be like Keith Richards is to Mick Jagger, or Clarence Clemons was to Bruce. He was brokenhearted about not being in *that* band. And he was very disappointed with what Mellencamp went on to be—he became a guy with a bunch of side players, and I think it broke Kenny's heart. If the *Blaze of Glory* project had been more of a record vs. a sound track, and I'd chosen to go out and do some solo shows, I would have had the opportunity to tour with Kenny.
>
> Every day at the end of recording, because I didn't have my regular band to hang out with, it was like, "Who am I going to hang out with? I'm gonna hang out with Kenny." We'd take Jeff Beck to the movies. It was funny, because if you talked to Jeff about music, he shut down, but if you talked to him about cars and movies, he became a giddy kid. So you had to find that commonality, and Kenny was able to broach all those kinds of different things, so I always included him in everything. That's why there was only one drummer on the album.

Jon Bon Jovi treated me with so much respect during those sessions. Every day when he walked into the studio, he would call out, "Handsome Kenny Aronoff!" And to this day, he'll say, "Hey, handsome, how you doing?" I always tell him, "Who the hell are you looking at when you say that? It can't be me."

After *Blaze of Glory*, Jon and I were friends for life. We are both intense work machines, and we both love music and NFL football. We did a bunch of projects together, and I love it whenever he calls me to do something with him.

Tama photo shoot after a Melissa Etheridge sound check on her 2004 *Lucky* tour. (Courtesy of Tama, photo by Paul Pugliese)

At Drum Paradise in front of their huge snare collection. (Photo by Robert Downs)

Onstage with Chickenfoot, St. Louis, Missouri, May 23, 2012. (Photo by Louis Countryman)

Recording session at Henson Recording Studios, Studio B. I used three different kits for this session. (Author's collection)

With John Fogerty, in St. Louis, Missouri, July 7, 2015. (Photo by Louis Countryman)

In my office in Studio City, California, with a small selection of Gold and Platinum records and CDs I played on. (Photo by Robert Downs)

Backstage passes and laminates from tours and shows I played. (Photo by Robert Downs)

My recording studio, Uncommon Studios LA, where I do a lot of my sessions today.
(Photo by EJ Linehan/Blacksheep Media)

My ever-growing glasses collection.
(Photo by Robert Downs)

Charts that I made for sessions.
(Photo by Robert Downs)

This photo was taken on the day of 9/11, four hours after two planes slammed into the Twin Towers. I remember being very angry during this photo shoot. I was on tour with Joe Cocker, and I couldn't fly to New York City to join them for the next show. (Courtesy of Klipsch)

Zildjian ad, 1995. (Courtesy of the Zildjian Archives)

Tama ad. The photo was shot in 1996, while I was on tour with the Smashing Pumpkins. (Courtesy of Tama)

XL Protector (Gator) cases at Drum Paradise, Los Angeles, where all my drums are stored for sessions. (Photo by Robert Downs)

I got my tattoo done by Corey Miller at High Voltage Tattoo, while being filmed on the shop's TV show, *LA Ink*. (Author's collection)

Years later, when I was back with Mellencamp, and Jon put Bon Jovi back together, we had dinner at a famous restaurant called St. Elmo Steak House after his sold-out show at Market Square Arena in downtown Indianapolis. At one point, Jon said, "Thanks for keeping Bon Jovi together," and I said, "What?!" I didn't know what he meant by that statement and naturally asked him how I'd kept the band together.

He explained that when I'd begun talking about my feelings about being unappreciated by John Mellencamp, it made Jon reflect about his success as a solo artist and the Bon Jovi band. He realized that being part of Bon Jovi was the most important thing to him in his music career. Those guys are his brothers and they have history, and doing it solo wasn't going to be the same or as good as being in Bon Jovi. I wish John Mellencamp and I could have been more adult back then to sort out our differences, but we were young and into our own worlds.

> **Jon Bon Jovi:** Kenny is and will remain one of my favorites. There's a category in the Rock and Roll Hall of Fame for sidemen, guys who aren't the artist, and I think without a doubt he's inducted, because I think he's that seminal. His body of work, much like all those great crews that were Booker T., the guys out of Detroit during the Motown era, Kenny's a seminal cat; he deserves the accolades.

As soon as I finished recording *Blaze of Glory*, Don Was hired me to record four songs with Elton John.

The thing about Elton, and I noticed it right off, is he always sings *perfectly*. He *never* sings off pitch, and I have never heard a male voice so loud in my life. Not Iggy Pop, not Mellencamp, not Fogerty, *no one*. It was unbelievable.

After recording with Elton John at A&M Studios, I went down the street and started a Bob Seger record at Ocean Way studios with Don Was.

I did a few more sessions in LA and then sessions in Indiana and New York before flying to Athens, Georgia, to record with the Indigo Girls for four days. It was a completely different musical experience for me, working with this group of women in the ultra-hip Southern college town of Athens.

This was also where R.E.M. called home, and I think I was the first drummer the girls had ever recorded with on their records. Scott Litt (R.E.M., the dB's, Carly Simon) produced and engineered their record, and I found the Indigo Girls' music was right to the point: it's about the blend of their voices, heartfelt but unpretentious lyrics, smart chord changes—and a great feeling that needed to be driven by a simple yet powerful rhythm section. When I listen to my playing on those songs, I can hear my energy, my excitement, and my personality come right through, even though my playing is very simple and direct. But it feels like just an extension of their music—there are no wasted beats or notes on their records, and that approach always works for me.

After four days of recording in Athens, I went back to LA to record with Bob Seger and Don Was again. *Bam, bam, bam,* I went from making a record with Jon Bon Jovi, then Elton John, then the King of Detroit rock 'n' roll Bob Seger, then the Indigo Girls, and back to Bob Seger. Now that's the music business the way I like it.

Bob Seger was Detroit royalty, from the same lineage as Iggy Pop and Mitch Ryder. He came up with Alice Cooper and Ted Nugent and MC5— he may have been known for these big radio-friendly hits, but he was very authentic, one of these guys who came up the hard way, working his ass off in bars and hauling ass from gig to gig, but fortunate enough to be a brilliant songwriter. He was very dedicated to old-school, 1950s rock 'n' roll, but knew how to write giant, Springsteen-esque anthems, but with a Midwest vibe. Bruce had New Jersey. John had Indiana. Bob had Michigan.

I did three records with Bob and later played with him on an entire US tour in 1996, running from January to June and ending with nine sold-out shows in Detroit. His set is just a remarkable run of timeless hits, songs like "Night Moves" (1976), "Old Time Rock & Roll" (1978, and the most-played single ever on American jukeboxes), "Hollywood Nights" (1978), and "Like a Rock" (1986), to name just a few. He really was the king of FM radio. Every song we played, everyone knew all the words. He was proof not only of the power of the radio, but of how to build a fan base. Back in the day, with the Silver Bullet Band, or when it was called the Bob Seger System, he'd do 250 dates a year. That is a fuck of a lot—and he did that for something like twenty years straight. He had built such a huge audience by staying on the road that years later when he took ten years off between tours, he still packed arenas. That is a hard core following. You don't get that just by having radio hits. And on top of it, Bob is one of the nicest guys imaginable. He knew how to get his point across to the band by being *nice*. I loved working with him.

Right after Bob Seger's record, Danny Kortchmar hired me to record a song with Hall & Oates, and then I was in the studio the very next day recording the old Dr. John hit "Right Place, Wrong Time" with Bonnie Raitt and B. B. King for the *Air America* movie sound track. Once again Don Was hired me for this session.

I sat right behind B. B. King when we recorded. Don loved putting everyone in the same room if he could pull it off technically, and also loves to record without a click track whenever possible to get that special unique human feel. After the first take, B. B. King said out loud without looking at me, "Drummer? Man, you are laying it down and I am *digging* you." Oh man, that made me feel good. Add to that Bonnie Raitt's sexy voice and silky slide guitar playing, and even after everything I have been talking about, everyone I was working with, this was on a short list of career highlights. It was *elevating*.

The sessions kept rolling. I recorded more Bob Seger songs, a few Neil Diamond songs, a Marshall Crenshaw record, the B-Force, Australian artist James Reyne, Adam Schmitt, and Will T. Massey in LA before picking back up with John Mellencamp, as well as recording with artists like James McMurtry, Sue Medley, and Henry Lee Summer in John's Indiana studio. Other highlights from that run included playing on a very cool Aldo Nova record (*Blood on the Bricks*) Jon Bon Jovi was producing in Montreal, a Les Paul tribute record at Electric Lady (Jimi Hendrix's legendary studio) with Slash, Iggy Pop, and Fernando Saunders in NYC, and recording and mixing a Breakdown record in Woodstock, New York. That kind of schedule always makes me smile, plus there was one very special session that I produced and played drums on, one of the most moving experiences in my career, recording two songs to raise money for the Ryan White AIDS Foundation in Indianapolis.

Jim Irsay, owner of the Indianapolis Colts NFL football team, a great friend of mine for almost thirty years, asked me to record and produce two songs to help raise money for the Ryan White AIDS Foundation. This was an amazing gesture of kindness by Jim to the White family, helping with AIDS research.

Ryan was a victim of a bad blood transfusion. He was not gay, as if that would matter, but he and his family were treated with disrespect by a bunch of bigoted assholes, and it was a very emotional experience for everyone involved. Ryan was just a child when he died.

I got to know Ryan White personally when he was still struggling to get better, and I helped get him a drum set. Jim Scott engineered the session for me, and Mike Mills from R.E.M. sang backgrounds on a song Jim Irsay wrote with Stephen Stills called "Colors." The other song we recorded was a rendition of "Amazing Grace" that Henry Lee Summers sang while I conducted a choir made up of Ryan's classmates and friends. I struggled to keep it together while I was conducting the choir. Everyone was crying their eyes out.

23

Fired, Again!

In 1991, John Mellencamp decided that it was time to make another rock 'n' roll record, but before we started rehearsing for *Whenever We Wanted*, I went to LA to record a few songs with Lyle Lovett, made a record with Billy Falcon that Jon Bon Jovi was producing at A&M, and recorded a song for the *Thelma and Louise* movie with Glenn Frey, "Part of Me, Part of You." I was also reunited in the studio with my first non-Mellencamp #1 artist collaborator, Belinda Carlisle, to work on her new solo album. And I squeezed in some songs for a Lisa Germano *and* a Henry Lee Summer record back in Indiana. I took nothing for granted, and I never felt like I had made it and could lay back and relax. Someone once said to me, "Kenny, why don't you stop and smell the roses?" I would always say, "I am smelling the roses every day, seven days a week. I am loving life. I love what I do. I had thought my career was going to hit the wall when Mellencamp stopped playing, but I was wrong."

My outlook on everything was different now that I was working as a session drummer. I loved being part of the Mellencamp band, but I felt more secure now because I had more options. I was able to make a great living doing sessions and drum clinics. The challenge now was how to keep everything going. I really wanted to do it all.

Months before we made the record that became *Whenever We Wanted*— not incidentally the first record that was credited to "John Mellencamp," with none of the Cougar bullshit—we had a meeting over at Belmont Mall Studio with John and the primary band members, Mike Wanchic, Larry Crane, Toby Myers, and me. The band got there first and we sat in the control room in the studio waiting for John, who arrived in one of his dark moods, when he wears dark sunglasses and doesn't look at anyone or talk to anyone. He just sat on the sofa in the back of the control room of his studio, chain-smoking in silence while we all awkwardly talked among ourselves, waiting for him to start talking. It reminded me of when my dad would call me and my brother down to the living room for a serious discussion. It always meant we were in trouble.

I remember John asked Mike to close the blinds (even though he was wearing shades). It was all very awkward. Finally, after forty-five minutes, he started talking.

The meeting was about a bonus John was going to give us for the thirteen years of hard work and dedication we had given to him. It was actually a lot of money. After John was finished talking, we obviously had some questions—it was all very unexpected.

The thing that ultimately set John off was when Larry Crane asked for everything John had promised us in writing. John stood up and confronted Larry face-to-face, as if they were going to go at it fist-to-fist, and he said to Larry, "You know I never put things in contracts." Larry told him, not unfairly, business being business, "Well, this time I'd like to have it in a contract." That's when John said, "Fuck all of you," and stormed out of the room.

About ten minutes later, his office accountant came into the control room and said, "John told me to tell you that you are all fired and to get all of your equipment out of the studio and rehearsal rooms immediately. I was told to pay you 'X' dollars before you leave today," and "X" dollars ended up being *half* of what he had just told us we would be paid.

We weren't wrong to ask questions, but it was never going to end on a happy note, not when John was in one of his shitty moods, and especially not when there was money involved. That always plays with people's emotions, and especially for an artist like John, who had been fucked over and screwed by managers and record companies. They usually never recover from those sorts of bad experiences, and money is a huge trigger point. That's the part we should have been smarter about, although now that I think about it, there was never going to be a good day to ask those questions.

Eventually, everyone came back into the band months later, except Larry. He took his check and left the band forever, which was a huge surprise to all of us because Larry grew up with John in Seymour, Indiana. I always thought he was John's Keith Richards. I figured he would be the last guy to ever leave the band, but that experience was a huge turning point for all of us. Things were very different after that day. My buddy David Grissom from Streamwinner replaced Larry.

Our first thoughts were, Holy shit, how is this going to work without Larry? But the reality is that we are all replaceable. Except for Charlie Watts and Ringo Starr.

John had also decided that he was going to produce this new record by himself. It would be the first time John didn't have a co-producer. That didn't really affect the band that much because we had so much input when we made records with John, but it put additional pressure on him to deliver.

One of the biggest changes John made was with my drum sound. I didn't like that idea at first, because I had become well known for it, especially my snare-drum sound. Instead of using an old brass 5" x 14" Ludwig Superphonic 400 or an aluminum 5" x 14" Ludwig Acrolite snare, he had me use an 8" x 14" wood Brady Snare, a totally different sound for me. And instead of recording my drums in the big room, John wanted to try recording my drums in a smaller room where the guitars usually had their amps. John always had a strong desire to keep inventing himself, but at the same time, he was aware of making music that was radio friendly.

We tried four different rooms and experimented with placing the drums in many different locations in each room. This is what was so cool about having your own studio and a significant budget to make a record: we had time to experiment, and if we didn't like something three weeks later, we could start the record all over again. It was possible and affordable back then. He also dropped the violin and accordion sound that had been our signature on *The Lonesome Jubilee* and *Scarecrow* records. This one was more aggressive, more in-your-face Stones-like rock, which I loved. John could be a moody son of a bitch, but he had great instincts.

The music business was booming at this time. I would get calls every week, or even every day, about recording on someone's record. It felt like Christmas morning all the time, you never knew what you were going to get. It was around this time I got the call to play on Meat Loaf's big comeback album, *Bat Out of Hell II: Back into Hell*.

This record ended up reviving Meat Loaf's career (my mom still calls him "Meatball," and to this day whenever we're talking and she asks me, "So, do you still record with that Meatball guy?"). It was the sequel to his wildly successful *Bat Out of Hell* album, and it featured the international chart-topper that would put Meat Loaf back in the public eye, "I Would Do Anything for Love (But I Won't Do That)."

Honestly, I thought we were wasting our time on that song because it was ten and a half minutes long, and I remember saying, "There's no way in hell radio will *ever* play that." What's even more crazy was a year after we'd recorded that song in LA, I got a call to come to NYC and record an intro to that song, which ended up making it even longer.

Jim Steinman, the genius behind Meat Loaf's music, always takes a long time making Meat Loaf records, and this took three years to finish. He was very methodical and detailed about everything. Meat Loaf was a perfectionist as well. But the results were spectacular, and unique to anything else out on the radio.

On that session in NYC, Steinman's intro (played by the brilliant Roy Bittan from the E Street Band) wound up adding two and a half minutes, and I kept saying, "You're wasting your time and money, no one will play a *twelve*-minute song on the radio." Boy, was I wrong, because that single ended up being #1 in fifteen countries all on the same day and eventually hit #1 in twenty-eight countries total. On top of that, *Bat Out of Hell II* sold 20 million records worldwide, and this became my fourth #1 single on the Hot 100 Singles chart in *Billboard*.

Hitting #1 on the Hot 100 Singles or Top 200 Albums in *Billboard* is the shit. To be #1 means you're the most requested on the radio, which means the most sales, which means someone is making a fuck of a lot of money. It's winning the race. It's winning the Super Bowl.

That year I also played drums on records by Patti Scialfa, Delbert Mc-

Clinton ("Roll with the Dice"), Corey Hart, Jaime Kyle, Sue Medley, Michelle Shocked, and Japanese TV/movie/rock star Tsuyoshi Nagabuchi. I produced an LA rock band called the Poor Boys and had a crazy two weeks recording albums with Patty Smyth and Chris Isaak.

I spent three weeks rehearsing and recording with Patty Smyth in LA (with producer Roy Bittan in A&M Studios, where I did *Blaze of Glory)*, and on the weekends I would fly up to San Francisco and record with Chris Isaak. So on Friday nights I would race to LAX and fly to San Francisco, then Sunday night I would race to the airport and back to LAX to get back to work with Patty and Roy. That became a familiar routine for me back then, and I loved it.

On Patty's record, I recorded a song called "Sometimes Love Just Ain't Enough," a duet between Patty and Don Henley, and I remember thinking this was a fool's errand because it was so pop-sounding. It was 1992 and the grunge music scene out of Seattle was coming on so strong. I didn't think radio was going to play it. I didn't think anyone wanted to hear this kind of song anymore. Everyone was listening to Nirvana and Mother Love Bone. But as with Meat Loaf, I was wrong, because "Sometimes Love Just Ain't Enough" went to #2 on the *Billboard* Hot 100 Singles chart and held that position for six weeks straight, and went to #1 on the *Billboard* Adult Contemporary chart.

I used to get *Billboard* and highlight all the songs I was playing on, on all of the different charts, and there was a time I was on twenty songs and fifteen albums in the same week on the Hot 100 Singles and Top 200 Albums charts. Eventually, I was on the country charts as well, and charting all over the world, especially in Canada, the UK, Germany, Australia, and Japan.

◄○►

In July, I got a call from someone asking if I would be interested in auditioning—with a bass player of my choice—for Mick Jagger. This would be for a record and then a solo tour, and of course, you know the answer: "Holy shit, when and where?!"

The best bass players are the ones with the biggest ears—they *listen.* They glue themselves to the drums and let me get right next to them. They are so tight with placement and groove, they are just part of my drum set. Michael Anthony of Van Halen, when I was playing with him in Chickenfoot years later—wherever I went, he was right there. It was like he was *hugging* me.

Bass lines define chords and harmony. They lead everyone to the next chord. Good bass playing is like the Bach of rock 'n' roll—perfect linear melodies in the low end, without interrupting the groove and the tonality. They can define the structure of the song. One of the finest bass players ever is Leland Sklar—he is an impeccable reader, but he never sounds like he's reading. His choice of notes is amazing. He has true musicality far beyond most bass players. James LoMenzo in Fogerty's band was an arena-rock guy, who played with Black Label Society, David Lee Roth, he was in White Lion and Megadeth, but he came up in clubs and really knows how to play *songs.* In Nashville, Michael Rhodes and Glenn Worf are two of my favorite cats. And I have done many sessions over the last fifteen years with my buddy Chris Chaney from Jane's Addiction. He totally understands both worlds—playing live and in the studio—and can really drive any band as hard or as nuanced as needed. Toby Myers from John Mellencamp's band was a very melodic player—like McCartney meets Sting, plus we were matched with a lot of energy. A few other great bass players I have worked with a lot in LA studios are Paul Bushnell, Hutch Hutchinson, Nathan East, John Pierce, and Bob Glaub, to name just a few.

I ended up bringing John Pierce, who I had done sessions in LA with for twelve years. The audition went like this: We went to SIR Studios. There were drums there, but I brought my favorite snare drum, bass drum pedal, sticks, and cymbals, the usual. Joe Satriani and Jimmy Ripp were the guitar players. Joe had an Afro back then, and he looked as cool with that explosion on top of his head as he does now with no hair. Actually he looks better now. The no hair thing is a good look.

My adrenaline level was pretty high when Mick Jagger came in the room. I mean, seriously, I thought this was as close to being in the Rolling Stones as I was ever going to get, and as soon as I set up, I just went into a funky beat without announcing I was going to start playing. You could call it an uncontrollable urge.

I still remember Joe Satriani looking at me with a surprised look on his face, but he just picked it up and the band fell in, just like that, and Mick started dancing, doing that thing I call "the Rooster Dance." It was all very surreal, seeing Mick doing his strut ten feet in front of me, without warning. I guess he couldn't control himself either.

John Pierce and I went out afterward and had three martinis while we waited for the call. We got the gig, but Mick's schedule kept changing and the project kept getting pushed back until I couldn't do the record or tour because I was still working with John Mellencamp, and no matter what, at that time, my loyalty was to John and the band, but that would be true of whatever work was already in the books. I always try to make it all work out so I can do everything, but sometimes you have to say no. Just not usually to Elton John or Mick Jagger. I hate that. It sucks and I never get used to it. I really want to please everyone, including myself.

24

Whenever We Wanted

The *Whenever We Wanted* tour started in January 1992, and we played arenas across America and Canada for three months.

The show opened up with me playing a powerful, funky rock beat I came up with for the song "Love and Happiness"—not to be confused with the Al Green song. The idea was to get the audience up on their feet and dancing before John and the band came out onstage.

Man, what an exhilarating feeling to walk onstage with 20,000 to 30,000 people just chomping at the bit to see us perform. People were ready to dance, sing, and party all night long with us. We delivered such a kick-ass high-energy show—three hours of nonstop hits. When I walked onstage, the audience would roar with excitement, screaming because they knew, and we knew, and the universe knew, it was going to be one loud, pumping, kick-ass show, and I got to start the whole thing off with an aggressively loud, *slamming* fuck-you funky beat. Oh man, what a rush.

Once I got everyone going, the guitar players came out from either side of the stage and ran to the front playing a smoky unison riff. Enter bass, background singers—dancing and singing—and eventually John came out playing maracas—and smoking a cigarette, of course.

After we played our show in Frankfurt, we flew to Hamburg and played a great show there. After the show, the promoter took us all to the famous Reeperbahn red light district, and we checked out some of the live sex shows. One of the promoters offered to set me up with one of the girls backstage for a private meeting, and I said, "Uh, no." It wasn't like every day I was being offered German hookers, but it was a good thing I took a pass because after a few drinks I started to feel a sharp pain in my lower back.

It was around 3 a.m., so I just went back to the hotel. When I got to my room, a switch clicked in my head as I realized I might be in trouble because this back pain reminded me of a kidney stone I had while I was making the *Scarecrow* record. There is no pain like the kidney stone pain, and there is no mistaking it.

I carried some painkillers that my doctor had given me just for this situation. I took one with a glass of water, but it all came up immediately, and I mean *immediately*. I wasn't sick, the pill and the water just came up and out. I tried it again and the same thing happened again. After another hour of intense pain, I realized I was seriously fucked, and I called our tour manager at 6 a.m., who then called our German promoter who was traveling with us, and fortunately for me he was staying in our hotel.

We climbed into the promoter's Mercedes and headed to the closest hospital, which happened to be back in the Reeperbahn, so you can imagine what their emergency room looked like, even early in the morning—a lot of hookers and junkies (and hookers on junk) and a crush of drunks worse for the wear after a night out drinking and whoring.

No one spoke English, and they wouldn't let our German promoter accompany me into the examination room to help translate. I couldn't believe it. I was on my own. Before they took me inside to a waiting area, the nurse said to our promoter in German that the doctor wasn't going to arrive to the Hospital until 9 a.m., and they wouldn't give me anything for the pain, even though I told them what was happening. I said I needed morphine, because that's the only thing that works, but when I said *morphine*, they looked at me as if I were a drug addict. The Reeperbahn hospital was full of them. How frustrating. I paced and paced in the waiting room, pleading to the nurses to get me something for the pain. They kept refusing me and the pain got stronger and stronger, so much so that I wanted to cry. I finally lost it and grabbed a nurse and pressed her up against the wall. I was really losing it. I told her that if she didn't give me something for my pain, I was going to destroy the hospital.

If you've ever had a kidney stone, you'll understand why I did that to the poor nurse. The pain is nonstop. It doesn't throb and go away, and is so intense it will make you do things you would not normally do. The first time I had a stone, I didn't know what it was and I drove myself to the hospital at 2 a.m. in Bloomington, and the whole time I was contemplating running my car into a tree just to stop the pain.

I freaked her out so badly that she finally gave me the morphine . . . *ahhhh.* I apologized and she turned out to be very kind and understanding, just not too quick to hand out narcotics in a room full of junkies. When the doctor came and later examined me with an ultrasound machine, sure enough I had a kidney stone, just like I had thought. They put me on a bed and rolled me into a room next to an old German man, wearing these old spec-like glasses, listening to Nazi-era music on a freaking ghetto blaster. I had an IV in my vein, with a saline drip to keep me hydrated. I kept dozing in and out, and every time I would open my eyes, that German guy would be staring at me, freaking me out. There was no way I could relax and enjoy the buzz.

One time I woke up and he was tapping the bottle of the saline solution. I was high on morphine, and I thought he was trying to kill me. I was thinking, Oy fucking vey, I am in a German hospital, and I am a degenerate Jewish rock drummer. I was definitely freaked out. Finally, my people showed up, woke me up, and said, "We are getting you out of here. Now, can you walk?" It was like something out of a war movie. Maybe not the *Great Escape,* but still, pretty fucking bold. Someone pulled the needle out of my arm, grabbed my clothes, and helped me out of the hospital into the Mercedes. I was so dizzy and nauseous that as soon as they started driving, I asked them to pull over immediately so I could vomit. After that, I felt a lot better. The promoter got me a private doctor, and I played the show that night. I told you, there is no calling in sick for this job.

Morphine and lots of water helped me pass that stone. Whenever I felt the slightest bit of pain, I would freak out, thinking that I was headed back to the hospital. I drank sixteen to twenty glasses of water a day, which helped alleviate the pain, except when that jagged, razor-sharp crystal stone finally flew out of my dick. That fucking hurt . . . and then it was over. But those days behind the drums with a kidney stone were brutal.

We toured for three weeks through Europe and our last show was in Paris. There was an end-of-tour party in the hotel restaurant, with the band and crew, but I didn't want to go. I had had enough and was chilling in my room when I got a phone call from one of our production girls, saying, "Come on, you've got to come down and celebrate," blah, blah, so I came down, and as soon as I started drinking, I was back into it. This was a Greek restaurant and the waiters did that Greek line dance with one hundred steps. The dancers would break plates over their heads like they were made of cardboard. Some of our drunk crew from the tour got up to join them and, of course, eventually I was dragged up there. I tried to do their dance and grabbed some plates and started smashing them on my forehead like the waiters did. As I was spinning around dancing drunk, I kept smashing plates on my bald head, laughing the whole time. It was a nice change from the beginning of the tour in the hospital with drunks and junkies. I noticed our crew was all laughing at me hysterically, and I thought I must have been putting on quite a show.

Finally, one of the girls pointed to my head, so I wiped my head, looked at my hand, and, holy shit, there was blood everywhere! All that sweat was *blood*. I had cut myself when I smashed the plates on my head. I was a mess. It looked way more serious than it was, but my people started running around to get something to bandage my entire head up, so now I looked like an idiot with a bloody turban on. I finally got back to the USA in one piece, but it hurt like hell in the morning.

◄○►

When we had breaks or days off, I flew somewhere for a recording session, including sessions with Corey Hart in Toronto and Bob Seger in Nashville, and another record with the Indigo Girls at Bearsville Studio in Woodstock, the legendary room where Bob Dylan, the Band, Alice Cooper, R.E.M., and the Rolling Stones have recorded. You know it is one thing to get *called*, it is another to get *called back*.

From there, I went back into the studio with Meat Loaf. On April 27, the Mellencamp band flew to LA and did *MTV Unplugged*, then took an all-night flight to Sydney, Australia. When we landed, we saw on the news—we had just missed the riots that broke out after the Rodney King verdict in LA. It was so completely bizarre, watching the National Guard in military vehicles, smoke in the air over the Sunset Strip—we had just been there, and this was exactly where I always hung out, or was driving through to get to a session or whatever. It hit home, even on another continent—I called some of my friends who lived near the Strip and they said they all had baseball bats, kitchen knives, and some had guns, ready to protect themselves in case some idiot tried to break in.

After we got home, we had a day off from our East Coast tour in Lake George, New York, and so the band rented two water-ski boats and the band went waterskiing. Toby, our bass player, Tracy (John's cousin, who also worked security for us), me, and our two pilots were in my boat. At one point, Toby and I were on this big inner tube that the boat was pulling. One of the pilots was driving, and he was trying to shake us off the inner tube by going fast over the wake, turning the boat around hard and fast. We were laughing our asses off, and Toby finally fell off and they stopped to pick him up. I wanted to go again, so they took off with me and, at one point, I decided enough was enough and just let go. And just in time—because the metal latch that attached the rope to the boat broke, and the rope and the big heavy broken latch came flying like a bullet right through the tube where the rope was attached. That was exactly where my hands and head were: one second more and I would have been split in two.

While I was contemplating almost getting my skull split in half, they started to pull the rope and the blown inner tube in the boat, but before the rope was in the boat completely, the pilot gunned the boat to come get me. Suddenly, I hear a scream and the boat stopped. I swam to the boat as fast as I could and I pulled myself in, I heard Toby screaming FUCK FUCK FUCK FUCK. . . . He looked at me in shock, and they were wrapping a towel around his foot. I looked around and, holy shit, laying by itself on the boat *was Toby's little toe*. When the pilots gunned the boat, the rope grabbed his toe and snapped it off.

We went to shore and I rode with Toby in the ambulance with his toe in a baggy on ice. I thought that was what I should do to preserve his toe. After the doctors examined him, it was decided that they would not sew his toe back on, because the chances of his toe staying on successfully and working correctly in a healthy way was very slim to none. So Toby lost a toe—I have no idea what they did with it. They should have given it to him as a souvenir. But the show went on. He played the rest of the tour sitting in a beach lounge chair to keep his foot elevated. Some bands do themselves in with drink and drugs. We had Greek dancing and motorboats.

◄○►

In September, I recorded and did some more live shows with the BoDeans. Then I did a drum-clinic tour and flew to LA to record a Stevie Nicks album called *Street Angel* with the amazing Glyn Johns (Led Zeppelin, Rolling Stones, the Who, the Beatles, Eric Clapton) producing.

Glyn is famous for being able to mic a drum set with only three mics, and he gets an amazing classic-drum sound. He's a true artist, a no-bullshit, super-intelligent, and very focused producer and engineer.

I love Stevie. She is an amazing artist and cool as you could ever imagine, super intuitive, gifted, a real rock star, *and* a great musician. But it was a tough time for her to be making a record because she was trying to quit everything all at once: smoking, drinking, and whatever else she was up to while making this record, and the toll that put on her must have been incredible.

There was no entourage with her, no one carrying black bags of cocaine or anything like that. Those wild days were way over for her. It was all very down to earth. She was very real, not like what you may have been led to believe if you followed Fleetwood Mac in the '70s.

And Glyn can deliver a record. He's as good as they come, but he hates wasting time. He wants to stick with the plan—he's a very scheduled guy and doesn't have a lot of patience for fucking around. If you are experimenting and it is producing results, he'll get you a glass of wine. He'll probably give you a hug. But if it's going south, he is like a general and he is going to start moving the troops in a different direction. At a certain point while we were recording, Glyn laid into Stevie and said in so many words, "I don't have time for what you're going through—I appreciate it, but we have to make a record." I felt bad for Stevie because she was definitely going through a lot, but Glyn had run out of patience and was trying to meet a deadline.

On the last day of recording, Stevie wanted to do "Just Like a Woman," the Bob Dylan song, and Glyn was not into it. Both Stevie and Glyn are great at what they do, and both have very powerful personalities—but the artist is the boss. At least when you are Stevie Nicks. So we recorded "Just Like a Woman."

Benmont Tench and Mike Campbell from Tom Petty's band were on the session, plus Andy Fairweather Low on guitar, and Stevie's background singers. We started jamming, trying to get the song together. I was experimenting with ideas and parts, and all of a sudden, Glyn started yelling into our headphones, specifically at me, "Go to the chorus! The chorus, Kenny."

I said, "Sorry! We're still working out the arrangement of the song!"

I took my headphones off and headed for the control room to try to get things sorted with the song structure and with Glyn, but before I got there, he came flying out, meeting me halfway. Smiling, he gave me one of his great hugs. We're cool. Everything is cool. We started again, and Glyn said something else in the headphones. Glyn was frustrated with the disorganization of everything, the song and people stopping by to say hi, which slowed the process down. I said out of frustration that the background singers weren't singing in the right place.

All of a sudden, the background singers' heads turned, and they looked right at me. They were not happy that I called them out. I was so embarrassed. I went to their room and apologized. I tried to explain that it wasn't about them. At all. Two of the singers laughed about it, but it took me a very long time to convince one singer that it wasn't about her. Stevie wanted this big, loose thing happening, exactly what Glyn didn't want. Glyn was about working and then talking. Stevie was about talking first and getting all vibey, and *then* working. Of course, Stevie had come up making records with Fleetwood Mac and was used to spending a year and millions of dollars in the studio to make a record, but that was never going to fly with Glyn. He wanted to nail the rhythm section and then move on. There was a lot of tension in that room—on the mellowest song ever.

Eventually Stevie and Glyn parted ways, and the record got finished by Roy Bittan. He called me a few months later and asked me if I wanted to come and record some songs for a Stevie Nicks record. That's the music business. You are dealing with a lot of personalities in this business, and a lot can go wrong without anyone really doing anything wrong.

There's no fault. It just gets complicated sometimes, which is why as a session guy, you have to learn to be *beyond* cool. If you get your feathers ruffled easily, this is not a good job for you.

◄○►

After our *Whenever We Wanted* tour, John Mellencamp started writing songs immediately for what would become his twelfth album, *Human Wheels*. Before we started recording, we flew to NYC to perform at Madison Square Garden for a Thirtieth Anniversary Concert Celebration honoring Bob Dylan, featuring heavyweights like Stevie Wonder, Eddie Vedder, John Mellencamp, Eric Clapton, Neil Young, Ron Wood, George Harrison, Sinead O'Connor, Kris Kristofferson, Willie Nelson, Richie Havens, and Lou Reed, to name a few, everyone performing Dylan songs. When Sinead O'Connor came onstage, the entire audience of 18,000 people booed and yelled at her till she started crying. The reason behind the hostility was she that she had just ripped up a picture of the Pope on *Saturday Night Live* as part of her musical performance, which did not go over very well, to say the least. Now, no matter how talented a singer and songwriter she was, every time she tried to talk to the crowd, they booed her. Mostly that's what they thought they were supposed to do, after all the media outrage at her performance on *SNL*, but finally Kris Kristofferson, gentleman that he is, came onstage, put his arm around her, and escorted her off. She had made a strong statement, she had to know there would be some consequences. Music is one thing. Art is another.

―◦―

It was sometimes a painful process making a Mellencamp record, where ninety-nine of one hundred ideas being suggested get thrown out, but that one great idea is worth all the shitty ones combined. It's a process—and in most cases you need to try all the shit ideas to find the gem. Unfortunately, this kind of experimentation rarely happens anymore, not in the studio on sessions I am on, because time is money, and there is no money, so there is very little time to experiment. *The clock is ticking, man. Deliver the goods now, or we will get someone else. . . .*

I went back to my 5" x 14" brass snare drum, and we put my drums back in the big room where I usually recorded. I still wanted to rock real hard, but I could tell that John was heading in a more introspective direction. I would drive ten miles to the studio in my SUV with the stereo blasting, trying to pump myself up, saying, "I'm going to kick this band's ass today," and in most cases, when we got to the studio, John wanted to relax and talk for an hour or more. By the time we started to record, all my super-pumped-I'm-going-to-kick-some-ass attitude would be deflated. It could be pretty fucking trying.

The first song we recorded was "When Jesus Left Birmingham," and I came up with a new idea that I had never used on John's records. My new approach was to play the percussion parts first and *then* lay down the big drum beat. I was basically playing my overdubbed parts first. That was my way of trying to reinvent myself, and John was into it.

I played a hip-hop type of groove on a tiny piccolo snare drum using a brush and a blastick (kind of half stick, half brush) to get a variety of tones. I played the beat softly on purpose, with the snare drum on my lap to make the drum sound muffled and tight, so the engineer had to turn up the pre-amps to get a strong signal to tape, which really made it sound very powerful, even though I wasn't playing loud at all. Then I overdubbed a bongo part and a shaker part to compliment that hip-hop snare groove. The engineer made a loop of my three parts for everyone to start overdubbing to.

John was excited—it was a new direction for us. We broke for dinner, and when we listened to what we had recorded two hours later, John said, "Nah, a swing and a miss. Hey, good try, let's try something else." I saw it completely differently: I thought it was amazing. It just needed my drum set and some electric guitars on top of my loop to add some power to these parts.

I asked John if I could overdub a Motown drumbeat groove on top of everything, and he said, "No, that's okay. . . . Let's do something else." I kept bugging him and pressed him harder because I had a vision for this song. I felt like we did the overdubs first and needed to play the foundational parts now, kind of in reverse of how it is usually done. Finally, John saw my enthusiasm and said, "Okay, go for it," and as soon as I was done and before anyone said anything to me from the control room, either Toby or Mike came out to overdub something, which meant John liked it. Touchdown, we were in business! I still think that's one of the coolest songs we have ever recorded.

We recorded from November 2 to 12 and then unexpectedly, on November 13, John Cascella, our amazing keyboard/accordion/saxophone player, died from a heart attack as he was driving home from a party in Indianapolis. Someone found him dead in his car in a cornfield.

That was a huge big blow. He was only forty-five years old.

We were a band that spent a lot of time together doing everything, we were a family. John Cascella had played with us for seven years, but I knew him for seventeen years. I was asked by John's wife to represent the Mellencamp band by speaking about John at the funeral. This was a sobering moment for all of us.

We had never experienced a band member dying. We were invincible, right? It wasn't like we were doing hard drugs or getting into gang fights. Maybe someone loses a toe waterskiing or smacks plates on their head until they are bleeding, but nothing *crazy*.

When we got back together to finish recording the new record, it was very lonely and upsetting to not have John Cascella in the studio with us. It was just a horrible feeling. John Mellencamp dedicated the album to John Cascella. He had made a big mark with us. He had reached millions of people doing what he loved, which I suppose is the best a musician can ever hope for. I think about it all the time—I'm very lucky to be doing what I do.

Before the year ended, I was asked to come to LA and audition for the Tom Petty and the Heartbreakers band because Stan Lynch—their drummer—had just left the group. The funny thing was Stan had come out to Bloomington to play on some Mellencamp tracks when I was not available to record, so we kind of did a switch with our bands. Stan told me when he was recording with John, he felt that they were trying to get him to sound like me, and eventually he said to John, "Do you want me to shave my head and tune my drum up high like Kenny?" Meanwhile, I felt that the Petty band and producer Rick Rubin wanted me to sound like Stan. Sometimes this business is just too weird to ponder.

25

Professor Aronoff

My motto has always been: *carpe diem*, seize the day, and seize opportunities as they come to you. There was a new scene growing in Nashville in the late '80s—it was becoming the third coast in the music business. More studios, more labels, more business, more sessions, more of everything. Larrie Londin, a great man, a physically huge man, and killer session drummer, kept trying to get me to come to Nashville to do sessions. He really wanted to help me, but I'd never had a chance to follow through and take advantage of his generous offer to help me out while he was healthy. He unfortunately had a stroke while performing a drum clinic in Texas and never recovered. He was a wonderful, big, kind man, but fragile, just like the rest of us.

Life is short and careers are shorter. I love being booked solid, seven days and seven nights a week for months on end. Downtime was *down* time for me. There was no rest for me, not if I could be playing the drums.

Spreading my session business into Nashville was a no-brainer—the business model was already there, proven and working. I just had to convince people that they needed me. So, in 1993, I decided to finally follow Larrie's advice and started reaching out to producers, managers, and label people in Nashville by calling or faxing them (no e-mail back then), and, thankfully, that worked immediately.

Being in the Mellencamp band had helped because country music, country pop music, and country rock 'n' roll music had totally embraced the Mellencamp style of heartland rock 'n' roll, so everyone knew who I was. I stored a couple of drum kits down there with lots of snares, cymbals, and percussion at a cartage company run by my friend Scott Davis, and I was in business. I remember Scott picked me up in a limo when I did my first session in town. It was a classy move.

Every successful business needs to grow in order to stay successful. A lot of producers and session musicians suggested to me many times that I should even move to Nashville.

When I started making records in Nashville, I worked with Bobby Carlyle, Vince Gill, and the Little Feat Band (with Tony Brown producing); a Christian band called For Him; Crosby and Nash produced by ex-Eagles member Bernie Leadon; Roger Alan Wade with producer Chuck Howard, Mac McAnally (also with Tony Brown); Billy Dean, and lots more. I also recorded a very special record that was being co-produced by Don Was and Tony Brown in Nashville, Memphis, New Orleans, and LA called *Rhythm Country and Blues.*

The concept was brilliant. It was basically putting Nashville and Memphis musicians and influences together. The album featured duets between R & B and country music artists singing classic songs, including Aaron Neville and Trisha Yearwood, Patti LaBelle and Travis Tritt, George Jones and B. B. King, Little Richard and Tanya Tucker, the Staple Singers and Marty Stuart, and Chet Atkins and Allen Toussaint. Sam Moore and Conway Twitty did an incredible version of "Rainy Day in Georgia." When Conway died a month later, no one could believe it. He had sang so well and was in such great spirits, having a laugh with Sam at the end of the track. The album debuted at #1 on the Top Country Albums chart and #15 on the Top R & B/Hip-Hop Album charts.

One day I got a call to meet with the head of the percussion department at the Indiana School of Music in Bloomington, where I still lived, and where I had gotten my degree in music. I was completely taken by surprise when they asked me to join the faculty as a teacher with the title of Associate Professor. Wow! IU was still the number-one music school in the United States and I was now Professor Aronoff. A professor of percussion!

They wanted me to teach and mentor five or six students a semester, but I was concerned about how much time it would demand of me because of my busy recording and touring schedule.

The percussion department was strong in four areas—mallets, timpani, multiple percussion, and snare drum—but lacking in drum set instruction. When I studied percussion at Indiana University, there wasn't anyone teaching drum set. IU was rated the number-one music school in the USA, and to be number one, it made sense that IU should offer drum set instruction, since that would be an obvious way for percussionists graduating from IU to make some sort of a living. There's not a lot of job opportunities for timpani players, unfortunately, and when someone did get a job in an orchestra, they held on to it until they retired.

I took on five students immediately and managed to teach at IU for four years: two semesters a year and three months off in the summer, so now my schedule was completely insane! I would fly home from LA or Nashville, or from somewhere on tour and sometimes teach at midnight! It was almost too much work, and I would tell my students, "I won't be able to teach you this week because I am doing the Letterman show. Watch it . . . there will be a quiz later!"

Shawn Pelton (Student): I met Kenny back when I was first going to school at Indiana University. Kenny was a great teacher because he'd been exposed to a lot of great teachers himself. He had a systematic way of focusing in on something that you were trying to develop, and it always applied practically to music and song form. He also had a lot of exercises that were kind of technique orientated and getting a big sound on the drums and stuff like that, how to read a syncopation book and applying different concepts that were sort of based on working with that whole Mellencamp style.

One of the exercises he had drum-wise that was interesting was he would just have us play one beat and then spend like twenty minutes focusing on the hi-hat and then twenty minutes maybe on the kick drum and then twenty minutes on the snare drum, which really relates to what happens if you're on a session, what really happens at the studio when you're working, as opposed to some abstract kind of drum shit that doesn't necessarily apply to making a living.

I tried to teach "Back in Black" by AC/DC, a masterpiece in simplicity, power, and groove, and they never really got it. I told them this was the stuff they were going to have to play if they ever wanted to work, but they had to fight through a lot of music-school training to get to the dirty rock 'n' roll. I remember one day I was working with a student on just that, and some opera teacher from down the hall came screaming into our practice room telling us not to play so loud.

―◄○►―

While I was in Bloomington, we finished up Mellencamp's *Human Wheels* record in March 1993, and the record was released the following September. We were listening to a lot of old and new stuff for feel, attitude, arrangements, or whatever. We weren't trying to sound like Sly Stone, James Brown, or the hip-hop that was on the radio, but it seeped into our sound, especially on "When Jesus Left Birmingham." "When I Came Knocking" and "Human Wheels" were more of what you might expect from us, and both of which went to #1 and #2, respectively, on the Mainstream Rock Track chart in *Billboard*.

We never did a *Human Wheels* tour. We promoted the record with press, videos, and TV appearances (Arsenio Hall, Letterman, MTV). John decided to wait to tour in 1994, after we recorded and released another album, two albums back to back. But we stayed relevant and visible by doing a few live shows in 1993: Farm Aid in Ames, Iowa; a one-off show in Indianapolis at Deer Creek Amphitheater with Blind Melon opening for us; and a sold-out crowd of almost 35,000 in Chicago, at the World Amphitheater.

This was the last show of the tour, and during the encore I threw all of my dripping wet clothes into the audience, except the boxer shorts that I was wearing. When I left the stage, I was handcuffed, arrested, and thrown into a room for indecent exposure.

Everyone backstage was freaking, except John, Mike, and the promoter because they were the only ones who knew it was a setup. They were all in on the joke. I had told John that I was going to strip at our last show, and this was his doing. I tried to convince the cop to let me go because I was an honorary deputy sheriff in Indiana, but he just said, "Indiana don't mean shit to me, son. You're in the state of Illinois now." I was really panicked. After I was thrown into a holding room, still handcuffed, in walked a female cop. I was still trying to explain my way out of this situation when she took her hat off and let her hair down, unbuttoned her shirt, and ... my girlfriend was standing right outside the door.

John Mellencamp and his wife, Elaine, came in to see how things were going, and they caught me—running away like a scared chicken from the sexy cop who was paid to do *everything* to me. She was very adamant. She told me it was her job. Sex, drums, and rock 'n' roll?

◄○►

As a drummer for hire, I was super lucky to continually get lots of great TV coverage, between Mellencamp performances and playing the *Arsenio Hall Show* with Patty Smyth and Jay Leno with Willie Nelson, I was very visible, which was great for business.

After the Mellencamp tour, I did a record in Milwaukee with the Bo-Deans, featuring the single "Closer to Free," which became the theme song for the TV show *Party of Five*. It's still their biggest hit ever, reaching #16 on the Hot 100 *Billboard* Singles chart. I toured with the BoDeans on and off all year.

In May 1993, Don Was hired me to do a show with Willie Nelson at the Roxy on the Sunset Strip in LA with a thirteen-piece band that also performed two songs on *Saturday Night Live* with Paul Simon.

I have never worked with anyone who sings as softly as Paul Simon. That's cool, that's his thing, but in order for him to hear himself, the monitor engineer has to turn his mic way up, which then picks up all the other instruments onstage. It's almost a no-win situation—turn Paul's mic up, it creates a new problem, and because he wants the band to turn down, he can't hear us. So he has everyone play super soft, and scrutinizes everyone's parts for hours in a sound check. The challenge for me was to drive this thirteen-piece band softly. It took a long time and patience to get it right—Benmont Tench, the keyboard player from Tom Petty's band and a mighty session cat in his own right, was on the gig that night, and during sound check Paul told him, "Everything you are playing is irrelevant." It was pretty shocking, since Benmont is one of the very best at what he does. He was so upset by Paul's comment, he had to take a time-out. Paul didn't mean to insult Benmont; it was just his way of saying "play something else," that's all. There are probably better ways to communicate, but we got it right, and there is no denying that Paul Simon is a genuine American master.

The biggest thing that can make a session go south is poor communication. When the producer and the artist aren't really prepared or very clear about what they really want to do, it can make things very difficult. And if the artist and the producer are impatient and demanding—well, that's the formula for a bad session. Demanding perfection when no one is prepared is the recipe for disaster.

Let's assume that all rock musicians are geniuses. Of course we are! But a lot of us might not have the skill set to handle our talent—or the personality, the communication skills, or the patience to work well in a studio with five or six other geniuses. Being a brilliant guitar player or drummer doesn't necessarily make you a well-developed human being. It's not always easy to be upbeat and happy for twelve hours while you're working your ass off in a recording session, but you have to stay patient and focused. It's a big part of the job.

The worst is when accountants and suits get in the way of musicians doing their job. They condescend, or don't understand the process to get the best results. Sometimes there is nothing you can do. In the early days, a lot of musicians were medicated, which didn't help either.

You never know when one song is going to end up on the radio for the next fifty years. It's serious stuff. You don't want to blow it. You don't want to miss a field goal in the last moment and end the season, and you don't want to fuck up a hit single. I'm not smart enough to know which song is going to be a hit, but I'm not taking any chances—seriously, if I knew, if the record company knew, if the artist knew, we'd all be billionaires.

◄○►

Willie Nelson's "Big 6-0 All-Star Birthday Party Celebration" in Austin, Texas, was at the old *Austin City Limits* venue. The show was being filmed and recorded, and I got to perform with Bob Dylan again, plus Johnny Cash, Waylon Jennings, Willie, Kris Kristofferson, Ray Charles, Travis Tritt, Naomi Judd, Neil Young, Clint Black, Marty Stuart, B. B. King, Emmylou Harris, and more. It's situations like these where all of my obsessive charting and practicing really pays off—so many different artists and styles, and they have fourteen cameras on you. You have to be flawless. The pressure is high—if you blow a gig like this, you never get asked back. I love it.

One day in 1990, I got a call from Slash, and he asked me if I would fly to London and record Steppenwolf's "Magic Carpet Ride" at Olympic Studios with him and Michael Monroe from Hanoi Rocks for the *Coneheads* movie sound track. It was great that I had time to do it—we had been hanging around since we were on Iggy's record together, and he had a day off from being on tour with Guns N' Roses to do this track.

After we recorded in London, Michael and I drove a couple hours out of London to the Reading Festival, where Guns N' Roses were performing for 70,000 people. Drummer Matt Sorum told me there was a part of the show where someone usually delivers a pizza onstage when they do the acoustic part of the show, and Matt asked me to be the pizza delivery boy.

I wanted to spice up my entrance a bit, so I took my pants off and wrapped a towel around my waist when I delivered the pizza, a joke based on the old porn movie myth that the pizza boy is going to get laid. What I didn't know was that they planned for me to play the congas with them after I delivered the pizza, which was fine, except my towel kept falling off. A bunch of girls in the front were pointing and laughing at me, and singer Axl Rose looked at me at one point as if to say, "Who the fuck are you, and what the fuck are you doing on my stage in a towel?" No sense of humor, but Matt loved it.

◄○►

At the end of June, I got a call from Cinderella's manager, Larry Mazer, asking if I would be into flying to Philadelphia to play with the band and audition at Kajem Studios for a record they were going to attempt to make for the third time.

When I heard the demos, I actually thought the drum tracks were great, but they were obviously looking for a different feel and vibe. I don't usually audition, but I didn't mind because I really wanted to make this record. It was hard and heavy the way I liked it, unlike anything I was working on at the time, and it sounded like a lot of fun, a good gig. The same week I recorded with Cinderella, I recorded a country record with Hank Williams, Jr., and two songs with the Buddy Rich Big Band.

Someone asked me in an interview once which style of music I preferred to play the most. My first thought was, I love all music and styles, but when he pressed me harder, I had to choose. I said, "Well, then I pick the music that rocks the hardest." I love Marshall stacks, lots of power and attitude and volume, that's me. And so, yes, Cinderella.

Tom Keifer is a badass singer-songwriter, and they had some very cool songs written for this record, *Still Climbing*. I rehearsed for a couple days and started recording with them two weeks later. I kept flying in and out to record for one week at a time because of my crazy schedule. Andy Johns (Glyn Johns's younger brother, who had worked with the Stones, Zeppelin, Van Halen, and Rod Stewart, among others) was the engineer and co-producer . . . until Tommy fired him later on.

Tommy and Andy had totally different approaches to making records. Tommy was all business, trying to finish this record, and Andy (the opposite of his older brother) was moving too slowly for him. It was too bad—Andy Johns got *the best* rock 'n' roll drum sound.

First, he took my front bass-drum head off and lined the inside of my 24" x 16" bass drum with tinfoil so he would get more ambience and attack from my bass drum. I heard he had done the same with John Bonham and Led Zeppelin. Andy also liked the front head of the bass drum to have no hole in it. He tuned both front and bass-drum beater heads up high to the same pitch. This gave you something close to that Led Zeppelin boom-

boom sound. He then hung a microphone in the middle of the bass drum. He did this by detaching a mic cable from a mic and dropping the cable through the air hole on top of the bass drum and re-attaching the cable to the mic when the mic was inside the drum, and then he put the front head back on the drum. Andy also placed a Sennheiser 421 mic in front of the bass drum and plugged it into a guitar amp that was eight feet in front of my bass drum, with a sound baffle in front of the amp. He put a mic in front of the amp speaker and recorded that as well. When he was done, it sounded like the voice of God.

We made a kick-ass record, but the timing for the releasing of this type of record was horrible. Polygram Records spent something like $1.2 million to make this record, and when it only sold 60,000 copies, Cinderella lost their record deal. A swing and a miss! *Bam!* The music scene in 1994 had changed—hair-band music wasn't out, grunge was in. The record never stood a chance. It's a shame, but it happens. They can't all be hits. You can still listen to it, though.

-◄o►-

I was constantly building my presence in Nashville, and I did as many sessions as possible given my crazy schedule. If you are an "A Team" first-call session player in any of the big cities, your schedule gets booked solid all the time. I was trying to be an "A Team" session player wherever I went, which is almost impossible. I was trying to juggle among the main three cities and Indiana, which made my life even crazier. I was always flying somewhere and had to turn a lot of sessions down. But you don't say no to Waylon Jennings.

Waylon is a Highwayman, an outlaw, a country superstar. He played bass for Buddy Holly and the Crickets, and gave up his seat on the ill-fated flight that killed Buddy Holly in Clear Lake, Iowa, in 1958, which may or may not make him the luckiest son of a bitch of all time.

We recorded at Ocean Way Studios in LA, where Don Was did most of his productions. Waylon was really excited to be recording in LA and not in Nashville, because he felt he could be more creative there. Earlier in his career he had been told by his label and producers what kind of record he *should* make. They told him what songs to record, suggested lyric changes, what musicians to use, and told him what the album cover should look like. No one should tell artists like Waylon Jennings, Willie Nelson, Johnny Cash, and Kris Kristofferson what to do with their music. Ever! These aren't *American Idol* artists. They are the real deal. Don Was totally understood that, so he created the perfect atmosphere for Waylon to be and feel creative.

Waylon and Don were both outlaws in their own way. But when Don played a demo of the first song we were going to record, it was a very traditional-sounding Waylon Jennings song.

I had to consider Waylon's style because his music is very defined, but I knew I had to bring new ideas into his traditional sounds to make a cool record for Waylon and Don.

Don hired me because he wanted me to come up with new ideas and create a direction that would excite Waylon and everyone in the room. The challenge was to be creative, but still honor what Waylon was all about. There's a fine line to how to do that—and no matter how many records or tours I had done up to this point, I was very clear about my position as a hired gun. I listen, I learn, and I lead, but I am very aware that I am not the boss.

This was the first day of recording, so it was important for everything to go right for Waylon and Don—the first day sets the tone for the entire session.

After making a chart (from just one listen to the demo), I went over to where all my percussion instruments were, frankly stalling while I was trying to figure out a fresh creative angle on this song. Eventually I grabbed a metal crasher (three strips of two-inch metal laying on top of each other in a metal frame) and attached that to a cymbal stand. I grabbed a string of tiny beads and made two cymbals sound like sizzle cymbals by hanging them on the cymbals. I put a djembe next to my hi-hat stand so I could play it with my left hand. I grabbed a Meinl cabasa (a plastic gourd with plastic beads all over the gourd, held together with strong string). I put castanets on my floor tom and played a vintage 1920s Ludwig snare drum with lots of snares, and turned the drum over so I could play the bottom of the snare. I played my drums with the Meinl gourd in my left hand, and a Vic Firth "dreadlock" (thick metal wire pronged brush-type thing) with my right hand.

My concept was to hold everyone together with that familiar Waylon Jennings 1-2-3-4 on my bass drum, but play all these cool, unpredictable sounds on top of the bass-drum groove. I was leading by example, and it worked. Mark Goldenberg on guitar, Robby Turner on pedal steel, Benmont Tench on keyboards, Tony Joe White on guitar, and Don Was on the bass all played very cool textural parts, while I played my trippy beat. At one point, Waylon came out of his vocal booth into our room with excitement. He was ecstatic. He loved working with Don, and Don hired the right guys.

After Waylon's record, I flew home to record a song with John Mellencamp for a movie called *Blue Chips*. I used some of the same creative ideas I had just come up with for Waylon's record in John's session, and it also set the tone for John's next record, *Dance Naked*, which we started recording a month later.

The song that I was most able to apply some of these new sounds and ideas to was a Van Morrison song we covered called "Wild Night." Me'Shell Ndegeocello played an amazing bass line, and John and Me'Shell sang the song as a duet.

I'm a huge fan of Me'Shell. She is so funky, sings great, and has so many creative ideas, not least of all that I should shave my head completely.

I said I wasn't ready to do that just yet, so she took me into the bathroom and convinced me to shave my head down with a clipper using a quarter-inch adapter. That got me warmed up for the final shave, when I said goodbye to all of my hair four or five years later. She was right, of course.

◄○►

Soon after that, I recorded a monumental last record with the Highwaymen—Waylon Jennings, Willie Nelson, Johnny Cash, and Kris Kristofferson. Of course, Don Was produced this historic record, and thank God (or Don Was) the session was filmed because it was the last time they would record together.

These guys were seriously badass motherfuckers. I spoke about communications skills earlier. Well, on this session, I didn't say much, and when I said something, I made sure it was important. That's another style of communication: *don't talk unless you have something to say*, and if a super-hyper drummer like me can learn that lesson, anyone can.

This was a very hectic time for me, because while I was recording with the Highwaymen, Meat Loaf started another record, and he didn't want to do it without me, so my schedule was like this: Meat Loaf Oct. 23–Nov. 1, and then the Highwaymen *and* Meatloaf Nov. 2, 3, and 4 together, which meant I recorded with the Highwaymen from 12 noon till 9 p.m. at Ocean Way Studios and then drove to A&M and recorded with Meat Loaf from 9:30 p.m. to 2 a.m. The really weird thing was that to me, this kind of schedule wasn't that weird at all. After the last Meat Loaf session, I took a red-eye to New York to perform with the Buddy Rich Big Band. This is what my life had become, and it was awesome.

Around the same time, the Mellencamp band got asked to be the featured entertainment in New Orleans at a famous club called Tipitina's for a Gavin Radio Convention. This was a convention for people who worked radio, MTV, and VH1, kind of a high-profile industry gig. Our management and label thought this was a great way for us to get radio, MTV, and VH1 into our new record, which was being released in a month.

John was seriously not into doing this. He was over doing kiss-ass industry stuff like this. He wanted everyone to like his record, release it, and make it successful. He wanted them to work for the money they were making off of him as an artist. The labels made most of the money off of John's record sales, and the manager got a percentage of John's net profits, so I could see why John felt that way. He worked like a motherfucker for his money and thought everyone else should, too.

While we were rehearsing in Bloomington the day before flying to New Orleans, the office accountant came in and said a few words to John, who then proceeded to go ballistic. When the accountant asked, "What should I tell the guy on the phone?" John said, "Tell him fuck you, we aren't coming!"

The reason John was so pissed was he had been promised heavy rotation of our new video on VH1 if we came to New Orleans to perform. John always followed up on people's promises. He wasn't seeing the video being played much on TV during the day, so he had someone research when our video was being played. Heavy rotation meant it was supposed to be played a lot, maybe seventeen times a day.

The bottom line was our video was being played late at night when everyone was sleeping. John got on the phone and went ape shit on our manager and hung up on him and came back into the practice room steaming. I loved that he wasn't afraid to stand up to these guys. VH1 ended up apologizing, and not only was John promised seventeen plays during the day, but seventeen at night as well, and the next thing you know, we are on a private jet to New Orleans.

The tour started August 1 in Montreal, and the next day after our show at Jones Beach, Long Island (one of the coolest venues in America), I got a call from tour manager Harry Sandler that we were going to cancel the second night because John was really sick with some weird flu. That was the first time we ever canceled a show because of any health issues, and it was all very strange. We've played with kidney stones and missing toes. The flu? That was not like John at all.

We took a few days off and finished that leg of the tour on August 30, but John had to shorten the show. He had very little energy and wasn't moving around as much, which wasn't like him at all. I was thinking, Jesus, what a powerful flu, if it could take down Mellencamp, fuck. I hope I don't get it.

When we got back home, John's doctor told him that he had experienced a mild heart attack on tour.

Heart attack? Holy shit, no one should have been having a fucking heart attack. We were like thirty years old. That was what he thought was the flu? It blew our minds. We thought he was invincible. *We* thought *we* were invincible. We ended up canceling the rest of the tour.

26

Melissa

When the doctor says you should stop smoking because it will kill you, you might want to start thinking about quitting. Not John Mellencamp. He still smokes, and throughout my seventeen years playing with his band, I've watched him smoke four packs a day, about the same as Jackie Gleason in his prime. He smoked nonstop, twenty-four hours a day. He would even wake up in the middle of the night a few times just to have a cig. The thing that he couldn't live without was the exact thing that might eventually kill him. That sounds like a bad relationship to me.

Honestly, the band was kind of bummed out that he had canceled the last three weeks of our tour, especially after the doctors told him he could go back as soon as he wanted. But he was freaked, as you could imagine. We weren't unfeeling, but on the other hand, we lost three weeks of work. It puts you in a hard place. You don't want the guy to keel over and die onstage, but playing those last three weeks would have reinforced to the band and our fans that the show must go on, and that he cares about our livelihoods as well. There's no workman's comp in this gig. The singer goes down, we all go down. We played with kidney stones and amputated toes; you don't get to call in sick. Maybe dead, maybe you get to call in dead. But that's it. And you better have a note.

But he was terrified. I never saw him like this. He was really scared to go back out onstage. For a hot second, he quit smoking, and then he started again. He chose another brand, an all-natural brand of tobacco, as if that was the *healthy* brand of cigarettes. He lived to smoke. He had to know that eventually it would kill him, but not to smoke would have killed something fundamental about him. Cigarettes were his fucking mojo. They were the longest love affair he had ever had, and he was not going to give them up. But we were watching him smoke and going, "Really, John?"

John finally decided to book some warm-up shows in the Midwest. I can only imagine the concerns and anxiety John must have had getting back onstage, physically and mentally, after his heart attack, but ultimately he was nothing but tough, and there was no way he was not going to get back on the stage, so in January 1995, we played a small club show in Grand Rapids, Michigan.

We were all concerned about that first performance after his heart attack. He must have been shitting in his pants wondering if he would have another heart attack right there onstage. He was excited to perform again, but worried he couldn't perform 100 percent without croaking, and it wasn't like John was going to come out and be less than 100 percent. That's not who he was. When the show started, John came out strong and cocky, and the small club audience loved it, but I knew he was going through a lot of stuff in his mind, honestly wondering if he was going to make it. It was pretty fucking brave, I have to hand it to him.

I was still flying all over the country like a madman doing sessions. I went to New York and worked with Andrew Lloyd Webber (the composer and writer behind Broadway hits like *Cats, Phantom of the Opera*, and *Jesus Christ Superstar*), then I went to Nashville to record with Billy Ray Cyrus, who is one of the nicest, coolest guys I have ever met. He is very humble and includes everyone in the creative process when you work with him.

I went to Philadelphia to work with Jon Bon Jovi on a new record he was producing for Billy Falcon, and wound up doing a two-page feature interview with journalist Tony Scherman on my momentum as one of the busiest session and touring drummers of the 1990s. It was published in the Arts and Leisure section of the Sunday edition of the *New York Times*.

I was on a roll, heading back to Bloomington to work with reclusive Guns N' Roses co-founder and songwriter Izzy Stradlin. He lived close enough, in Lafayette, Indiana, and decided to come to Bloomington to work with Mellencamp's guitarist, Mike Wanchic, who was going to produce some stuff for him. I don't think it ever came out, but it was a fun session. He was trying to be creative, really trying to find himself post-Guns N' Roses.

From there, I was whisked off to Willie Nelson's Pedernales Studio, thirty minutes outside of Austin, Texas. It was originally Pedernales Country Club, and Willie turned the main reception building into a recording studio, and there is a nine-hole golf course there. He bought the property and built a house on top of a hill, but when he is off the road, he still lives on his bus, even when it is parked outside his house.

Sometimes I played golf with Willie when I wasn't recording. It was surreal, playing golf with Willie, puffing on one of his joints. You could never say no when he offered you a toke. That would be rude!

Around that time I was recording with Willie in LA, Don Was was producing, and one day Willie came in and said he had to leave early to play a charity event at which Frank Sinatra was also performing. Don immediately said, "You have to take us!"

So Willie, Don, Reggie Young (Willie's guitar player), Mickey Raphael (Willie's harp player), and I jumped into a limo and headed for Palm Springs to be Willie's band. We were in such a rush and things were happening so fast, we actually went to the wrong hotel. The car took off and we were stranded there looking like *Spinal Tap* meets *The Beverly Hillbillies*. Finally we made it to the venue and played behind Willie.

I was listening to Frank Sinatra way before I ever heard or saw the Beatles. Frank was the rock star for my mom's generation, and his records were always being played in my house when I was a kid.

Frank was amazing to watch up close: his style, swagger, and, of course, his voice. On top of the personal highlight this was for me, we were actually opening what would be his last live performance ever, although he didn't know it yet. The whole experience had been Willie and Don Was's idea, and the three of us were standing on the side of the stage, with our heads just about touching like the Three Stooges, trying to get a better look at Frank.

After the show, I flew to Houston to play the Houston Rodeo with Hank Williams, Jr., which was a slightly different musical experience.

My typically insane schedule took me back to NYC to play *Late Night with David Letterman* with the Highwaymen. From there, I found myself whisked back to Indiana to enter the studio with John Mellencamp for what would be *Mr. Happy Go Lucky.*

Once again, John wanted to introduce some new ideas for this record, so he brought in a very cutting-edge, well-known DJ/producer named Junior Vasquez, who'd worked with Madonna, Whitney Houston, and Janet Jackson. What that had to do with John's music, I have no idea, but he was getting into loops and dance grooves, far away from the what-you-see-is-what-you-get Americana.

I didn't get it—I thought Vasquez was a cool dude, but what were we doing chasing Madonna?

Everything starts with a great song. A great production can help present a song better, but a great song is where it all starts. You can't shine a turd. This wasn't who we were. We weren't a dance pop band. Chasing trends was nowhere—it never worked for the Stones. Mick seemed like he always wanted to update the sound of the band or play whatever was hot, and it never worked. People may have tuned in because it was the Rolling Stones, but drum loops for Charlie? No one wanted that. It certainly wasn't Keith's bag. I heard the story that they hired Babyface, the hip-hop producer, to do some looping and mixing, and Keith walked in and said, "So you're Babyface? You're gonna look like Fuckface after Mick's done with you."

I was totally open to being hip—and I think John was great for trying, and he went out and got the best dance mix guy in New York, but I didn't think Junior really brought enough to the party, and I don't think it made sense with John's style of music. John was always about songs. This felt like a desperation move, which doubly made little sense because he had earned a great following the hard way, with sweat and hard work. He didn't need any tricks.

The record got mostly good reviews, but it was definitely a departure. It turned out to be the last record I would work on with him.

◄◦►

Back in my world, the race was still on. Fresh from Mellencamp's record, I was off to do a Rod Stewart session. It never stopped—I'm leaving out a ton of gigs and sessions—the phone was always ringing. Never in my wildest dreams did I think it would work out this well.

And every day was a surprise. I flew to LA to record a Tom Petty song, "Leave Virginia Alone," which Rod Stewart was going to sing for a movie sound track. When I got there, I ran into Melissa Etheridge's guitarist, John Shanks, who was talking to Hugh Padgham, the producer behind Sting, the Police, Genesis, and one of the architects of that massive "In the Air To-night" drum sound. As soon as they saw me, they both burst out laughing, simultaneously, almost cryptically.

> **John Shanks**: I'd been playing with Melissa for a long time, and we were working on *Your Little Secret*, and Hugh Padgham—who was producing the record—he and I were sitting in Studio B at A&M and were talking about drummers who might work on a song we were struggling with, and I said to Hugh, "You know, the perfect drummer for this fucking song is Kenny Aronoff. It needs that kind of energy." Hugh loved the idea and asked, "Do you know him?" And I said, "Yeah, I've met him a couple times, but I don't have his number. . . ." Now, this was 1994, so it was pre-cell phones and the Internet, and I could have gotten ahold of it, but right at that moment didn't have his number, and oddly enough, right then as we were walking from Studio B, there's Kenny, literally walking down the hallway! But that's Kenny to me: the right guy who's always there at the right time.

They couldn't believe it, though they couldn't tell me anything about any of this at the time because they hadn't discussed any of their ideas with Melissa yet. This was the peak of Melissa Etheridge's career: she had tons of hits on the radio, videos all over MTV, and had been touring on and off nonstop for three years. They were still on tour and were recording this new album while they were on breaks, doing what any smart artist should do when they are hot: keep the momentum going. She was staying relevant and on top of it. No slacking.

I was a super fan of Melissa's music, and could relate to her singing and her energy, and was ready to bring my own to her next record. I began two months later.

Amid all of this, I somehow kept up with teaching my students at Indiana University. I had to constantly make up lessons because of my crazy schedule, but to make it up to the students, at the end of each teaching year, I always had a wild party at my house. I had the basic cookout with lots of food and booze, but the thing that made my party different was my invention, Kenny Croquet, which was two croquet sets combined and set up pretty much everywhere except the living room, and at every wicket there were instructions that the players had to read and follow. Things like: "Do a shot of Jack Daniels, do ten push-ups, and slug someone in the arm," or maybe you had to sink three baskets in my basketball court before continuing to the next wicket. A lot of people got stuck because they were pretty drunk from the previous wickets. And then you got to the wicket at the trampoline; you had to get on the trampoline and bounce up and down with your ball and somehow hit it off the trampoline to move on. Finally, near the end of the game, you had to play through a few wickets with your pants around your ankles (female percussionists were exempt from this). I have no idea why this never became part of the accepted curriculum. Seems like somewhere in there are some pretty valuable lessons. I was preparing them for the real world . . . at least the rock 'n' roll world. You have to do a great job, even when you're drunk with your pants down around your ankles. The neighbors would drive by and wave, with that half smile I was getting very used to, as if to say, WTF is Kenny up to now?

─◄o►─

Heading into the studio with Melissa to record *My Little Secret*, I had a feeling this was going to be the beginning of an amazing relationship with her, and it was everything I had hoped and more. She blew me away with her singing, her music, and her heart of gold.

We recorded in one of my favorite rooms at A&M (Henson) Studio B, which had this big crystal in the wall. That room is great if you want a powerful, ambient rock 'n' roll drum sound, but the cool thing is that Studio B room isn't so big that it's unmanageable. You can deaden the room or keep it super live, but even when it's super live there's just enough ambience, but not too much. It was perfect.

The first song we recorded was "I Want to Come Over," which became one of the record's biggest radio hits. I remember I went into Melissa's vocal booth and asked her to sing and play the song on acoustic guitar so I could make a chart and get an idea of what beat to play before we started tracking together, and I have to tell you, she is one of the best rhythm guitar players I have ever played with, and when she sang it, she sang it as if we were in a stadium performing live.

I love it when musicians go for it when they are recording. I was so moved by her I could barely control myself. She excited every cell in my body. She inspired me to play at the highest level possible. It was just one of those crazy things. Lightning in a bottle. Stars lining up. It happens. We still talk about that first recording session and how we motivated each other.

After four days of recording, I told her and her manager, Bill Leopold, that I wanted to play live with her someday—after the studio nearly melted me, I needed that experience. Bill playfully cautioned, "Be careful what you wish for." I thought, Bring it on, bring it on.

> **Melissa Etheridge:** Oh my God. Kenny has such a powerful way of playing that any other musician is in danger of being overpowered by it, but he and I had so much fun because we would just push each other further and further, and as far as he could go, I could go, and as far as I could go, he could go. I come from a bar-band background; that's where I learned to play—years and years in the Midwest playing bars. That's where I learned dynamics, and Kenny took those dynamics with me—when we would start kind of low and move into those big choruses, when I went

to look for another gear, he was always there, ready to go one step higher. It was amazing.

The way he hit the snare drum was above and beyond anyone else who was playing drums at that time. You can tell, there's not many drummers where you can listen to a recording, and go, "Oh, that's Kenny," just because of the way the snare drum sounds. *He* was the sound of the late '80s and '90s, *that* was Kenny. He was a force to play with, to harness, and the first time I ever played with him, I turned around, looked at him, and said, "Whoa, you gotta be my drummer!" He was amazing.

Melissa was the amazing one, and this was just the beginning for us. Meanwhile, I was about to be blown away by the next in a series of life-changing phone calls, this one from one of the undeniably greatest songwriters in American rock 'n' roll history, a cat as badass as anyone who ever shook a guitar.

27

Blue Moon Rising

John Fogerty was the mastermind behind Creedence Clearwater Revival, the singer, writer, and guitar slinger behind their amazing string of hits, including "Proud Mary" (covered most famously by Ike and Tina, but also Elvis Presley and a ton of others), "Travelin' Band," "Fortunate Son," "Who'll Stop the Rain," "Lookin' Out My Back Door," and on and on. I was always crazy about them, since I was a teenager rolling joints on their album covers.

But it had been years since John played any of his Creedence material. John's lousy record deal with Creedence and Fantasy Records is legendary, and he held a grudge against his old label by never playing those songs so Saul Zaentz, the motherfucker who owned some of the rights, would never get another dime out of him.

I was the thirtieth and final drummer John Fogerty had asked to record on what would become his Grammy Award–winning *Blue Moon Swamp* record. It took him five years to record that album. *Five years.* Talk about perfectionists, Fogerty was way beyond anyone I had ever met. Five years and thirty drummers to make a rock record?

Playing on *Blue Moon* was a new experience for me. I'd never recorded an album before the way John did: first of all, I was told only to bring my sticks, no drums, no snares, no cymbals, etc. That was a very unusual request, because bands and artists always wanted me to bring my equipment, so I would "sound like Kenny." But John was very knowledgeable about all the instruments and the individual detail it took to make each instrument sound the way he likes. I have seen John ask a bass player or guitarist what pick they're using, and where they're hitting the strings on the neck of their individual instruments. He played both instruments incredibly well, along with drums, and his favorite snare drum was a 1962 5" x 14" Ludwig Supra Phonic 400 snare drum with a Remo Coated Ambassador head on it tuned very specifically. John would also pick places on the top head to glue moleskin, to get rid of certain overtones and undesired ringing. He was trying to make it sound *perfect*.

Luckily for me, that has always been my favorite snare drum (until I designed *my own* signature snare drums, made by the Tama drum company, and modeled after that old Ludwig snare). In the studio, John personally tuned one of the snare drums every day and changed the snare heads every night after each session. He went further with the snare-drum obsession than any drummer or producer I had ever met. We even discussed where my stick struck the snare drum.

The first song we recorded was "Rambunctious Boy," and I immediately understood where he was coming from. We didn't record with a click track, but the engineer played a click to us through our headphones before every take to give us the correct tempo, and then John would count off the song. Bob Glaub played bass, and John sang and played guitar. I eventually realized that John was *only looking to get the drum tracks*. We would record a song two times, and then we would all go into the control room and listen to what we had done. We'd repeat this process over and over again, playing that same song for three or four hours. John's songs are simple and brilliantly right to the point, but he had to record a lot of takes to get *exactly* what he was looking for.

John Fogerty: It had been sort of a frustrating journey for me making *Blue Moon Swamp*. I think when I was young, I just thought if a drummer or any musician grew up and became competent and good, he could play anything, but it kind of doesn't work that way. I had literally been through thirty drummers on my album, some of whom had actually played well and so I kept what they had. But what I would usually do on the record is I'd have two or three or four songs, and I'd invite a drummer in and then we'd work a little bit on each of those songs that I had in mind, and I'd try to find the one he was best suited for, and of course, many times it turned out the fella wasn't suited for any of them. So I'd be very frustrated. I had met Kenny and known about him—the first time when I'd played at Farm Aid with Mellencamp when Kenny was his drummer at the time—and I thought he was pretty doggone good. We did a Roy Orbison tribute where I got to do a song or two, and Kenny happened to be the drummer in that band, and I thought, Wow, that guy's pretty good; he seems to get this. So after having been through so many drummers on *Blue Moon Swamp*, I said, "Okay, you know what, I'm gonna call Kenny." I had a song called "Rambunctious Boy," which is sort of a driving, straight-eight-to-the-bar kind of thing, and it turned out he played it really well, and his feel was exactly what I wanted.

In most sessions, I would have said I nailed it in one to three takes, but John was looking for something—and I didn't know what that was yet. After a short lunch break, we recorded a second song and repeated the same process that we did with the first one, for hours at a time. Now, here's the amazing part: we recorded the same two songs the next day, then the same songs on Wednesday, the same songs on Thursday, and finally the same two songs on Friday. I had never recorded so many takes of a simple song in my life, but the bottom line was this was a process that made John Fogerty happy and satisfied.

John Fogerty: I've come to learn that what's really going on with Kenny is, he's playing right in time, but there's a sense of push—certainly the backbeat and the kick drum—and it feels like the music is *leaning*, as Bill Monroe used to say, "They gotta put the lean to it." Turns out that bluegrass very much depends on that same feel that rock 'n' roll—or at least the kind of rock 'n' roll I like—depends on, so having done that first song, the next time I had a song I was ready to record, I just called Kenny rather than going through a phone book and trying everybody that I'd already tried. What I said years later was, I just sort of progressed through the remaining songs of the album—I think there were five of them yet to be recorded—and Kenny played well everything that I threw at him.

We were a good match for each other because we both are workhorses, perfectionists, and never completely satisfied. He wanted lots of takes, which seemed crazy but was fine with me—I always thought I could do it better anyway. This was the beginning of a relationship that has lasted over twenty years and is still going on, making records and staying on the road—which with John means you spend about as much time sound-checking and rehearsing as you do actually playing in front of people. He still wants it perfect, every time.

After the Fogerty session, I did two songs on Celine Dion's *Falling Into You* album at the Hit Factory. Her record came out in 1996 and sold *32 million* copies worldwide, and went to #1 in fourteen countries, including the USA. And then I flew from there back to Indiana to rehearse for the mother of all stadium rock concerts: the grand opening of the Rock and Roll Hall of Fame at the Cleveland Baseball Stadium.

Bruce Springsteen opened up the show with Chuck Berry, spinning on a circular stage. I played second with John Mellencamp, and when the show was done, I stood on the side of the stage for almost eight hours just watching. The highlights for me were John Fogerty—who I wasn't touring with yet, even though that was soon to come—Al Green, and the Pretenders with Chrissie Hynde singing "Going to Ohio"—she grew up in Akron, which is right next to Cleveland—and the local crowd of about 80,000 went nuts for her.

I ran into her after the concert, backstage at 2:30 a.m. She was sitting on a road case holding a bottle of white wine. I approached her and told her that I was a huge fan and asked her why she had ignored me when I saw her before in the elevator earlier that day—when we were the only two people in the elevator. I told her, "I felt like you were blowing me off as if to say fuck off." To which she immediately responded by saying, "Oh, darling, it's not *fuck off*, it's probably I want to *fuck you!*"

28

Mellencamp—the End

Bob Seger production rehearsals had started in early January 1996 in Ann Arbor, Michigan, with our complete stage setup with sound and lights. We set up in a big venue in order to tweak everything for the arena tour. So far, Mellencamp was cool with me touring with Bob Seger, as I could give him one week in April to finish up the *Mr. Happy Go Lucky* record that we were still working on. Miraculously, the week Mellencamp wanted me to record fell exactly on a week Bob Seger wanted to take a break from touring. It all seemed like it would work out.

Seger's dress rehearsals for the 1996 US tour were supposed to be January 3 and 4, with the next two days off (I booked a session in Nashville for those two days—I really hate days off) and rehearsals continuing on January 7. On this tour, I negotiated a deal that paid me for each workday, but not on days off. This made it possible for me to keep doing sessions while on tour, which worked in my favor, most of the time—during the session on January 5 and 6, a huge storm rolled in. All airports within a 400-mile radius were closed. My only hope to make it back to Detroit in time for Seger's rehearsal was to drive through the night in a blizzard on highways that were closed—seriously, I could have fucking died out there and no one would have found me for days. There were twelve inches of snow on Highway 65, and I was slamming through it all in order to get to an airport that was open so I could fly at 6 a.m. It was a full dress rehearsal with sound and lights. This was no casual band practice; this was the final run-through for a sold-out arena tour. Seger hadn't done a tour in ten years—this was huge. Stress level was 200 percent. It was a total fucking nightmare. Everything went wrong for twenty-four hours. I never should have taken that session in Nashville—I ended up risking my life for some unsigned songwriter because, typical of me, I can't say no. I made it to the dress rehearsal literally fifteen minutes before Bob walked in.

When Seger finally took a break from tour in April, I recorded some tracks with Mellencamp in Indiana, and while we were recording, John mentioned to us that our record label, Polygram Records, was having their annual corporate week-long conference in Hong Kong and wanted him to be the entertainment on the last night. Elton John had performed the year before and U2 the year before, so it was an honor and a very big deal to be invited. John didn't want to go all the way to Hong Kong, but he couldn't turn this down, especially because it would help get the label behind his new record. Basically we had to do it.

I think John secretly was hoping I couldn't go to Hong Kong because of my tour schedule, and that that would be his way out, but there happened to be a perfect five-day break on the Seger tour, which allowed me to make the trip. But it was a bit risky because the commercial flight back from Hong Kong I ended up taking landed in Detroit, Bob's hometown, on the afternoon of a Bob Seger show day. It was the first of three shows at the 23,000-seat, sold-out Palace Sports and Entertainment Center. There was no showing up late, not on this tour.

I didn't feel comfortable telling Punch, Seger's manager, about this Hong Kong gig because I knew he would freak out—it was cutting it close. If there were any delays, I would have fucked everything up. Before telling Punch about any of this, I started gathering as much information as possible. The big question was, could I arrive in Detroit on the morning of the Seger show *and* have some back-up flights available? Always have a Plan B.

Mellencamp's management seemed to think it was very possible for me to get back to Detroit in the morning, because they believed some record company executives would be flying in and out of Hong Kong on their corporate jets. They thought I could most likely jump on someone's jet after the Mellencamp show and start my journey back to Detroit.

The other idea was Mellencamp might be able to start 30 minutes earlier than scheduled, so I could race to the Hong Kong airport and catch a commercial flight to Paris or Holland, and connect there and get to Detroit by 9:30 a.m. the day of the Seger show. I felt confident that Seger's management would be cool with one of those scenarios. Turns out I was *wrong*. They were not happy at all.

Things weren't falling into place: Apparently there was a law in Hong Kong that said no corporate jets were allowed to park at the Hong Kong airport, and Polygram did not want us to play thirty minutes earlier so I could fuck off back to Detroit. I couldn't get a break: if I spent the night in Hong Kong and took the earliest flight back through Tokyo, that would get me to the Detroit Metro Airport at 2:45 p.m. the day of the show. It would take at least ninety minutes to drive to the Palace, not to mention the time it would take to go through customs. I would miss sound check for sure, but at least make the show.

I had to tell Punch the bad news. Punch said he was actually going to have to look into an insurance policy with Lloyd's of London to cover that one show in case I didn't make it. Oh man . . . I was feeling caught between rock 'n' roll and a hard place, between two very big artists, one who had been my boss for seventeen years, even though I hadn't been on retainer since the late '90s. I ended up on the phone with Mellencamp's manager, who just screamed at me. He told me I had to get on that plane to Hong Kong, and fuck anything and everyone else.

The night before I had to fly to Hong Kong, I was playing with Seger at a sold-out concert at Market Square Arena in Indianapolis, and Punch told me right before the show that Lloyd's of London finally came back to him with a huge quote, and it was more than I would make for the *entire tour*. I immediately called Mellencamp and told him what Punch had just told me, and John replied, "There's no way they will make you pay that much." I told John that it sure seemed like Punch wasn't fucking around when he told me; that it seemed very real and believable to me, and I didn't want to gamble with that possibility. John's response wasn't surprising: "Just do the right thing." I thought, "What is the right thing?" I wanted to hear from John or his management, "Don't worry, we got your back," and I wanted to hear from Seger's people the same thing, but no one was saying that or giving me any sense of relief.

Well, I played the Seger show, and the next morning at 8 a.m. I was on a private jet from Bloomington to LA and then a commercial jet from LA to Hong Kong. I drank and slept the entire way, and as soon as we got to the hotel in Hong Kong, I went right to the big ballroom in the hotel where we were performing and did a five-hour sound check. I finally went to my room to eat some dinner and relax, but fifteen minutes after being in my room, the phone rang and it was Punch calling from Detroit. He said the insurance policy to cover that first show in Detroit with Seger was now only $3,400 because the Detroit Pistons had been beaten in the NBA playoffs, eliminated sooner than anyone had expected, so now there was an open night at the Palace if Seger needed it.

This made sense. Now, if I somehow got in later and Seger had to postpone the first show, instead of the make-up date being a month or more later, we now could use the open date and still play three in a row. But I had fifteen minutes to decide whether to take the insurance or not. I asked Punch if I could call him back in ten minutes and immediately called John's management in NYC to ask if they would pay the insurance bill and cover my ass because I had done "the right thing," to quote John. No one would say yes, so I called Punch up and said, "Get the insurance," and sure enough, they ended up deducting $3,400 from my salary. But now that I think about it: I never saw the insurance bill. Why didn't I ask to see the bill?

I was fortunate that my flight landed on time in Detroit and my bags came out fast, but someone stopped me at customs and wanted to know what was in my Anvil case. Another customs guy interrupted and said, "Hey, man, let Kenny go. He's Bob Seger's drummer and he's got a show tonight at the Palace!" Then a third customs guy jumped in and said, "He's not Seger's drummer. He's Mellencamp's drummer!" They almost got into a fight. I had to laugh, but between the both of them, I was out on the curb in about thirty seconds, where someone met me and took me to a helicopter to fly from the airport over the city to the Palace, to make up for the ninety minutes I'd have spent in traffic, which could have meant missing the sound check, which was not at all acceptable.

That was a first for me. It was like flying in a glass bubble, like at the end of the first Willy Wonka movie. I could see the Palace way off in the distance past the city. We landed outside in the parking lot. It was so rock 'n' roll, or like something out of a James Bond movie. I was actually *early*. I remember Bob had a big smile on his face. When we were in the home stretch of the show, playing a string of up-tempo hit songs, Chris Campbell—Seger's bass player—walked up onto my drum riser and said, "Come on, Kenny, admit it, you're tired!" I just smiled at him and played harder. I would never admit to anyone that I was tired or jet-lagged, or anything, except that I was Superman.

―◦―

My relationship with John Mellencamp was becoming more and more strained by now, and we eventually had to have what was the inevitable conversation about my position in his band. It was June 1996, and I was in Detroit, performing with Seger.

I spent four days in a hotel room writing a letter to John that I never sent. I wish I had kept that letter—I wrote the type of things I was afraid to say to John face-to-face.

It was hard to be around John at this time, because he was always angry or in a bad mood. I mean, why would I want to be around that, especially when I had options? And I had options! I was over it. Time to move on. I felt he didn't appreciate the band he had, a very fucking good one that was very loyal to him. The entire thing was awkward and uncomfortable. I loved being in his band, and we all worked our asses off for him. We were a team. But when you're working your ass off for the cause, and you're getting yelled at, or put down, you have to ask yourself, "Is this still worth it?" We helped create his sound. We loved him and would have gone to the mat for him. But there were still a lot of hard feelings that needed to be addressed.

I had already visualized my future as a session drummer when John had announced his hiatus. I had been training for this for years, with the crazy schedule I was keeping in and out of John's band, and I was confident about heading out completely on my own, but still, writing that letter helped me find the best way to express myself when I actually spoke to John.

Leaving John's band after seventeen years felt like a divorce. I had spent more than a third of my life in John's band. We spent more hours in a year together than we did with our wives, girlfriends, and family. That's what being in a successful band is all about. Leaving wasn't an easy thing to do.

I always know what I want to do emotionally, but the conflict with me always lies between what I feel like doing . . . and what I think I should do.

When I finally spoke to John on the phone, I was nervous and very uncomfortable. But as it turns out, he was very polite and not angry like I expected. This completely undermined everything I had to say. There was no argument, no fighting or bitterness. He was as nice as he had ever been, and it kind of deflated me. It was genius on his part—I was all set to take it on the chin (if I didn't find the nerve to confront him)—but surprisingly he was super cool. He was very capable of blind anger and just fearsome yelling, but I think we had both come to the same conclusion that it was time for me to leave the band. He said, "Let's look at it like we are two ships passing on the sea. . . ."

And I was just happy to avoid the confrontation.

Tensions had been steadily building between John and me since we took a break after the *Lonesome Jubilee* tour in 1987 and I started doing a lot of sessions. My schedule became busier and busier, and John felt that his band wasn't the priority in my life anymore. He was probably right, even though I may not have seen it, because I was still a very loyal soldier. Nothing came before Mellencamp's band, not Elton John, nothing.

But my role had changed: *Kenny, the drummer in the John Mellencamp band* to *Kenny Aronoff, the drummer who plays in John Mellencamp's band, the session drummer for everyone.* John had to have *hated* that. My income was coming from three different places now—touring, sessions, and drum clinics. John watched me grow from the guy playing in local clubs to performing in arenas with him all over the world and getting press of my own. And when it was all over, I had recorded many more records and many more #1 hits with other artists.

The hardest thing about leaving John's band was I wasn't going to be playing with the guys anymore. And those drum parts made me feel as if they were my songs as well—how many drum breaks do audiences actually know as well as the choruses?—and it was hard to give up the identity of being the man behind them. Then again, touring wasn't like it had once been. I wasn't always on the prowl, wasn't in it just for the girls and the partying anymore. I was having a blast just by *playing*, and making a lot more money doing it.

I was in such high demand outside of John's band by then that when he decided with no notice that he wanted to record a song or make a video, I was usually in LA or Nashville working and had to fly home to Indiana and then right back out of town again. I had grown independent, and this began to cause a lot of friction between us. I wasn't on a retainer anymore, so I felt I could justify saying, "No, I can't come to Bloomington right this second because I'm recording with Hank Williams, Jr.," or whomever, "but I can come tomorrow or next week." I remember when we actually had that conversation, his first response was, "Well, you just tell Hank Williams, Jr., you have to come home."

I learned a valuable lesson from that experience about the importance of sticking to your commitments, which might sound basic, but in the music business, your word is *everything*. No matter how big the offer might have been, if I started leaving studio sessions for a bigger arena gig here or there, with John or anyone, my reputation would have turned toxic overnight, destroying years of working for a rock-solid rep for reliability. You can never be wrong if you keep your word.

John Mellencamp: Things got to the point where I'd say, "Kenny, I need you to come," and he'd say, "I can't, I got a session booked," and I'd say, "I don't give a shit about your session, Kenny," and he'd be like, "Well, I can't tell these people no, I've already said yes." And I understood that: that he'd made a commitment, but we were young guys, and if we were doing it today, I think we would have handled it differently and had better communication skills, and all of that. But we were young guys, and I was particularly domineering at the time. I remember what did it with me with Kenny—just knowing we had to part company—was I needed him to play on something, and he was supposed to go down and play on a Hank Williams, Jr., record, and I said, "What? You think I care about Hank Williams, Jr.?" Once that happened, I knew our days were numbered, and shortly thereafter is when we parted company.

I was always happy for Kenny, even when I was disappointed that he'd left the band. Did I think he made some wrong decisions? Yes. I wouldn't have played for some of the people he played for, and I wouldn't have screwed up the deal with this band. I would have tried to figure it out with me, but we were both too immature. I'm not blaming him, by any means. I blame myself. But don't get me wrong, I'm perfectly happy with the drummer I have now. It's not like, "Oh, I wish Kenny's back in the band," because Kenny wouldn't fit in my band now, because we don't do that music anymore, and I don't consider myself a rock musician anymore, nor do I want to be. I was basically angry at him and I both for not being smart enough to make it work. This is where Kenny's ambition and excitement got in the way. But of all the guys that were in my band that broke out on their own, Kenny was the only one that survived, because he really had the ambition.

I am very grateful to John Mellencamp. Being in his band launched my career. He put me on the map. I now realize he was right about a lot of stuff when I was in his band, and I was just too immature to see it. It's similar to the kid who thinks his father is full of shit, but later on realizes that he was spot on.

Playing with John's band gave me an amazing stage to become Kenny Aronoff. We are connected by our music forever, and we are connected by our life experiences, in the studio and on the road during one of the greatest periods in rock 'n' roll history. We are good friends again, and when we get together, it's like the line from "Cherry Bomb": "When I see those guys these days / We just laugh and say do you remember when . . . ?"

29

I Can Breathe Again

The next question for me was, Do I stay in Indiana, or move to LA or Nashville? Do I do just sessions? Do I look for another band? I really liked it there. It was home. And after traveling around the world on tours, and hopping from one city to another doing sessions, it felt great coming back to Bloomington. I grew up in a small town, and even though Bloomington was a city of 100,000 people, it still had that feeling of family and community. The cool thing was I didn't have to make any serious decisions right away because I was working all the time, and I was being flown everywhere from Indiana.

We traveled in luxury on Melissa's tour: The US tour began in 1996, one month after the Seger tour ended. We had our own small, eight-seat private jet, and the cool thing was, we were based out of one city for two or three weeks at a time. We stayed in Boston for three weeks and flew from there and back every night we had a show. As soon as the show was over, we would run off the stage to a van, then to the jet to take off, land in our city, into a van (where I would change out of my sweaty stage clothes), and back to the hotel. We were based out of hotels like the Ritz Carlton in Atlanta, Georgia, and a Four Seasons in Dallas and Houston.

I loved playing in a small, four-piece band. On the road, Melissa never did a sound check, but John Shanks, Mark Brown, and I would jam nonstop for a few hours every day. We were all into sounding better *together*. Because Melissa was headlining arenas and actually had *two* stages—we played her hits, but we also jammed a lot, and during live shows, she loved featuring the band. At one point in the show, she would leave the main stage and head to the small stage in the back of the room, way out in the audience while the three of us kept jamming on the main stage.

When we saw her pop up on the other, smaller stage, we would end our jam, and Melissa would do a few songs by herself on an acoustic guitar. The audience in the back of the arena would go insane because they suddenly had the best seats in the house.

While she was playing her solo set, John, Mark, and I would leave the main stage and make our way back to the small stage through the halls of the venue where no one could see us. We would then join Melissa on the small stage for a few songs. After we played a few songs, we would all leave one by one back to the big stage through the audience. It was a gauntlet of crazy fans trying to grab us as we walked or ran past them. There were a few times when her fans would grab us so passionately that they would rip our shirts off—I loved her audiences, they were the very best, loving in a way that many fans are not. They really adored her.

One night, when we didn't fly after our show, I was hanging out in the hotel bar with some *extremely* hot fans of Melissa's. I eventually said good night and headed for the elevator to go to my room. But when I got on the elevator, they were already there. And when I got off, they got off. My Spidey Sense was tingling. They were a couple of gay chicks, and I was a guy and . . . wow . . . okay. Turns out one of the women was into girls *and* boys, and her partner was only into girls, and so . . . I resisted at first, but eventually, because they were so persistent and convincing, I gave in. It was *me and her*, and then *her and her*, and then *me and her and her*, and then finally just me alone thinking "Wow, did that just happen?"

Just as suddenly as they'd been there, they left. It was like a big storm rolled in and rolled out, and there I was all alone in the calm *after* the storm. I ended up checking out of that room and getting another one because there was too much energy in that room—I would never have fallen asleep. I actually had to leave the hotel and go have a drink at some bar before I came back to sleep.

Melissa Etheridge: Touring with Kenny is probably one of the greatest experiences I ever had. He would never play the same thing twice. I mean, we would play the songs, but whenever we went into any sort of jam or into the choruses when we kick it up, he was always looking for something different, and he would play stuff where my jaw would drop because I couldn't even think these parts in my head. They were so intricate and musical and astounding, things that I don't even know if anybody else could play, and he would do it with such enthusiasm and energy. He's one hyper dude, *unbelievably* hyper. One of my favorite things he used to do was, during the height of the tour in 1996 when we were playing huge arenas, I would end the show with one of the songs from *Your Little Secret*, this sort of obscure tune called "This War Is Over," and I would leave the stage first because I wanted to highlight all the musicians. So then the guitar player John Shanks would solo, then he would leave the stage, then it would be just the bass player Mark Browne and Kenny left, and I told him, "Kenny, this is your time, you do whatever you want," so Kenny would do this *insane* solo, and I used to stand backstage and wait just to hear what he would do, and it was truly insane, so out of this world. Then at the end, he would stand up on his stool and jump back over his drum set, off the riser, onto the stage. Oh my God, that's his energy, and he and the crowd both loved it so much!

One night while I was performing, I got some nasty muscle spasms in my back and chest area, so bad I could hardly breathe. I always played very aggressively, and I was lifting weights pretty intensely on my days off, so I thought maybe I pulled or tore some muscles.

The tour was a physically rigorous one—we did a two- to three-hour sound check before each gig, and then did a three-hour show with no opening act. So I was losing my breath with these muscle spasms while I was playing, and the audience was cheering us along with no clue I was in this kind of pain—I had to keep playing as though nothing was physically bothering me. That's just being a professional, and at points during these spasms, I literally found I couldn't breathe, even though I could keep playing. It was the strangest thing—my lungs would just lock up like someone had knocked the wind out of me, and this would go on for thirty seconds at a time, and it frankly scared the shit out of me. I went to the doctor after the show, but he wasn't sure what it was. He had me apply hot and cold packs six times a day and gave me some painkillers just to keep me going.

Finally, we landed in Dallas, and I went to the Dallas Cowboys' chiropractor. She did some X-rays and came back to me and said, "You've got three ribs that are out of place!" They had been putting pressure on my lungs and causing these spasms, and she had to make a fist and push really hard into my back to get them to pop back into place. It was like a fucking miracle cure. She had the position she did with that team for a reason—I walked out of there feeling like nothing was wrong, but it took an NFL bone crusher to fix me.

That year became my most successful earnings year to date, and beyond that, it was a huge year of growth for me in so many ways. I left the Mellencamp band that year, but managed to tour for eleven months with Bob Seger and Melissa Etheridge, and on my days off I did *twenty records*. And just when I didn't think it could get any better than a good night on tour with Melissa, the phone rang, as it does.

Don Was wanted to hire me to play on a sound track he was producing with Tom Hanks. Tom was not only acting in the film but writing and directing it as well. It was about a fictional early '60s rock band called the Wonders, who had a runaway hit with a song called "That Thing You Do!"

We were instructed during the session to record many different versions of the song, because Hanks wanted many different stages of the Wonders playing the song throughout the movie—everything from the band learning the song in their garage, to playing it in the makeshift studio where the band recorded the version of the song that wound up on the radio, and then live versions as well. It was a unique process, doing so many versions of the same song, but if you watch the movie, you get the idea of how a band grows and how the music grows with them.

After hours of recording, we finally went into the control room at Ocean Way Studios—and there was Tom Hanks sitting at the big mixing board! He spoke and acted totally like the character he played in the movie, and when he saw me, the first thing he said to me (in his manager voice) was, "Nice job, Kenny, but where's your beret?" I was stunned, and gestured to Don in silence, What the fuck is he talking about? Don laughed at me in silence and eventually pulled me aside and told me that Tom was actually inspired to create this movie from the John Mellencamp "R.O.C.K. in the U.S.A." video that I was in. In that black-and-white video, I was playing the drums dressed as a beatnik and was wearing a beret. Tom had even asked Don if he could get someone "like Kenny Aronoff" for the session before Don told him, "Like Kenny? No. There is no one *like* Kenny. So I hired Kenny."

30

Bill Clinton and the Rolling Stones

By 1997, I had performed at so many different events, I didn't get nervous anymore, but playing thirty feet from President Bill Clinton—who was looking right at Jon Bon Jovi and the band—was a real trip. You always hear about how he can own a room with just his eyes. It is very true.

It was the Presidential Gala to benefit the Ford Theater in Washington, you know, where Lincoln got shot (I even got to check out the exact booth where Lincoln was sitting, and I have to admit it was a little creepy). The show featured Bon Jovi, Natalie Cole, the tap dancer Gregory Hines, plus a magician and a ventriloquist. Seriously. A magician and a ventriloquist. At least they didn't get top billing, like the puppet show in *Spinal Tap*.

As soon as we finished our number, I was so pumped and hyper from playing for the president that I ran off the stage and accidentally walked into the wrong room. I knew because it was filled with the baddest-looking Secret Service guys imaginable, his A-Team, loaded to the teeth with serious weapons. No one was smiling at me. It looked like they were deciding how they were going to kill me. Smoke was coming out of their noses. Their necks were like the size of my waist. I backed out of the room, slowly.

When the show was finally finished, and I had been properly identified as one of the performers and not a threat, everyone came back onstage. President Clinton and the First Lady came down and shook everyone's hands with conviction—they really knew how to make you feel important. I guess it is their gift. The president especially, because he is a real rock 'n' roll fan. I got the idea that he was genuinely thrilled to be there. The very next year, I got to do the same gig with Fogerty, and the president was obviously a huge Creedence fan and got off being around the guys in the band.

After President Clinton and the First Lady shook everyone's hands, he came back over to the band. In a moment of hyper-excitement and confidence, I told him that I had just been recording in NYC and LA, and everyone wanted me to tell him that they loved and supported him. This was at the peak of the Monica Lewinsky scandal, and he was getting a lot of shit thrown at him. The president smiled at me, shook my hand, put the other hand on my forearm, pulled me in real close, still looking me straight in the eye—it felt very genuine and heartfelt, and he made me feel like I was his best friend. That was his gift. He said, "You know, they've been trying to get me out of office for six years, and it ain't gonna happen. Ain't gonna happen."

At the after party, a lot of congressmen and senators came up to me, at first they all wanted to say, Hey, great show! But what they really wanted to know was what the president said to me. Apparently they didn't get as much face time with him as I did.

◄◌►

After a few sessions in Nashville, I flew back to LA to finish up John Fogerty's *Blue Moon Swamp* album. We spent one more week recording two more songs for his record—and this ended up being the last week of *five long years* of recording drums.

I really liked working with John. I liked how every note I played had to be perfect, and he asked me if I would be into touring with him. This was going to be the first time in at least seventeen years he would perform the Creedence Clearwater Revival songs that had made him famous.

This was a big deal—*everyone* wanted to hear those songs. People loved him, but he couldn't really put over his new stuff without playing the hits. I know people who claim not to like Mellencamp or Iggy Pop or Bruce Springsteen or whatever, but no one doesn't like Creedence Clearwater Revival, *no one*.

Could you imagine writing "Proud Mary" and not playing it on your gigs? And when he finally did, his audience just exploded. There was a real hunger to hear him do the old stuff, and the best thing is he had not lost a shred of his intensity. He was singing and playing guitar as well, or better, than he did in the '60s and '70s. Maybe even more intensely—he drove me as hard as anyone ever has, telling me to push the beat harder and harder, making it much more aggressive than Creedence ever was, really slamming the beat, just pummeling the drums.

John Fogerty was Creedence Clearwater Revival. He was the songwriter, the arranger, the producer, the voice, the guitarist—he masterminded the entire thing. He had an astonishing vision, and I love the way the drums feel and sound on those original recordings, but he wanted me to incinerate the older groove. So much that I'd get a lot of shit for it by the critics, who can't get past the old records. I remember a bad review in the *Los Angeles Times* criticizing me for pushing too hard:

> Fogerty and his muscular five-piece band . . . often steamrolled over the evanescent qualities that made the original versions so infectious. In particular, celebrated session and touring drummer Kenny Aronoff pushed beats forward rather than remaining a microsecond behind to give the songs room to breathe. Fogerty often seemed challenged to fit all the words in at the accelerated pace, and many of his inspired guitar riffs consequently got short shrift. Faster and louder doesn't necessarily equate with better.

But what the critic missed was that's the way John *demanded* it. He's the boss, not me. It's his decision to play those songs like that, not mine. But no one has ever cared more about how the drums sound than John. He's very focused and determined, and he won't stop trying until he gets what he is hearing in his head. It's his band, not mine. I'm just the engine in his car—he's the one driving.

I have been making records and touring with John since 1996, and I have done sound checks on a show day that have been as long as six hours because he wasn't happy with the way the PA or his monitors sounded, or how his guitar sounded, or how the drums sounded. Twenty years later, we are still rehearsing "Proud Mary." The guy just does not stop trying to make everything *perfect*.

John is especially particular about the drum sound, both live and in the studio. When we are on tour, John will spend thirty minutes of our sound check every day making sure my snare and kick drum sound the way he wants them to.

When we sound-check, he'll walk the room while I groove by myself, and then with the band, then by myself, and again with the band. It's amazing how much John knows about sound and frequencies, and I love his devotion and uncompromising care to detail. I rotate between two of my signature snare drums that are tuned to the same pitch until he picks the one he likes the best. John and I discuss mic placement and tuning every day. John prefers the sound of my snare drum—he likes my 5" x 14" signature Tama snare drum—with a die-cast hoop versus a triple-flange hoop, because the die-cast hoop gives my snare more attack and crack when I hit it. It also centers the pitch of the drum. He can hear the difference between the two different metal hoops. Not a lot of people can. In the studio and live, he loves a Tama 22" x 18" maple kick drum with a Remo fiber-skin three head on it. He usually likes the front head off in the studio with a packing blanket folded a certain way touching the beater head. After years of recording and playing live with John, he lets me do all the tuning now, and he trusts and likes what I do, but back then, I had no problem deferring to his ears entirely. I was in the hands of a master.

John knows that drums drive the music, and he wants me to push the band from the first note of the show to last note. He *never* wants me to lay back on any song we play. John likes me to place the snare drum right on the beat, or just a bit on top of the beat. It is definitely not what he recorded on the CCR records.

John Fogerty: The main thing is, Kenny always plays the drums like he's excited. It's like a little kid just discovering a new drum fill he wants to try

out. It truly does come off that way: that he's excited about what he's doing and that's very much a contagious thing. It really helps keep you fresh
when you're playing thirty-five, forty dates in a row. You never want to
feel like, "Okay, I'm just going to stand here and play this same old guitar
lick." I'm an excitable boy myself. . . .

The *Blue Moon Swamp* tour with John Fogerty was huge. No one had
heard John play or sing those CCR songs for almost two decades, and on
top of that, John was finally releasing the record he had been working on
for five years, and before he actually recorded it, he had spent five years just
getting *ready*. This period was truly the rebirth of John Fogerty.

In most cases, if an artist or band took just two years off, their careers
would be over, but not in John's case. He had a lot of fans, a real legacy, and a
lot of good will toward him. He was a legend, the real deal. When we played
cities like Los Angeles, NYC, and Nashville, lots of well-known musicians
came out to see us perform. We did the David Letterman show three times
that year, *VH1 Story Tellers*, *VH1 Hard Rock Live*, *Good Morning America*,
and *Late Night with Conan O'Brien*, and John won a Grammy for Best Rock
Album. We also played at my old stomping grounds, Farm Aid, this year in
Chicago. I remember it as being one of our best shows. John Mellencamp
was also performing at Farm Aid that year as a headliner.

This would be the first time I saw John play live when I wasn't playing
drums behind him. Which was kind of weird for me. It was like being married to someone for almost twenty years, going through a divorce, and then
seeing that person a year later in a bar with someone else.

On my way to the venue, I ran into his tour manager, who told me that
John said, "It would be okay if I did *not* say hi to him. . . ." I guess it was too
soon for us to be friends again. I honestly felt a little hurt by that, but that's
John. I still love him.

◄○►

Right before I began rehearsing with Fogerty, I played the drums on a new

Joe Cocker record, and during the first two weeks of rehearsals, after I re-hearsed with Fogerty from 12 p.m. to 6 p.m., I drove twenty minutes to Rumbo Studios in the valley and recorded a Catie Curtis record with Roy Bitten from 7 p.m. to 11 p.m. But wait, there's more. From midnight to 5 or 6 a.m. I recorded with Charlie Watts on his solo record, and also with the Rolling Stones on their *Bridges to Babylon* album. Now *that* is a full day of recording, Kenny Aronoff style.

The Rolling Stones gig happened very naturally. One night after record-ing with Catie, I stopped by Ocean Way Studios at midnight because Don Was had invited me to drop in and say hi. When I got there, Keith Rich-ards was recording in the big room in Studio One with Charlie Watts, Ron Wood, and a few other musicians—Jim Keltner on percussion and Waddy Wachtel on guitar. Mick wasn't there. I was told Keith had some musicians record with him to help inspire him and the other guys when they were recording.

Mick recorded his tracks on the days Keith wasn't recording. They were doing their own thing separately, but they would decide which songs were going to end up on the record together. Meanwhile, Charlie Watts was in the small room, Studio Two, in the back, recording his solo jazz record when he wasn't recording drums with Keith or Mick.

The first night I came by Ocean Way, I saw Jim Keltner and Charlie in the lounge eating some food. Dinnertime was usually at midnight, when Keith was recording. Everyone would arrive at 7 p.m. and work until 5 or 7 a.m. I was staying at the Sunset Marquis Hotel, where Keith, Ron Wood, and some of their crew were also staying. I could hear them from my room in the back of the hotel when they came in at 7 a.m., laughing and cackling like crows at each other.

In the studio, Keltner introduced me to Charlie Watts(!) and suggested to Charlie that I play some percussion on his solo record. Jim had already been recording percussion on Charlie's album, and Jim and I both played drums and percussion together on the Joe Cocker *Organic* record, so he knew we could work together as a team. Charlie was totally cool with that idea(!!!), so I went back and recorded percussion until 6 a.m. that first night.

I played weird percussion, like a steel bucket with brushes, an African drum with my hands and sticks, brushes on a plastic Meinl gourd with beads, a tiny snare drum with a splash cymbal on it, and lots more. Charlie loved what I did, and he kept inviting me back to record more (!!!!!!!!!!!!!!!!!!!!). I ended up on three tracks on Charlie's solo record, and one night after rehearsing with John and recording with Catie, I came into the studio and there was Mick Jagger, Ronnie Wood, Charlie Watts, Benmont Tench from Tom Petty's band, and some other killer musicians setting up in Studio Two. Engineers and techs were running around trying to get everything set up and ready to record.

Don had finally convinced the Stones that to make a *Stones* record, it was important to record with the principal players all together in the studio at the same time. So it was Mick, Charlie, and Keith, with me and Jim playing percussion, and Benmont on keys, and Don Was on bass. Ronnie was just hanging around—drinking a Guinness and maybe some whisky, but definitely present, creating his own party.

For one track, I was playing a brush on a gourd that had beads on it, and after a few takes, Mick came up to me and asked me to make sure I didn't mess with the feel of Charlie's hi-hat part. Charlie has a unique feel and style. What he plays is way more special and nuanced than you might realize when you casually listen to a Stones record, but when you are in the same room with him, it's like nothing you have ever heard before. He is unpredictable, not quantized, and impossible to imitate or copy.

It was positively fucking surreal. I was playing with the Rolling Stones. Not Charlie's jazz record (still the coolest thing ever), not a Mick Jagger solo thing (which I got to do, later), the actual *Rolling fucking Stones.*

31

The Smashing Pumpkins

H ello, Kenny? This is Cliff Burnstein from Q-Prime Management. I'm calling about one of the bands we manage, the Smashing Pumpkins." The Pumpkins were going on tour that summer and they needed a drummer. Would I be interested in auditioning with the band for their upcoming tour?

Two years before, in '96 when I was out on tour with Bob Seger, I had heard that the Pumpkins' drummer, Jimmy Chamberlin, had left the band. I told Cliff that I had faxed my resume to his office, but I never heard back from anyone. Cliff laughed and said he remembered hearing about my fax because my forty-page resume took thirty minutes to transmit, and a lot of people in the office were pissed because they had to wait until it all came through. They wanted to send me a bill for the fax paper.

Cliff also said that he and his partner at Q-Prime, Peter Mensch, both had come to see me perform live with John Fogerty in NYC on the *Blue Moon Swamp* tour and for many reasons thought I would be perfect for the Pumpkins' tour. He said Billy Corgan was in NYC finishing up mixing the *Adore* album, and he would let me know when Billy wanted to have me audition. At this point in my career, I usually didn't audition for a tour because the artist or band already knew me, or at least they knew the way I played.

> **Billy Corgan:** Kenny is a true professional. That's why through the years,
> he was one of the highest-paid studio musicians, because if you called
> Kenny's number, you knew exactly what you were gonna get, and you
> could literally book it to the minute—that's something that's not always

appreciated in the music business, but as you get older, you look at these things maybe from a different perspective. Maybe it's like a baseball manager who goes, "Okay, I know I can slot that guy in at third base every day," because you know what you're gonna get, and it's beyond solid. It's probably the least appreciated thing in rock 'n' roll—you have to understand that it has *everything* to do with the way they played that beat.

Nik Aronoff: When my dad got the call from the Smashing Pumpkins, I knew their music—that was my age demographic and generation—we were listening to all the grunge bands: Nirvana, Soundgarden, Smashing Pumpkins, the Pixies, anything we could get our hands on that was that huge, punk, grungy rock 'n' roll that destroyed the '80s. So my room was up in the attic of our house, and I heard my dad yell upstairs to me one day, "Hey, Nik "—and he'd never done this before—I couldn't believe it because I was only fourteen—but he asked my advice about what he should do about joining the band, and I was like, "What?!" For me, it was like, "Wow, my dad's going to be playing with somebody that's *actually cool to me!*" I was fourteen at the time. I didn't care about John Fogerty and Melissa Etheridge and John Mellencamp because that was not what I listened to, and it was, so he was asking my opinion, and I said, "Dad, you've gotta do the Pumpkins! This is really relevant. It's what *we're* listening to."

I was really excited about auditioning and wanted to do the tour, but I was a bit concerned because my style of drumming was so different from Jimmy Chamberlin's style of playing. A lot of the Pumpkins' songs seemed to be built around Jimmy's beats and grooves. I wasn't sure if Billy wanted me to play like Jimmy, or be more myself, or a combination of both. It's impossible for any drummer to replicate another drummer, especially if that drummer was a big part of the sound of that band. I was not worried about playing Jimmy's parts. I was more concerned about what Billy was looking for so I could win the audition.

I started making very detailed charts of all the songs from the three Smashing Pumpkins albums, *Gish*, *Siamese Dream*, and *Mellon Collie and the Infinite Sadness.* I wrote all of Jimmy's drum parts out note for note and set up a very strict practice routine in my studio in Bloomington, Indiana. My process of learning and memorizing songs for a tour is very methodical: I start memorizing five songs a day, then the next day I review all of the songs I had memorized and start memorizing another five songs. On day three, I review the ten songs I memorized and start learning five more. On day four, I review fifteen songs and start learning five more, and I do this until I have the entire set down. Repetition and persistence is the way I learn. There are no short cuts. I worked eight hours a day, taking short breaks to eat and clear my mind.

It helped that I was already a huge fan of the Pumpkins' music, but the more I played the music and lived with it, the more I got wrapped up in it. I felt like I was an actor learning a heavy part in a movie, and the movie was Smashing Pumpkins.

A week before I flew to NYC, Cliff told me that Billy was not interested in me learning any Smashing Pumpkins songs. "Oh no! Wow. . . . Okay. . . ."

I asked Cliff, "What is Billy looking for? How should I prepare for the audition?" He told me, "Billy said don't try to sound like Jimmy Chamberlin. Think more in terms of *Pink Floyd.*"

I got it immediately. Besides being very intelligent and having a photographic memory, I saw that he always did things in a uniquely Billy Corgan way. He wasn't just *alternative,* he didn't just do things a *little bit* differently—he methodically and intellectually chose to do things very unexpected—but still easily understandable and attractive to the masses.

While I flew six hours from LA to NYC for my audition, all I did was listen to the Smashing Pumpkins albums, trying to embrace the vibe of their music and Billy's way of thinking. It was pouring rain when we landed, which seemed to be fitting. There was definitely a dark side to their music.

When I got to the rehearsal studio, I was met at the door by a 6'8" guy named Gootch who worked for the Pumpkins. He was cool and said Billy was running late, so I went over to the drum set and started adjusting the kit. I saw D'Arcy talking on a pay phone, having an intense conversation and totally in her own world. She didn't even realize I was there. Then, super quiet and cool, James Iha came up to me and politely said hi and shook my hand, and that was it.

Eventually, Billy showed up, came walking into the room with a lot of confidence, wearing a long trench coat. Smiling, he came right up to me and said, "Hi, Kenny, Billy Corgan. Sorry I'm so late. I have been mixing our new record. You know how that goes." But he got right to it and picked up his guitar and said, "Kenny, we already know how to play loud, fast, and hard. I want you to think more colors, Pink Floyd and maybe Grateful Dead when you play." I thought, "Cool," but wasn't really sure what he really meant.

Billy Corgan: This is me speaking, so you can interpret this how you want, but I think Kenny was an extremely skilled and gifted musician who wasn't appreciated as an extremely skilled and gifted musician. He was so good at what he did that maybe he was taken for granted, and certainly some of the stories he told me later reflected a sense of feeling like he was being overlooked. Like what he brings to the table is something that maybe people—including somebody like me—wouldn't appreciate on first blush. And having been so intrinsic in that success that he'd had with Mellencamp, I could see that there was a side in his musical playing that he really hadn't explored, which is pulling from kind of an emotional place, which—as strange as it sounds—I don't think he'd really done before.

Sometimes musicians who are very, very skilled, they don't have a lot of intellectual attachment to what they do: they can just do it. So if you listen to a recording of Kenny at eighteen, he was probably very, very good right away. Obviously he's worked very, very hard, to be *one of the best drummers in the world*. But whatever it is, Kenny brought that to the table, and sometimes people say, "Oh yeah, keep doing that," and there's not a lot of intellectual work that goes into that. And so I think I appealed to him in a way to approach music in more of an emotional point of view, and I don't think he'd really ever thought of it like that. Like I'd talk to him about things like dynamics, and dynamics to Kenny is ten. He plays on ten. I was trying to get him to understand the emotional journey that I wanted him to take, and then once he understood that, then his playing, vis-à-vis the music we were playing, got a lot better.

—◦—

When people say to me, "Play like this" or "Play like that," you never know what they really mean. Whatever they are hearing in their head may or may not have anything to do with the song. It may just be some sound or vibe they liked from another record, so I always go to the Kenny Aronoff Philosophy of Drumming, which is:

1. Establish a beat.
2. Keep good time with that beat.
3. Make that beat *groove* and *feel* good.
4. Add creative ideas to that foundation of beat, time, and groove without fucking up rules 1–3.

Billy started playing a kind of psychedelic thing on his guitar that definitely made me think of colors, a moody non-rhythmic sort of thing. So I started playing rolls and quiet vibey parts on my cymbals, colors with no defined rhythm, then added timpani-like rolls on my toms while still playing my cymbals. Then I played cymbals and toms together, adding my snare drum with the snares off. I was trying to develop a repeating rhythm phrase that everyone could identify with and follow. I found the beat, found the groove, and pulled everyone in. And *then* I started to add creative ideas to that foundation. We eventually built that jam into a powerful Pumpkin thing.

After we finished, I said to Billy, "Is there anything you would like me to play differently to make it better?" He smiled and said, "Just do more of the same." We did one more jam, and that was it. The audition lasted thirty-five minutes. I remember thinking while we were jamming that I probably wasn't going to be touring with the Smashing Pumpkins. Their faces were like poker players: I wasn't getting any feedback from anyone while we were playing. There was zero interaction between the musicians.

What I didn't realize was that this was the Smashing Pumpkins' way of doing things. It was their way of communicating. D'Arcy was looking away from everyone to the right as we jammed, and James was looking away from everyone to their left, and Billy was in front of me rocking hard, playing with emotion, focusing on his guitar and really feeling what we were doing. It didn't feel like there was a band vibe or that anyone wanted to connect or engage with anyone else. I didn't realize till I was on the road with them that that was the Pumpkins' way of interacting.

The next day at LaGuardia Airport, while I was at my gate waiting to board a plane to fly back to LA, I got the call from Cliff Burnstein delivering the good news: "You got the gig! Billy really liked your playing, and he would like you to be the drummer on the *Adore* tour this summer." I was super happy, but really surprised I got the gig—I had no indication from anyone how the audition went.

Billy Corgan: We tried out some fantastic drummers, and having played with obviously a very skilled and flashy drummer in Jimmy Chamberlin on the surface, you would think Kenny would be kind of the opposite pick. But it made total sense to us, having grown up on John Mellencamp music, and knowing the kind of musician Kenny was, and getting to know Kenny as a person.

We were coming off of a massive wave of success where we'd been on tour almost continuously, and we literally went studio/tour, studio/tour, studio/tour, and I often tell people I think from 1990 to 2000, when the band broke up, I think the longest period of time off was two weeks in that entire period of time. So you had people who were kind of just living that weird oxygen, and Kenny kind of parachuted into that and got it sort of full on. I think it says a lot that I trusted him to be a stabilizing force in that, which is maybe the greatest compliment we could give him.

If I had to pick one thing that really sticks out is: D'Arcy, our bass player, is the type of person who is very black and white with people, and she just adored Kenny. She just adored Kenny, and I don't know if she felt comfortable with him or safe with him, but it was very rare to see her open up and be herself in front of somebody who was, to a certain extent, an outsider. And I really remember there was one time where D'Arcy knocked all the glasses off a table and was dancing on a table somewhere—God knows where we were—and I just remember looking at Kenny's face and saying, like, "This is what you signed on for, you're in the circus here." I think at times under difficult circumstances, his person, the beautiful spirit that Kenny is, it was nice to see that D'Arcy could connect with him and open up a little bit, because she hasn't always had that relationship with *me*.

Before I started rehearsing for the Pumpkins' tour, I got a call from someone in LA saying that John Fogerty was thinking about going on tour in June or July or August, but nothing was definite. I started to panic right away fearing a conflict. I hate that feeling—I didn't want to say no to anyone, and I especially didn't want to disappoint John Fogerty. I had to make that phone call to John and explain that I wasn't going to be available that summer to tour with him if he decided to tour. As we were discussing everything, I heard his wife, Julie, in the background yell out, "Oh no!," when she realized what me and John were talking about.

I felt horrible. I felt like I had just disappointed my dad or a coach. As I was talking to John, I ended up sitting cross-legged on my kitchen floor. I explained to John that I had pursued the possibilities of touring with the Pumpkins two years ago, and it was a definite tour this summer, and since there was no definite Fogerty tour, I took a guaranteed gig. It was just business. John was very disappointed, and I really felt like I had hurt his feelings, like I had let him down, and that was the last thing I wanted to do. We were becoming good friends, personally and as musicians. John did eventually go on tour that summer, and I missed that one. It broke my heart, but I was back in his camp eventually. And I got to play with the Smashing Pumpkins.

I rehearsed with the Pumpkins in Chicago for one month. Every rehearsal was recorded, and every night I would go back to this amazing apartment I was staying at on Michigan Ave. A couple of my best friends, John and Missy Butcher, let me stay in their amazing apartment that was connected to the Four Seasons Hotel. I had two views, and both looked out on Lake Michigan, and I would sit there and make detailed charts of everything we had rehearsed that day. I was living like a king.

I would also learn songs that I still hadn't learned yet from the *Mellon Collie* CD. Writing charts was the only way for me to remember all the new songs and new arrangements. Billy has a photographic memory and can remember everything—even if we hadn't played a song for two or three weeks. I am the opposite: my method is to write it down, then memorize it. Sometimes people make fun of me for making such overly detailed charts, but as you know, chart writing has been a life saver for me in so many live and recording situations. I definitely do not ever want to be the person slowing down a rehearsal or recording session.

There have been sessions where the music is so complex that writing a detailed chart is the only way I can record in the limited amount of time I have. The biggest challenge is to make it sound like I am *not* reading music, like I have been playing those songs for ten years.

The *Adore* album and tour was a departure from what the Pumpkins had been doing on their previous three records. Billy wanted to play every song on the new record, so we only played three songs from the previous three Pumpkins records: "1979," "Bullet with Butterfly Wings," and "Today."

Another big change was Billy added Mike Garson on keys (who had played the great avant-garde piano solo on David Bowie's "Aladdin Sane") and two percussionists, Dan Morris and Stephen Hodges. Lisa Germano (on violin) did some rehearsals but never joined the tour. So not only was the *Adore* record a huge departure from the Pumpkins' previous records, but the way we played the album's songs live was uniquely different from the record. That frustrated some of the fans who wanted to hear the hits, but the super-fans loved what we were doing. There was so much rhythm going on between the percussionists to my right and left, my goal was simply to keep everyone playing in time and locked into a groove, but there was a lot of overplaying going on between the two percussionists. They had massive setups, and both guys were super creative, but, wow—I was right between them, and there were times when their grooves were totally different from each other, not to mention what I was laying down. At one point I asked them if they could hear each other in their monitors and they said no. I said, "No shit." That's exactly what it sounds like, two lawn mowers running at two different speeds, and I could hear them both. Eventually it got sorted out, but for a while there I was going crazy. Where's the fucking groove? Billy never heard any of it because he was standing in front of his wall of Marshall amps.

We did one warm-up show in Chicago at a famous club called the Metro before heading out on tour. I had my fourteen-year-old son, Nik, with me. He was a huge Pumpkins fan and was pumped to be there. I was wearing a tight, elastic black short-sleeved T-shirt, with a half-inch bright yellow stripe going from my neck down across my shoulders and down each sleeve.

This was just the beginning of a new look: Just as I was walking to the stage, Nik took off his big yellow-lens Urban Outfitters goggle-like glasses with thick black frames, handed them to me, and said, "Wear these, Dad, they match your shirt."

The next day in the Chicago paper, the review talked more about those goggle-like glasses than how I played the drums. I have now been wearing sunglasses whenever I perform for almost twenty years. Actually, at one point, I thought, Fuck the glasses, and stopped wearing them, but I got so much *shit* for not wearing glasses that I went back to wearing them again.

> **Nik Aronoff:** I became inadvertently responsible for his whole sunglasses look. Urban Outfitters had just blown up all over the country, and so I had these huge, black-framed with yellow transparent lenses, like sharp-shooter yellow. So I was standing on the side of the stage, and my dad went, "Those glasses are cool!" And I asked, "You like them?" Took them off my face and put them on his head, and he went out and played on live television wearing them, which started his wearing sunglasses full-time onstage.

Billy Corgan: But I got him to shave his head! He was kind of working the donut thing going around the head, and I was like, "Dude, not for Pumpkins, you have to shave that."

Between the glasses and my shaved head, I had a new look, a new vibe, and I immediately got hit on by girls everywhere, naturally validating those changes in an extremely positive way. It made me look younger, I guess. Younger and *harder*. Of course I didn't mind any of this at all. I started to create a new look, *my* look—not an easy thing to do, but very important in the music business. I came to it late, but the most important thing is, it has to be *believable*. It has to be you, who you are as a person. It has to be real or it will die quickly. This was definitely me.

—◦—

We flew on a big G-4 jet and did one show in every country except the US and Canada, where we did a whole leg of the tour. But in Europe, it was a whirlwind: Germany, France, UK, Greece, Russia, Belgium, Spain, the Netherlands, Sweden, Denmark, Italy, Canada, Argentina, Brazil, Chile, Mexico, and Ireland. There was one day we were in three countries: after our show in Dublin, the next day we flew to the Netherlands and performed at the Bospop Festival, and afterward flew to Paris.

In Moscow, I did something at the end of the show that I have never done before, and, boy, did I pick the wrong show to do it. As we were ending the last song, I stood up and started beating my cymbals with my fists (with drummer gloves on) as I beat my kick drum with my foot. In the spirit of Keith Moon, I kicked over the drum set. I kicked the drums off my riser onto the stage where Billy was, and then Billy kicked the drums across the stage.

I was laughing my ass off as I ran off the stage, and out of the building onto a small bus. What I didn't know was as I was knocking over the expensive, hard-to-find in Russia, Tama Star Classic drum kit, my drum tech, Tracy, had been trying frantically to stop me. Since I never destroy drums when I play them, he had no idea that I would do that in Moscow, and he was right. Or it would have been any other night.

I had no idea that the kit belonged to the son of a KGB officer, both of whom just happened to be on the side of the stage watching me as I kicked their kit off the riser. They had asked Tracy if I would take good care of the kit, and he'd said, "Are you kidding? Kenny is the coolest and would never do anything to mess up your kit. He's not that guy," So when I did kick the drums, the KGB officer made a gesture toward Tracy that he was going to slit his throat!

After the show, the promoter came storming up to our 350-pound tour manager/enforcer, Charlie, and yelled in a thick Russian accent, "Your drummer, he breaks the drum set!" Charlie said, "Where? What? Show me!" And after the promoter showed him two broken cymbal stand tops, he says, "Here, this your drummer . . . he breaks." In classic rock 'n' roll road manager fashion, Charlie pulled out a huge wad of rubles, and said, "How much?" After Charlie paid the promoter off, the promoter waited till he was holding the cash, and said, "Your drummer, he breaks a microphone," and they went through the whole routine again, Charlie demanding the promoter show him, because he knew it was a shakedown at this point. "This microphone isn't broken," he told him defiantly, and the promoter insistently continued, "It's broken," so Charlie pushed back again, "Where, how?"

When the promoter again simply responded, "It's broken," with no further explanation, Charlie had had enough. He picked up the Shure 57 microphone and beat the shit out of it! With the promoter's eyes and mouth wide open, Charlie told him, "Okay, now it's broken. How much do I owe you?" and rolled out more rubles and paid him off. This is why Charlie got called to do all the big international tours, because he knew what to do and how to handle these people. We made it out of Russia with no problems from the KGB and flew on to Greece.

◄◦►

On tour, Billy would change the set list thirty minutes before each show, and not just change the order but make *huge* changes on what we played in certain sections of our songs. He would give me all the changes in his dressing room. I would write them down and then go tell everyone else in the band—that became our ritual. The guitar techs would scramble to get all the guitars tuned and in order for the new set, and because I wrote everything down, I would usually play all the changes perfectly. The thing was—most people would forget the new stuff because they were playing the songs from memory, and some of the changes were *huge*. For example, a typically loud chorus in a song might now break down to just one guitar, vocals, and me on the hi-hat. Billy wanted certain songs exactly the way we had been playing them, and other songs he wanted us to improvise or do completely different.

The challenge for me was always trying to figure out what he wanted at any given moment. Sometimes it seemed that everyone in this business was nuts: the only thing that was predictable about Billy was that he was so *unpredictable*. I just committed to what I thought was right. I would go to the hotel after every show, listen to the show we had performed that night, and rewrite certain charts so I would remember what the latest arrangements were for when we played that song the next time. Sometimes we wouldn't do a song for two weeks, and Billy would always remember the arrangements. He could even remember all my fills and cymbal crashes. His memory was truly amazing.

Billy Corgan: Before Kenny had played with us, we'd done some really, really long tours, and I'd found that a band that doesn't have something to work on gets bored, and then eventually, that stale feeling creeps into the sets. So it became a habit of me or the band to always tweak so that every night that you walked onstage, there was that little bit of anxiety, like, "Oh, I've gotta remember this, I can't forget that." It keeps people on their toes, in a good way—it keeps them musically engaged, because they just can't check out, because a really good musician can check out. My father was a gigging musician for thirty years, and he was so good I know there were nights where he probably thought about what he was going to do as soon as the show was over, so I was asking Kenny to stay connected on that level every day. And we would change arrangements backstage, not even during sound check, like we would be walking onstage and I'd go, "You know that part at the end of the song? Only go two times instead of four," and he'd look at me like, "What?" It was just the way we worked. It wasn't a conscious thing as much as it was a device to stay current with what we were doing.

In Greece, I remember he made nine big changes in nine songs right before the show. I played every change perfectly, except for one that we had not discussed. His cue for his new idea was just turning around and looking at me. That was it: just a look with no expression. I couldn't figure out what that meant—it didn't come with musical notation—so I guessed and I guessed wrong, and he wasn't too happy about that. Then, in Stockholm, there was a complete train wreck at the end of the song "1979." I stopped where I thought we were supposed to stop so the guitar could do the re-intro lick again before the band would come back in. I stopped, but the band kept going. I immediately jumped back in and ended the song as we always did. That was the last song on the main set, and it must have pissed Billy off something terrible because before playing our encore, he went up to his mic and yelled in it, "Aronoff, you're fired, you're fired!"

I couldn't believe he said that *right into the mic to the audience.* I had never experienced anything like that, even on my worst days with Mellencamp. I was pretty pissed off and I told him so the next day.

The next day when we were in Denmark, I mentioned to him that what he said on mic really bummed me out, and he smiled and said, "Oh, that's just Corgan humor, it's not personal." I told him honestly, "Oh, wow, that went right over my head, because no one ever fired me onstage before."

The last live show I did with the Pumpkins was Halloween night at Dodger Stadium in Los Angeles, opening up for KISS. Since it was Halloween, we thought it would be cool to dress up in costumes. We settled on dressing up as the Beatles, with Beatle wigs and my bass drum head sporting the Beatles logo on it. Our keyboardist, Mike Garson, tried to resemble Yoko Ono with a long black wig, but he didn't look anything like her. Right before we played, we were announced as the Beatles and then played "Money"—the old Motown song that the Beatles had played as part of their early sets when they were still primarily a rock 'n' roll band. I remember the audience looking at us completely baffled. As soon as we finished the song, we did the traditional Beatles bow, took our wigs of, and went right into the Pumpkins song "Zero," and that's when the crowd really went nuts—45,000 people had come out to see the show, and most of the fans were dressed like KISS, and they quickly got the joke and into the spirit of it all. It was truly a Halloween concert to remember.

—◦—

The Smashing Pumpkins tour was over, but I spent the next two days with Billy Corgan and legendary Black Sabbath guitarist Tony Iommi for Tony's first solo record, *Iommi*, in one of my favorite drum rooms in LA, Studio B at A&M Studios (now called Henson). Bob Marlette was engineering and producing the record. Billy played bass, co-wrote the songs, and overdubbed vocals later. We spent thirteen hours each day recording with only one forty-five-minute break for dinner.

When I got to the studio, early as always, Iommi was already there sorting out his gear with his guitar tech. I immediately liked Tony. He had a very relaxed kind of vibe to him, very friendly, no ego at all. I thought his quiet English-gentleman demeanor was a huge contrast to the dark, haunting hook lines he created for Black Sabbath. It didn't all match up, and that was really cool. He was totally open to anyone's suggestions, but still very clear about what he liked or didn't like. Everyone was really into working hard for him and we were very focused. I love that.

I got drum sounds right up until Billy walked in, and typically, he said hi to everyone and got right down to business. Tape started rolling immediately.

Billy asked Tony to play one of the new guitar licks he'd been working on, and Tony busted out an amazing, heavy riff that sounded like classic

Sabbath. Billy picked up a bass and played it back to him. Billy then said, "What else do you got? Play me another hook line." Tony played a second amazing hook, and Billy once again played that one back to Tony on his bass.

Next, Billy looked and pointed his finger at me, then pointed out to the big room where my drums were, telling me in sign language that he wanted me to go to my drum set to start rehearsing and arranging the song. Tony and Billy recorded in the control room while I was out in the big room, where the drum sound was the best. We basically constructed a song from scratch right then and there, and I remember there were all kinds of sections that I gave names to on my chart: dark section, heavy section, blue section, half-time section. It was very Sabbath like.

I never heard any vocals until the record came out. I just watched Billy, Tony, and producer Bob Marlette discuss parts, but couldn't hear what they were saying unless Bob or Billy held down the talk-back button in the control room. All I could hear was their instruments when they played, and after Billy got frustrated with me about not understanding what they had been talking about, I got off my drum set and walked into the control room and handed the assistant engineer $20, and said, "Every time these guys talk, push the talk-back button down so I can hear what they are saying," and walked back to my drum set. Problem solved.

We spent a day and a half on the first song, called "Black Oblivion." It was an intense session, but super creative, with four creative people trying to create a masterpiece from scratch. Later Tony had lots of special guests play with him on different songs—Dave Grohl, Henry Rollins, Phil Anselmo, Skin, Serj Tankian, Ian Astbury, Ozzy Osbourne, Peter Steele, and Billy Idol all came by. The one thing we all had in common was that we loved Black Sabbath.

> **Billy Corgan:** I think "Black Oblivion" was a seven-minute-long take, and I was playing guitar, with Tony on bass, and Kenny obviously on drums, and when I was listening I couldn't believe it. . . . I mean, you're talking about a man playing drums live, two live musicians, and you're

used to hearing it speeding up and slowing down. But as I was listening back to Kenny, I go, "There's no speeding up or slowing down, it's just kind of weird," so I asked the engineer I was working with to get a metronome out and we got the tempo—it took a second to get the tempo of the track—and I set the metronome and hit play to lock it to Kenny, and again, you're playing to *live human beings*, and he literally was *on the click*. I mean, that is unbelievable. I was stunned, because I kept waiting for him to drag a fill or something and then go off the click. He was playing to his own inner meter! That is like *inhuman*! That's one of the most stunning things I've ever seen in a studio.

That was the last time I ever recorded or played with Billy Corgan, but it was not the last time I would record with Tony Iommi. Six years later, I made a killer record with Tony and Glenn Hughes called *Fused*. It was one of the coolest records I ever made. We actually became a *band*, Tony, Glenn, and me, with Bob Marlette co-writing, producing, and adding some guitar parts.

We recorded in Monmouth, Wales, in a big farmhouse that was converted into the studio where Sabbath would rehearse and record. I stayed in Geezer Butler's room.

I spent a week there. Tony, Glenn, and I would record live bass, drums, and guitar with no vocals. Everything was tracked live. Once we got a drum track, we moved on to another song. The idea was to get all the drum tracks, then Glenn checked all his bass tracks to make sure they were perfect, Tony overdubbed all his guitars, and then Glenn put on all the vocals. This was the real deal, a band living together in a band house, recording, and becoming a closely knit group—a classic power trio, but with our own sound.

We were planning on touring and recording some more, but very soon after we got started, Sharon Osbourne put Black Sabbath back together, so our power trio never happened and it was back to normal life: For the rest of 1998, I played *Late Night with David Letterman* with John Fogerty, promoting the new *Premonition* live DVD we made on a movie set in Burbank. I recorded some music with Joe Cocker, Rod Stewart, Meat Loaf, and

Corey Hart in LA, and with Deana Carter and Randy Scruggs in Nashville. I toured with the BoDeans and performed with Richie Sambora, a second time on *Letterman*, *The Jay Leno Show*, and at the Gavin Convention, and then I got a call to play with Lynyrd Skynyrd. That's Kenny Aronoff normal.

32

What Song Is It You Want to Hear?

I 've always loved Lynyrd Skynyrd. I never felt they were ever trying to be cool; they were just born cool—they reminded me of the Rolling Stones in that way. They are the real deal, and they welcomed and accepted me from day one, as if I were in the band, and you know, I love being *in the band*. No matter how many sessions I do, there is nothing that can replace being part of a gang. I got that as a kid when I was putting together my first bands, and I felt that from the Mellencamp experience—until I didn't—but I also got it from Seger and Fogerty and Melissa Etheridge. With those guys I never felt like a gun for hire. I felt like family.

Skynyrd was recording *Edge of Forever* at Ocean Way in Nashville, and they did not waste any time. It helped that we were working with a legendary producer in Ron Nevison, who has worked with everyone from Led Zeppelin and the Who to Ozzy Osbourne, Heart, KISS, Chicago, and on and on. Ron had asked me to record with Skynyrd because he felt comfortable working with me there after we did the Jefferson Airplane album together.

He specialized in bands like Skynyrd: *real bands that played,* that had their own sound, and he did a great job of capturing that sound. They weren't trying to reinvent the wheel, no loops, no tricks, just that classic Skynyrd personality. That's what the fans wanted, and it is what they were best at.

Every day they would drive to the studio in three cars from the hotel they were staying at, just outside of Nashville, go right to their instruments, and start playing and recording immediately, live on the floor. Leon, Billy, Gary Rossington, Rickey Medlocke, Johnny Van Zant, and Hughie Thomasson all recorded at the same time, and I loved that. That many people recording together in time, in tune, and making it feel like a band that has been playing together *forever* is not as easy as it sounds, even if—maybe even especially, if you actually have been playing together forever, like Skynyrd. Or the Stones. It's a tribute to them that they were able to all be in the same room together and get along together and work so well. It went great—Skynyrd could really play, and therefore there was no reason to fix everything, or put the tracks on a grid and auto-correct every note, put samples on the drums, etc. This wasn't about fixing mediocre shit; this was about playing great rock 'n' roll. No frills, all thrills.

Billy Powell and Leon Wilkeson—original members of Skynyrd—told me about the famous plane crash that these guys had somehow survived, one of the single worst moments in rock 'n' roll. I mean, this shit was harrowing, and it wasn't something I ever would have dared ask them about, just out of respect for the band members who died in that crash. But they wanted to tell the story, so I listened. I mean, seriously, I could not believe I was being told about the Lynyrd Skynyrd plane crash *by guys who climbed out of the wreckage.* No matter how many rock stories I've been told, by the biggest rock stars in the business, this one cut straight to the bone.

One night after recording all day, Leon called me up and wanted to play me some music that he was working on. The only place we could listen to his music was in my car, so as we're sitting there listening and talking and drinking whiskey, Leon started talking about the crash. In 1977, their Convair CV-300 jet crash-landed in a field in Mississippi. Six people died, including their singer, Ronnie Van Zant. The drummer crawled through a swamp busted in a hundred pieces, just a broken-up human being, to try to get help. When he finally found a farmhouse, he was greeted by farmers with guns who wanted him to leave immediately because he looked so fucked up.

Twenty people survived, and I realized, holy fucking shit, this was no Buddy Holly plane, it was a *commercial jet*, completely unbelievable that it would crash. Stuff like that scares the shit out of me—I've had my close calls, landing gear not working, devastating drops in midair, plane stalling in midair, small jets battered by storms, plane wings catching on fire when taking off . . . stuff that definitely put me one step closer to God, but nothing like a *fucking jet crash-landing into a swamp*. And let me tell you, the guys—and gals—that played and ran with Lynyrd Skynyrd were the toughest fuckers in the world, real badass Southerners who used to kick the shit out of each other for fun. I don't know of any other band that would have literally come crawling out of the wreckage.

Leon told me that after the plane crash, the first thing he remembered was he was in a cloud, in heaven, and he saw Duane Allman and Ronnie Van Zant sitting on a bench. One of them had a fishing pole and the other had a guitar, and they said to Leon, "Hey, man, you think playing music is cool, check this out. It's amazing up here," then *bam*, Leon said he was suddenly in a hospital bed with tubes in him and nurses all over him. He didn't have any idea what had happened, just that a big steel piece of metal went right through his midsection and somehow he had survived. He figured it wasn't his time yet.

When I met him, he was a happy, smiling dude and had a very cool style of playing bass. We got along great, and when we were almost finished recording their record, they asked me to tour with them, but I was already committed to Melissa Etheridge's next tour, supporting her *Breakdown* record, which I had played on.

When I wasn't on tour with Melissa Etheridge that year, I did drum clinics across the USA and did my usual variety of sessions, including Amanda Marshall's second album, Japanese artist Miyuki Nakajima, Garth Brooks's "Chris Gaines" album, and a session with Eddie Money, who I really love. I've worked with Eddie many, many times, and every time I record with him, if I don't play a drum fill that excites him on the *first* take, or if I play too much, he'll hold down the talk-back button and say to me in my headphones, "Kenny, Kenny, Kenny . . . man, don't give me the cheap fills. I want the expensive ones." Eddie sounds like a New York City cop, so I listen to him—he actually was a cop before he hit with "Baby Hold On" and "Two Tickets to Paradise."

Then I flew east to Nashville to play with Philip Claypool, then on to the Washington, DC, area to record with country music star Mary Chapin Carpenter. My road trip from there took me onward to New York to work on Celine Dion's new album, and then finally to Boston, where I connected with Stryper singer-songwriter Michael Sweet to play on a solo album called *Truth* he was recording with Bob Marlette.

On the last day of the year, December 31, 1999, I flew to Washington, DC, to perform with John Fogerty on the steps of the Lincoln Memorial, facing the Washington Monument, for a huge event called "America's Millennium Concert." It was nine degrees the night we played, but it felt like it was nine *below* zero. I was the only member of John Fogerty's regular band that performed with him because the show's producer, Quincy Jones, wanted to have a super-group onstage for our segment. My band mates that night were Edgar Winter, Slash, and Vernon Reid from Living Colour on guitar, and Eric Clapton's bassist, Nathan East—who had played with everyone from Barry White and the Love Unlimited Orchestra to George Harrison, Elton John, Sting, and on and on. He played the bass line of Daft Punk's hit "Get Lucky," which won the Grammy for Record of the Year in 2014. It was definitely a heavy group.

Besides the excitement of performing right in front of Bill Clinton and the First Lady for the third time, there were many celebrities in the audience, backstage, and on the stage, plus over a million people standing outside in the cold watching us perform, not to mention the millions watching all over the world. There was a lot of tension in the air because we kept hearing that terrorists might want to take advantage of this huge event—there definitely was a sense of concern, and a slight fear in the air, and I have to admit that it was definitely on my mind. It was hard not to be reminded of the threat—there were snipers on the roof of the Lincoln Memorial, and security was very, very present: military, police, and my old friends, the Secret Service, everywhere.

After the show, we all were all invited to the White House for drinks. Getting into the White House was a huge event itself, because of the very intense security check points we had to go through.

As I was about to get on one of the yellow school buses to take us to the White House, I noticed Jack Nicholson and his girlfriend, Lara Flynn Boyle, were standing in line right in front of me. When we got on the bus, they went right to the back of the bus, like the cool kids, and it felt like I was in high school again. I sat in the aisle and my girlfriend, Liz, sat inside against the window, while my son, Nik, decided to sit one row back on the other side of the bus. I think he wanted to be independent of us and be his own man. Nik was a teenager by now. I knew where he was coming from.

After we found our seats, I looked up and Robert De Niro cruised by me and Liz, took a look at Nik, stopped as if he were going to sit next to him, looked at him and grunted "Nah," and then sat behind Liz. Then Bono got on the bus and decided to sit next to De Niro, right behind me, and we all (Bono, Nik, and me) talked about the new Smashing Pumpkins record *Machina*, which I hadn't heard yet, but Nik had, so it was really him and Bono talking while I listened, never mind that I had actually been in the band. Mary Tyler Moore(!!!) got on the bus with director Martin Scorsese. Anthony Hopkins, Sam Waterston, Kris Kristofferson, and Tom Jones all were on the bus.

At one checkpoint, we were stopped and security people looked under our bus with mirrors to see if there were any bombs. Dogs sniffed the outside of the bus, then came on our bus, where security people were asking for everyone's identification. It was funny because when they got to Martin Scorsese, he told the female security agent that he had forgotten to bring his wallet with his driver's license. She told him he couldn't go to the White house, and he said, "Come on, isn't it obvious who I am?" Jack Nicholson and other actors started defending Scorsese, and finally someone at the front of the bus started quoting De Niro in *Taxi Driver*: "Are you looking at me? Are you talking to me?" It was like a bunch of high school kids on a school bus, acting like high school kids, on a school bus. Some things never change.

◄○►

Another phone call: Bob Marlette called me up and asked if I was available to play on Alice Cooper's record, but I was already booked. Bob couldn't wait for me, so he went ahead and started Alice's record at Henson with a young drummer. I think he tried one drummer and that didn't work, so he tried someone else and that wasn't working either. After a few days of recording, Bob called me back up and said, "Can you come over after your session and listen to what I am recording and tell me what you think?" When I got over there and listened to a bit of what they'd been working on, I could tell the drummer wasn't getting it, he sounded tense and uptight.

Bob has a very meticulous way of working. After the drummer did a take, Bob would give him this grocery list of ideas or changes he wanted the drummer to make for the next take, and the drummer—who I guess had never worked that way before—was a bit intimidated and nervous under the pressure, and because he couldn't write detailed charts, he wasn't able keep up with Bob. If a drummer feels intimidated or nervous, he will sound intimidated and nervous when he plays.

I told Bob what I thought, and that was that. The session I was doing ended a day early, so I immediately called Bob and told him I was available now, and he asked me if I could start recording the next day, and was I cool with recording four songs a day, which meant a lot of catch-up. I said of course, but I didn't have the music in advance, so I was walking in cold.

After hearing the first song, I told Bob and his engineer that I would need about forty-five minutes to make a detailed chart of it. The drum programming on the demo was very detailed and extremely well thought out and crafted. All the guitars, bass, keyboards, and vocals were crafted around these drum parts. There is no way I would be able to record four songs in one day without my own charts, so I sat at the console and ran Pro Tools as I wrote them. Once I had a song charted, I went to my drum set and practiced playing the song until I was ready to record it with confidence. If Bob wanted a change, I'd write it on the chart, and the next take he got exactly what he wanted. Next!

Alice Cooper came by the studio that first day to say hi and check me out. He listened to what we were doing and he was happy—and then we never saw him again. A lot of guys work that way, just coming in to do vocals, with no real connection to the musicians who are playing the music.

From top left, clockwise: Working with Al Pacino at Ocean Way Recording studios in Hollywood for his movie *Danny Collins*. Rehearsing with John Legend and Alicia Keys for *The Night That Changed America*, the tribute honoring the Beatles for the fiftieth anniversary of their appearance on *The Ed Sullivan Show*. Catching up with Billy Corgan at the NAMM show in Anaheim, California. Hanging with the amazing producer Don Was. Hanging with Melissa Etheridge backstage, 2015. (All photos: Author's collection)

From top left, clockwise: Recording with Little Richard on Jon Bon Jovi's *Blaze of Glory* record in 1990 at A&M Recording Studio, in Studio A. With Dave Grohl, watching the LA Kings in the playoffs. I flew in from Europe, and he flew in from Hawaii that day. Backstage at a Grammy rehearsal for the Highwaymen segment. Merle looks serious. With Nathan East, outside Letterman.
(All photos: Author's collection)

From top left, clockwise: Hanging with super drummers Ringo Starr and Jim Keltner after performing with Ringo at the El Rey Theatre in Los Angeles. Jeff Bridges and I took a picture right as I was walking onstage to perform with John Fogerty at Sturgis Motorcycle Rally. Jeff performed also. An after-party at the Kennedy Center Honors with Yo-Yo Ma. Recording a Brian Wilson record at Ocean Way Recording studios. (All photos: Author's collection)

From top left, clockwise: In the Kennedy Center Honors greenroom with Robert De Niro right before he gave a speech honoring Dustin Hoffman. Elton John and Jon Bon Jovi at Henson Recording Studios in Los Angeles. An after-party at the Kennedy Center Honors with Sting and my wife, Gina. Sting had been honored that evening. With Peter Frampton, Keith Urban, Steve Lukather, and John Mayer at rehearsal for *The Night That Changed America*. Hanging with Slash somewhere in LA. (All photos: Author's collection)

I was on the phone, and Bob Marlette was lying on the couch playing an acoustic guitar, when Paul McCartney popped in. Actually, Paul knocked on the door, which was open, he was so polite—I just saw his knuckles, and I shouted, "Hey, c'mon in." I had no idea who it was. Really, it was that casual. "Hi, I'm Paul. Is Alice around?"

Bob jumped up like the president had just walked in the room, and we were standing there like two little kids next to each other just giggling. It turned out that Paul was recording in the studio next door to ours and was stopping by just to say hi. He was very nice and shook our hands. He had a great sense of humor, and at one point he said, "The last time I saw Alice, Linda and I were out to dinner with him and his wife. Elton John joined us for dinner, with this guy who he said had a twenty-inch cock." Bob and I looked at each other, and I know we were both thinking the same thing: Paul McCartney just said "twenty-inch cock"! All three of us were cracking up!

We hung out for nearly an hour, just laughing, and talking about the Beatles' new release *The Beatles 1* that was #1 on the *Billboard* charts and how the Beatles were on the cover of *Rolling Stone* magazine thirty-plus years after their heyday. Paul McCartney—a Beatle, my hero. Amazing! I had to keep pinching myself. I'll never forget that.

33

Scammed!

I was going so fast, I thought I was invincible.

I never saw it coming. I had never experienced anything like this before. Crimes of this magnitude have ruined people's lives forever. I'm lucky it didn't cripple me forever. Actually, it made me stronger, and more powerful, more successful, and far wiser. This was a huge life lesson in getting knocked down, getting up, and learning to let go.

I was scammed out of a lot of money—six figures worth of session and touring fees, gone. But not before I heaped four years of legal bills on top of that, and another pile of dough on private eyes. Eventually the FBI got involved. And I never saw one dollar of the money I lost.

It was a lot like a Bernie Madoff scam—and how many really smart people got taken in by him? Lawyers? Business people? Movie stars? The New York fucking Mets? Even though I consider myself a fairly astute business person after running my own brand and business for the past thirty-five years, I didn't see this scam coming. I guess I was in good company, if nothing else.

The DiBruno family were controlled by father Joe, Sr., and had scammed over 600 families over thirty-plus years. They were professional con men, real heavyweights. The scary part is they didn't see themselves as people doing anything wrong, even as they robbed seniors of their retirement plans and savings accounts. And they'd been in plenty of trouble before. As far back as 1989, the SEC busted them for issuing fraudulent stock, but somehow they always seemed to skirt by without getting tossed in jail, and then they just did it again.

It was a simple enough scheme: The DiBrunos took money from investors—and you have to understand they put on an incredible show to make everything look legit—and then put the money in their own pockets.

Once the investor money was deposited in any of numerous banks, they would slowly make withdraws, just under $10,000 so a red flag wouldn't go up to the IRS. They were experts in moving money around—and spending it as quickly as it came in. The family would meet every morning and split any money they had between them, like Ma Barker and her gang. They destroyed a lot of people. Old folks just wiped out. I had heard of a few victims hanging or shooting themselves after they realized they had been fleeced. It was fucking grim.

Like everything else, for me, it began with a phone call, although how was I to know that this was a *seriously* wrong number?

They were working with a singer-songwriter, this cat named Jody Lee Hager, who didn't even realize that he was being scammed as well. He actually lived with the DiBrunos for a while—they claimed that he was on the verge of signing a multi-million-dollar recording and publishing deal.

He was a key witness later in the civil suit I had filed against the family—he had seen how they operated—and testified that one afternoon he saw someone come to the DiBruno house to tip them off that that local sheriffs were on the way. This was right before their fraud was uncovered and indictments started flying, and the tip gave them the chance to start shredding documents and to literally escape from police pursuit through the back door! It sounds like something out of a crazy crime-caper movie, and what followed really did play out like a *Dateline* or *48 Hours* special.

The DiBrunos had convinced people to invest as much as $2 million in Hager—he was going to be the biggest thing in Nashville. Like father, like son, Joe DiBruno, Jr., the guy who eventually scammed me, set up a fake publishing company, a record label, and offices to make everything appear professional and legitimate.

I originally flew down to Charlotte to play drums on a session—the studio owner/producer had reached out to me through the Internet. I had never heard of him before, but the fee was good and I was available, and you know I hate to say no, so I went. He was a partner with Joe DiBruno, Jr., on some other projects, and when I was there, I remember Joe, Jr., was very friendly and quiet. Now I realize he was sizing me up as a mark.

He showed us a lot of flash money, as they say, taking eight of us out to Morton's Steak House numerous times and picking up the bill with cash. He drove a Hummer and came by the studio during the day on any number of custom Harleys. He acted like he had millions. He *looked* like he had millions, the very picture of success.

He kept in touch with me by phone after that first trip and told me in passing while back in LA that his dad, Joe, Sr., had some involvement with the United Nations and was involved with supplying a healthy milk product to Third World countries. His dad had actually scammed a well-known scientist into appearing on CNN to talk up this low-cholesterol milk product, called "Dairy Trim." They did an interview in the *New York Times* based on a fake press release he sent out. He and his son were really believable—there wasn't even a formula for the product, but they had $10 million dollars worth of phony stock certificates and family members shilling as happy investors. Eventually they bilked real investors out of millions before the SEC shut them down. You can Google Joe DiBruno and get the whole story.

If I knew about any of this, obviously I would not have been flying back to Charlotte to record for Joe, Jr.'s fake label. He was still throwing a lot of cash around while he courted me, but I didn't see what he was doing. It all seemed normal enough. I've met tons of rich dudes in my business who just want to be around musicians and love throwing money around at steak houses and showing you their hot rods and toys.

One night while we were eating at Morton's, Joe overheard me on the phone trying to figure out a way to get to Nashville from Chicago, after flying from Switzerland to Chicago, in order to make a rehearsal for Willie Nelson's seventieth birthday bash. It was another close call, like my Hong Kong to Detroit trip. Joe, Jr., pulled me aside after I was off the phone and said, "I can help you make your connection. My dad is super connected and probably can get you a private jet." And by the next day, he had made arrangements to get me to Nashville on a private jet. When I landed in Chicago from Switzerland a month later, one of the pilots met me at the gate, and we flew to Nashville in time for me to make my rehearsal. That just lets you know how well oiled a con these guys were running.

After that, Joe would call every so often and ask me about the music projects I was working on, and tried to figure out when I was free to come back down to Charlotte to record for his label. During one of these conversations, he mentioned his dad had a new product—unbelievably, another milk product (talk about fucking balls). This milk used some sort of low-calorie sweetener so kids would like it better, and they said that the New York school systems were going to be their first big customer (that's a lot of milk), and they're going to be listed on the New York Stock Exchange. The company was called International Food Technologies (IFT), and Joe, Jr., sent me links of his dad and the scientist on CNN and in the *New York Times*, along with some brochures. It seemed like a safe investment—selling better-tasting milk to kids seemed like an idea whose time had come—eventually I made a substantial investment in the company. Joe had said numerous times that I could get my initial investment back *immediately* anytime, whenever I wanted it. Maybe I was naïve to think that was possible, but that really made me feel safe about making the investment.

I realized I was being scammed while I was down in Charlotte, recording for what would be the last time. I was sitting in Joe's office when my wife, Liz, called and said, "Hey, as long as you're sitting there, I want to ask him some questions about the investment."

Liz had worked as an auditor for a large firm with offices in the World Trade Center. She knew what she was doing. So I put her on the phone, and she knew what questions to ask him. I watched as Joe started to get nervous and sweat. He started pacing and continued to fumble with all the questions she was asking. She later told me that they were basic bookkeeping questions that he should have been able to answer easily. I began to get a very bad feeling.

As the days went by, I felt a mix of emotions as I absorbed the fact I had been fucked: violated, devastated, and utterly helpless. Mostly I felt stupid. But I figured I would get all my money back—at the time, it didn't occur to me that I wouldn't get anything back at all, and that it would wind up costing me tens of thousands more in legal bills.

This was just the beginning of a long four-year tour of hell.

It was a ton of work that my lawyers, and Liz, had to stay on top of daily for four years. But I was like a running back. I just kept on going no matter what they threw at me. I never slowed down. It was like having another full-time job, but I kept flying all over the world, touring and playing sessions, and then coming back to deal with this bullshit. I hired a law firm in Chicago to work with me, and eventually a private investigator to begin probing the DiBruno family more deeply, and was even in touch with the FBI.

A civil lawsuit was filed in Indiana, which I eventually won, and I sued Bank of America because they had mishandled the money I had "invested" in IFT. My checks had never been deposited in the correct accounts, and they allowed this to happen without following standard procedure, which was to notify my bank that checks made to IFT were deposited in *different* corporate accounts.

The day I realized I was being scammed by the DiBrunos, I called a friend for some professional advice, and she told me to walk away, cautioning me, "You will never see your money, ever. Just walk away."

Naturally, that was the opposite of what I wanted to hear, and there was no way I was going to just walk away. I wanted to take these guys down. I wanted my money back first and foremost, but I also wanted to see these degenerates put in jail for scamming me and everyone else they had swindled over thirty years. But she was ultimately right. You rarely find the money.

In a telling moment before all the trials, I had met with Joe, Sr., face-to-face in a large corporate conference room at my lawyer's office in Chicago, because Joe, Sr., wanted to work things out and avoid a trial.

He showed me a bunch of new investment brochures and promised me that I would get all my money back if I invested in *these* companies. It was unbelievable. I threw it back at him, slammed my fist down on the table, leaned forward like a cat about to pounce on his prey, looked him straight in the eye, and said, "I don't give a fuck about you or your fucking son." I looked at his lawyer and *his* lower lip was quivering, but none of this fazed the old man. He remained cool and actually threw his son under the bus, saying he was really sorry that *his son* had scammed me and that *his son* had emotional and physical problems. It was really incredible, the dude was a complete sociopath.

My lawyer pulled me into a side room and was suggesting we should settle. I said fuck no—Joe, Sr., had no intention of giving me back my money. Any kind of settlement was useless. I was shocked my lawyer even suggested a settlement. The whole thing sucked.

I never recovered a penny of a six-figure investment and spent almost as much in legal fees, but at that point, it had become a matter of principle for me. The FBI said they really felt for my situation, but the agent I talked to also said they were focusing on terrorism and murder, and money scams were not at the top of their list.

What finally got the FBI hot enough to get involved was a TV story about the DiBruno family and how they had been scamming people for thirty years. They really didn't give a fuck until it was on TV. Joe, Sr., and Joe, Jr., eventually went to prison as a result of their investigation, but somehow the mother and the other son got off.

During my lawsuit against Bank of America, my first witness was Joe DiBruno, Jr., and I was flooded with emotion watching him hobble into the courtroom in chains (ankles and hands) in that orange prison jumpsuit. I listened to the chains rattle with every step he took. Adrenaline rushed through my body; my mind was racing. I wanted him to look at me so I could say, "You fucking asshole, all you had to do is give me my money back . . ." *Ching, ching, chang* went the chains, but he never looked at me. I had my two lawyers to my left, Bank of America had four lawyers to my right, and there was a twelve-person jury and a judge in front of me watching him walk to the podium to be sworn in. He took the Fifth on every question my lawyer asked him. He walked toward me before leaving the courtroom, but he kept his head down. *Ching, ching, chang.*

For his crimes, he had been sentenced to something like twenty years with no parole. His old man wound up dying in prison.

Joe, Jr., went back to jail, and Bank of America eventually got off on some technicality, and that was the end of that. The judge stopped the lawsuit on the third day in court. I was stunned.

I walked around the courthouse for about thirty minutes reflecting on the last four years. I was embarrassed, frustrated, and angry, but I also felt some relief and was already moving forward. Thank God I had that built into my DNA. I'm like a shark—if I don't keep moving forward, I can't breathe. It was time to move on.

While I was walking around the courthouse, I ran into about half a dozen separate jurors who all told me how bad they felt for me—they said they totally understood why I would have made those investments, and one very wealthy woman in a fur coat, dripping in diamonds, said she would have probably made the same investments. One person was a schoolteacher, and another was a very successful lawyer, and they all said they wanted to award me my money, and they didn't understand why the judge ended the case abruptly. I realize now how foolish it was going after a bank as big as BoA, even if I was right. I learned so much about the system I could probably write a book about just that. There is a lot of corruption, and there is nothing you or I can do about it. It wasn't like they were ever going to be worried about a fucking rock musician.

Even if I had won the case, BoA would have appealed it, and I would have been back in court spending tens of thousands of dollars trying to defend my win.

The day before the very last day I could have appealed the Bank of America verdict, I finally decided to let go so I could get on with my life and not pour any more money or time down the drain. Letting it go meant I could rebuild and focus on moving forward with my life. The DiBrunos were done with. Not much more I could do.

I learned so much from this situation—*when you can let go, it's way more powerful than the thing that you let go.* That was an important lesson.

I try not to be humiliated by this story, but it isn't easy. I can see now that I was moving so fast between tours, sessions, drum clinics, and parties, living this crazy life that I didn't even see the long con. I was probably missing a lot, moving the way I do. This was a message to slow down, but honestly I am just no good at it, slowing down. I hardly ever sleep through the night. My brain is always switched on.

My editor tells me my book is making him dizzy—"Kenny, it's too fucking much. It's like you are *always* in fifth gear. I'm gonna have a heart attack just *reading* it."

This book may be ridiculous—see Kenny run from session to session! Mellencamp and Seger, Iggy Pop, Meat Loaf, Bon Jovi, Tony fucking Iommi, Elton John, Melissa Etheridge, Smashing Pumpkins, John Fogerty, Lynyrd Skynyrd, Stevie Nicks, the Rolling Stones (not to mention Charlie's and Mick's solo records), Alice Cooper (not to mention Cinderella and Stryper). Celine Dion, Johnny Cash, Waylon Jennings, Willie Nelson, Hank, Jr., and every other happening cat in Nashville, LA, New York, and on and on—it sounds obnoxious when I hear myself tell it!

But if I am going to stay relevant, I have to get up and get in the ring every day. No one cares about a has-been rock star. But I'm a fighter. I worked like an insane person to get here. I never think about slowing down, and I hate the word "retire."

I was never a full member of any band. Nobody handed me millions. But I will say this about Mellencamp: He taught me the fear. Fear of failing, fear of not staying relevant in a business that changes with the weather. This shit can be all over in two seconds—and I've already heard the vultures. I thought the vinyl LP was going to be forever. Somehow we got sold on CDs, and now they're a fucking relic of the past as well. Free streaming—who saw it coming? The industry leaders had their heads in the sand and let it happen with hardly a whimper. But like I said, you have to stay positive. Positive mental attitude, no matter what. If you let the bastards get you down, you can't win.

34

The New Pop

In 2000, right around the same time I was dealing with the DiBruno family, I got a call from my old friend John Shanks, who I had played with in Melissa's band. He wanted me to overdub some powerful drums on a new, young, female pop artist he was producing.

Usually the goal is to get a drum track first and then build everything on top of that, but this was a new way of recording, overdubbing drums *after* everything else has been recorded. The challenge was to try and make it sound like all the musicians were playing together at the same time.

This was the beginning of a whole new thing that would take over pop radio in the early '00s. I was kind of getting in at ground zero.

Shanks produced Michelle Branch and was a co-writer on a lot of her songs, and he was brilliant at helping create this new sound that the radio just loved.

Michelle had it all. She was ridiculously talented, wrote great songs, had the look, played a little guitar, and with Shanks, she was unstoppable.

Producer John Shanks: This was an era where Britney Spears and the Backstreet Boys were blowing up—the initial Max Martin period—so it was very *programmy*, that kind of Swedish pop thing, and when I met Michelle, being a big fan of singer-songwriters but also someone who likes electronic music and hip-hop and beats, and in the sense of that production, I thought, Wow, how do I work with somebody and make her relevant and keep it kind of pop? I always knew in the back of my mind the last thing I would do is use Kenny because he was sonically advanced enough as a musician to be sensitive to what we needed to do on each song—meaning creating interloops, like a little hip-hop kit in the verses and the B-section, and then a big kit in the chorus.

The first song I recorded with Michelle was "Everywhere," and the big challenge for me was how I was going to get the right drum sound with the right parts to fit on these tracks, because there were so many guitars, loops, vocals, keypads, and bass that we had to sonically figure out where to place the drums, and how to tune them so they fit into this new way of making records.

We were definitely experimenting in the studio, working hard and fast, and I remember thinking I had nailed a take, but when I looked into the control room and I saw no reaction or excitement, I knew something wasn't right. I got off my drums, walked back into the control room, and I asked John, "What's going on?"

He said, "I don't know, listen and you tell me." When I listened back to what I had just recorded, sure enough, I heard a discrepancy between the drums and rhythm guitars. I asked the engineer to play just the drums with the click track. I was tight with the click, so I told the engineer to add the loops, and everything still sounded great. So I asked John, "Are you keeping all those guitar parts?" And when he told me he was, that's when I realized it doesn't matter where the click is. I needed to play with John's rhythm guitar parts to make the track feel great. I figured they were going to bury the loops or keep them in the background anyway and keep the guitars loud.

When I got back to my drums, I adjusted my mix with my mixer so I could hear lots of guitars. I got rid of the loops and turned the click down a bit, and *bam!* I got a take immediately and everyone in the control room was smiling.

I had started making my own loops in the early '90s with Mellencamp, but using loops with a wall of guitars and other instruments became even bigger in the '00s. And recording with Pro Tools, producers now had infinite tracks at their disposal. After twenty years of being a successful studio drummer, I was still trying to stay relevant and adjust to where the business was heading.

Michelle Branch's single "Everywhere" launched her career. That song went to #12 on the *Billboard* Top 100 Singles charts, #5 on Top 40 Mainstream, and #9 on Adult Top 40. John Shanks and I did the World AIDS Day/Staying Alive concert on MTV in Seattle with Michelle. This was the first time I performed with Michelle live, and it helped me make my decision later on down the road to go on tour with her. It was a great preview into how touring this new hybrid-pop sound was going to work live. It was kind of a crash course for what would go nightly on a bigger tour.

One thing I am sure of is that you have to adapt to survive. I did it in the late '80s and early '90s, when I'd started my second career as a session drummer, and here I was doing it again in my third decade. The world changed, the business changed, you had to change, too, if you wanted to stay on top.

Michelle was becoming the new cool thing, especially for young girls coming up on pop music. Having John Shanks co-write and produce her songs helped a lot—this was definitely his niche, creating these fantastic radio-friendly records. They were a perfect team, and John was now being recognized as a great contemporary pop writer and producer.

Things worked out so well that John asked me to record Michelle Branch's second record, *Hotel Paper,* which was a smash hit and produced two more hit singles. "Are You Happy Now?" became a Top 20 hit on the *Billboard* Hot 100 Singles chart. "Breathe," her second single, was a Top 40 hit as well.

I made videos for both of those singles with Michelle and her band. I liked the idea that I was part of the complete package, creating the image that she had a band, and that some of the band (namely *me*) also played on her record and toured with her. That was a great marketing call by her management—it made her look like the real deal, not simply manufactured. I was part of the sound; I was part of the band. It was authentic. I felt very connected to the music and got along great with Michelle. For me, it was like a rebirth. I loved every fucking second of it.

Michelle's music was pop, but I was able to rock like I always do. I was also able to use my funk, hip-hop, and R & B influences in her show—there were tons of dynamics. I was also very into the idea of running Pro Tools from the drum set on tour, combining the loops, keypads, and whatever else was created in the studio that we could not replicate live with my acoustic drums and the rest of the band. If this was the future, I wanted to be a part of it.

The Are You Happy Now? Tour went all over the world, starting first in the USA, opening up for the Dixie Chicks in arenas. Michelle's sound was a hit with audiences everywhere we went, from Europe to Australia to Japan to Hong Kong and Canada. The tour started in May and ran through December, and my visibility with Michelle was enormously important in keeping me current and relevant in the eyes of yet another new generation of rock fans.

Because budgets for real studio time had been diminished so much by then, John Shanks was trying to get as much work done in one session with me as possible. While I was on tour with Michelle Branch, I flew from Boston to LA to record thirteen songs *in one day* with John Shanks at Henson Studios—eight Alanis songs for her *So-Called Chaos* record, two *Anastasia* songs, one Gwen Stefani song, a Johnny Rzeznik song, and finally a Melissa Etheridge song, "This Moment." I have never recorded that much music in one day. After the session, I took a red-eye to New York to do the *Regis and Kelly* TV show with Michelle Branch—we had to be there at 6 a.m.

We did a lot of TV—when Michelle Branch's fans got home at night after a show, they could see us on *The Tonight Show with Jay Leno*—which we played twice. We were everywhere: *Jimmy Kimmel Live, Late Night with Conan O'Brien, Last Call with Carson Daly, MTV Beach House/Total Request Live, Pepsi Smash/WB Network, MTV Hard Rock Live,* the *Radio Music Awards*, and even major live televised sporting events like the *Monday Night Football* halftime show, the Major League Soccer Cup 2003 halftime show, and Michelle had heavy rotation on MTV—back when they were still showing videos.

◄◦►

In 2001, I played with Vasco Rossi, Italy's equivalent to Springsteen or the Rolling Stones. I am talking *massive* popularity—he sold out three stadium shows in Milan in thirty minutes. The audiences were insane—in Rome they chanted "Vasco, Vasco, Vasco" for forty-five minutes before we hit the stage and threw bottles filled with piss at the opening band. The first show I performed with Vasco was at Imola racetrack. About 120,000 people attended, and the audience threw bottles at Alanis Morissette and her band while she performed before us. I could not believe it. Everything about Italy was out of control. That tour was like *Satyricon* and *Caligula* combined.

Global business was good—it wasn't just American stars I was working with. Years later I did a record, *Fly*, with Zucchero (who was also a massive Italian star) with Don Was at Henson Studios. I also recorded at Henson with Lee Seung Hwan, the South Korean superstar, and played a live show with him at the Olympic soccer stadium in Seoul, Korea. I recorded with superstar Jimmy Barnes from Australia, Krokus from Switzerland, huge superstar Miyuki Nakajima from Japan (thirty-seven studio albums!), plus Mumiy Troll and Stas Namin and the Flowers, both from Russia.

◄○►

It's kind of weird when I think about it. I got into this playing and studying timpani and aspiring to be in a prog-rock or jazz-fusion band, and now I'm playing on pop hits by Kelly Clarkson, Avril Lavigne, Hilary Duff, P!nk, Ashlee Simpson, not to mention an album with Alanis Morissette, who started her own revolution.

It was good stuff, getting the call to work with these ass-kicking young women. It definitely kept me visible and kept the Aronoff brand vital. I guess what's even more surreal is that right after playing with these young artists, and recording music for *American Idol*, I was back and forth working with John Fogerty, who was still making great records fifty years after his first hit. He wrote songs that never got old. That's a miracle in this business.

How long could this career of mine possibly last?

I never ask that question. Other people ask it, not me.

Guys like Fogerty, Springsteen, Seger, Dylan, and Elton John have lasted over four decades and have been on the road their entire lives, making ten lifetimes' worth of hits. These guys may be the old classic rockers, but they still have the power as leaders in the music business.

These days the record companies think *they* are the rock stars—the labels, the accountants, the managers, the money people, most of them don't play a lick, and they think the musicians work for them.

Recently I've been hearing a lot of "Take it or leave it—this is what you get paid." There isn't a lot of discussion: "If you don't want the gig, there are a hundred people dying to play."

Young artists often don't get what it means to have the best sidemen in the world, and even if they do, the record labels these days don't generally care. It's the old way of doing things.

No label or manager would dare tell Bruce Springsteen who should be in his band, or tell them what they think they should get paid. If someone ever made a stupid suggestion like that to Mellencamp, he would tell them to fuck off. I saw him do that many times, and I loved that about John—he fought for himself and his band. Mellencamp wasn't always the nicest guy, but it was *his* band, and he could push back against the record company to get what he wanted. Michelle Branch is an absolutely fantastic talent, but no way in hell was she going to be able to get away with that. No young pop star just coming up could.

Of course people are now making entire records on their computers—"In the box," they say. They aren't even bothering with an actual person in a room playing actual drums. Sure, you could sample my snare drum, but you cannot sample my attitude or four decades of making hits and solving problems. You cannot sample my soul.

But as long as people keep buying this stuff, they're going to keep making it. And it's not just music—we live in an economy where people want more for less, want the same thing for free, or are just willing to settle for less. Ask any writer who used to work for a living. Ask any photographer who spent a lifetime perfecting their art and now has to compete with every would-be Annie Leibovitz with an iPhone. And everything has suffered.

It's not just the arts—people go online to get medical advice instead of going to a doctor. These are truly some crazy times.

For me, playing the drums is bliss. Like I've said, it is sexual and visceral and spiritual. It is liberating and positive. It is also habit forming—once you've had the high of being behind the kit in an arena with a great band, or come out of a session knowing you just made a smash hit, you can't get enough.

When I take a vacation, which is not often, every fiber in me screams to get back behind the drums. That's where I belong. But I still had no balance in my life, and due largely to my insane hurricane of a lifestyle and career, eventually it effected my relationship with my second wife, Liz.

It was a wonderful relationship, but when you are as busy as I am, non-stop, running from session to session, from tour to tour, doing drum clinics all over the world, living the rock star life, it's easy to lose perspective and difficult to be present in a close relationship—unless you make the effort and make your relationship a priority.

Sometimes I was on the road as much as eleven months out of the year, and that can be hard on any relationship.

﹣◇﹣

About fifteen years ago, while I was teaching in Banff, Canada, a Native Indian showed me his ritual powwow drum. It had an animal skin stretched over it and written on the drum was "Truth and Honor." When I saw it, I just stared at it—the meaning of those words hit me hard in my heart, forcing me to drop my head and reflect. I realized at that moment that I wasn't living my life with truth and honor. I wasn't that guy *yet*, but I wanted to be that guy *now*.

Many years later, after having worked on becoming a better version of myself, I decided to have "Truth and Honor" tattooed on my arm, on the *LA Ink* television show, by Corey Miller, an amazing tattoo artist in Los Angeles. I really bonded with Corey because he is a drummer, too, and we had a lot in common. The tattoo design he put on my arm is a much better version of the hand-engraved design on my signature snare drums made by Tama.

I was in the tattoo chair for four hours, and to distract me from the pain and to keep me focused while I was being interviewed, I involuntarily grabbed my crotch to stay focused. "Truth and Honor" is now tattooed on my arm forever, and this is the way I try to live my life now. I can't walk away from it.

When I was twenty-three years old, my dad told me something that was so spot-on. I was living at home with my parents after I graduated college, practicing my ass off on the drums eight hours a day, trying to figure out what my next move was, while I was seeing three different women from three different cities at the same time. That seemed normal enough to me, juggling women: one was from Boston, one from NYC, and one from Baltimore.

My dad saw all of this happening, and he said to me, "I don't want to tell you how to live your life, but maybe you should spend a little more time getting to know yourself first before you have all these relationships."

I got all defensive and tried to explain myself, but it just sounded like "Blah, blah, blah." I laugh now because I get it. If I'd had my shit together back then, I might have replied, "You know, Dad, you're absolutely right, but I'm going to fuck up all my relationships for the next thirty years before I get my shit together," which is exactly what I did.

When I saw "Truth and Honor" on that powwow drum in Canada, I woke up. It was like being pulled out of the *Matrix*. Until that moment, I had spent most of my life focusing only on being a great drummer. I was having a blast.

I knew in my heart and my soul that I wasn't going to slow down with my career, but I realized now that there were other parts of my life that needed just as much attention.

Liz always supported my career, and my insatiable passion to tour and make records every day, but when you're gone as much as eleven months a year, that is not a great formula for a marriage.

Liz and I were very fortunate that it wasn't a hostile or angry breakup, and we were able to talk about what we had to do to move forward with our lives. We have remained friends.

I am a workaholic. I can't say no. Bon Jovi calls and my only question is, "What time is sound check?" Meat Loaf calls and I'm halfway out the door before I even hang up the phone. I was still behaving like a high school or college kid, just running on excitement. I had been handed the keys to the candy store *and* the toy store. I was living in the moment with no boundaries. Nothing was off-limits.

It must have been impossible to live with me back then. I was acting like a lunatic, taking red-eyes between gigs, never sleeping, and in a gang fight with the DiBrunos. Among all this craziness, I honestly believe that playing the drums kept me sane. It is the best mental therapy in the world.

You could imagine how I felt, with my back up against the wall, the fear of becoming a rock music anachronism being very fucking palpable.

35

A Little Piece of My Heart

The Grammy Awards are still the music industry's biggest music event every year, the golden standard for music award shows. If you are in the music business, just being in the audience is a big deal. But if you get to perform at the Grammy's, it's fucking huge.

In 2005, Melissa Etheridge and Joss Stone were asked to perform two Janis Joplin songs to honor Janis for her Lifetime Achievement Award. Melissa performed "Piece of My Heart" and Joss performed "Cry Baby."

This was a super-emotional return for Melissa, now bald and beautiful, but also tired and beaten up from chemotherapy and radiation treatments. Nevertheless, in spite of her physically weakened condition and concern over how the crowd would react to a bald breast-cancer survivor, there was no way she was going to sit at home and watch someone else fill her spot honoring Janis Joplin—Janis was such an important influence and inspiration to Melissa, and Melissa, like Janis, was as tough as they came.

So she came out onstage in front of a global television audience—not to mention the Staples Center, packed with industry heavyweights who could not take their eyes off of her—and turned in one of her greatest live performances. I saw a lot of people in the audience crying, and they gave her a standing ovation. Even the band was emotional. She made a huge statement for women who had lost all their hair during chemotherapy, to never be ashamed, and she inspired thousands of cancer patients and their friends and families.

It took everything she had to get through that performance—physically and emotionally—but you wouldn't know it because she came across so strong and powerful. She told me later that that there were moments while performing that she was concerned she was going to pass out. I was just a few feet away from her, and know her very well, and I never would have guessed. She is all guts. Melissa's and Joss's performances are now considered one of the top ten Grammy performances. It was astonishing.

Melissa was dedicated to reaching out to women, to educating and sharing everything she had learned going through her battle with cancer. We did a special event with Lifetime Network's *Women Rock* cancer concert, and Melissa invited Patty Griffin—one of my favorite singers, who I'd made a killer record with in Nashville (*Flaming Red*)—to perform with us because when Melissa had been bedridden from the horrible chemotherapy, she experienced a calm, peaceful feeling listening to Patty's voice and records. She said she will be forever grateful for Patty's music for helping her get through some pretty rough times. Melissa explained to me that at one point while she was going through chemotherapy, she was bedridden for two weeks, unable to move or talk, but she could think and hear everything that was going on around her. She was a prisoner in her own body, and at times she felt like she was losing her mind.

Later that year, we performed with Melissa Etheridge on *Late Night with David Letterman*, *Good Morning America*, and *Live with Regis and Kelly*.

Melissa Etheridge is my fucking hero.

◄○►

After another Fogerty tour, a few months with the BoDeans, a Santana session (with Michelle Branch, no less, which represented two worlds coming together and not colliding), and a fill-in gig with Joe Cocker, whose drummer had to miss a gig, I did six weeks of Tama drum clinics through the US, Canada, and Europe.

Indianapolis Colts Owner Jim Irsay: Any young person who has the privilege to be around Kenny Aronoff has just been given an endless blessing, because the thing with Kenny is his heart is so big, man. I mean, he'll never turn a young, aspiring drummer down who has questions and wants to learn what it's about. Thank God for people like Kenny, because he shares his gifts and he's willing to teach. Let me say this: when I gather my team up before a game in the locker room, and we're going out to battle, I mean, I wanna tell you something, I put everything I have on the line for greatness. I have done everything I could to make that circle of men as strong as it can be before we go out there to do battle, and I mean a commitment that you're willing to give it all. And I think every time Kenny takes the stage or puts those drum sticks in his hands, it's like he's committing all he has in you with no holding back, for your art. That is something greatness is found in, whether it's music or sports or business. It's talking about that level of commitment, and he brings that intensity to his playing, that's what it's about. He's an all-in guy.

Teaching is a big part of what I do, along with touring and sessions. I perform drum clinics mostly in music stores or small theaters, unless it's a big drum festival with lots of drummers. Sometimes, though, these drum-clinic tours can be huge. When I did a Yamaha DTX electronic drum-clinic tour with Bob Terry through Europe, I had my own tour bus with two drivers, a four-man crew, and we carried our own PA and drums. I performed in nine countries in eleven days.

My drum clinics are very well organized, over two hours long, with speaking and performing segments. I play along with some of the hit records I have recorded, and some less-well-known songs to support what I am speaking about. I have a keynote presentation with over fifty pictures and a few short movies.

The Zildjian cymbal company sent me all over Asia, Australia, Germany, and Russia on one long drum-clinic tour. So many countries and cultures, all because I play the drums! Everything was first class, and I worked harder than I do when I am on tour with a band, because in this situation, I am the band! I am everything.

I was in a different country every day: China (Shanghai), South Korea, Japan, Thailand, the Philippines, Singapore, and Malaysia. I stayed in gorgeous hotels, with no days off on the entire trip. Once I landed, I would go straight to the hotel to chill for thirty minutes, and then to the venue to set up and do my sound check. After sound check, I did interviews, photo sessions, TV, then finally the drum clinic itself, focusing on music, technique, and how to become successful *and* stay successful in your life and in career—it's much more than just about playing the drums.

Then an autograph session, more interviews, dinner with the people hosting us, and finally back to the hotel for maybe four hours of sleep before the whole circus started all over again—getting on the plane, getting off the plane, going through customs, it was nonstop. It was especially weird flying over Vietnam—it was such a scary place when I was in high school when the war was on, and now I was zooming over it on a drum clinic tour. Crazy.

The last stop on the Asian tour was in Sydney, Australia, then back to the USA, and then nine cities in nine days across Germany, *bam bam bam*, and finally my last two clinics were in Moscow and Novokuznetsk, Siberia. It was December 5 and I had never felt so cold as I felt in Siberia. I slept in our five-star hotel with my ski hat on, fully dressed with long underwear. I had the heater on full blast but still froze my ass off. The cold air cut like a razor blade. Even though it was a five-star hotel in Siberian terms, it was like a two-star hotel the USA. In the bar, there were these decrepit businessmen picking up the scariest-looking prostitutes ever. The front desk had an old-fashioned switchboard, where they would have to manually connect calls with cables—it was like being flung back to 1950.

When we landed in Moscow, we went to Red Square for a photo session and then to the venue. My name was on the outside of the building where the clinic was being held:

* * * KENNY ARONOFF TONIGHT * * *

I was really surprised to see my name on the building in huge letters, but Aronoff is a Russian name, and I guess that made me kind of a big deal. The place was sold out, 1,000 seats all filled.

There were a ton of interview requests, and I did my first interview with a gorgeous Russian female journalist. Between her accent and how hot she looked, I felt like I was in some James Bond movie. She was terribly sexy and spoke with an accent that reeked of sex and the Cold War.

My next interview was in a bigger room, and as I entered the room I was blown away because instead of one person, it was twenty-five reporters, all with tape recorders. It was like a presidential press conference, with a million microphones sitting on the table in front of me and people clamoring to ask questions. The first question I got came from a heavily bearded man with a thick Russian accent, who asked me, "So, Kenny *Aronoff*, that's a Russian name, you from Russia, no? Tell me how your Russian blood makes you such a good American drummer."

It was the most awkward question, especially considering my relatives had to flee Russia to come to America to escape being killed. But the people asking questions were great, and they loved that I had Russian heritage, and they treated me like rock royalty. I answered the question like this, "*Pazeba!* Thank you! But of course my Russian blood has made me the best American drummer—with Russian passion, strength, and power!" They drank it up like cold vodka.

◄◦►

Mark, the artists relations person for Tama UK, asked me when we started our UK tour if I would mind doing an interview with an online publication focused on women drummers, and of course I said, "Sure"—I felt it was important to encourage young women to play the drums. Playing any musical instrument can really build self-confidence and can really help young people in making friends and finding themselves. The drums especially—to me, at least—were great for women to play because women can bring such a fantastic energy and spirit to something so tribal.

During my sound check at the Barnsfield Theater in Exeter, a very beautiful, blond-haired woman with pigtails walked into the theater with a ten-year-old boy. I thought at that time they were probably brother and sister because she looked so young and only stood five feet tall, and because—generally speaking—hot chicks don't usually hang around drum clinics and definitely not at sound checks. Along with every other dude in the place, I turned my head when she walked in. Everything about her was hot.

When I finished my sound check, Mark came up to me and asked if I was ready to do that interview he had told me about a week earlier, and that's when he introduced me to Gina and her son, Connor.

Gina was incredibly smart and quick thinking with a great sense of humor, and her interview questions were really good—better than most guys who usually want to just talk about gear. She had a lot of insight, and I loved that she was really into playing the drums and was taking lessons and playing in bands all around Exeter. I was kind of blown away by that.

At the very end of the interview, she said with a smile, "I have one more question that I always ask drummers when I interview them. Do you wear boxers or briefs when you play the drums?" I started laughing and told her playfully, "I wear neither."

After the clinic, I signed some autographs, and a bunch of people, including Gina and Connor, were hanging out in my dressing room. I was drinking some beers, and by now I wasn't even pretending not to flirt, and she was laying into me with her sarcastic British humor. I could feel a chemistry instantly between us, and I wanted to see more of her, so before we left for our next destination, I invited her to come to the *Rhythm Magazine* drum festival four days later near London.

Gina and Connor left after all the gear was finally loaded into the truck, and I jumped into a car and drove off with Mark. We went right past them, and I caught Gina looking back over her shoulder at me.

I was thrilled when she came to London. She had never seen Thomas Lang, Terry Bozzio, Jimmy Chamberlin, and some of the other great drummers playing at the festival, so when she got there, I introduced her to everyone and she had a great time.

Gina was really serious about playing the drums. It wasn't a hobby to her at all, and I loved that. She was really into watching the other drummers, and we talked about drummers, drumming, drumming styles, music, gear—she had a brand-new Tama drum kit she was excited about, and I was totally turned on by this woman who was so into playing the drums.

While we were watching Jimmy Chamberlin perform, I slid my arm around her waist and she didn't object. Then I went a bit further and I slid my hand into her back pocket, like a high school kid and. . . . It was one of those moments where I was either going to get a look, a gesture to stop, slapped in the face, or something, but everything was still cool.

Eventually it was my turn to rock. After the event was finished, Gina had to drive the three hours back to Exeter, and I had to head back to the USA the next day. But before she left, I gave her a hug, and I clearly remember thinking, Should I kiss her good-bye, you know the friendly kiss, real quick? Then I thought, *But what if it's longer than a friendly kiss . . . hmmm I better not . . . But maybe I will.*

Kissing is a very powerful thing. It tells you a lot about a person—and if the kiss is amazing, it can fuck with your head afterward. You never know. That's where that phrase "I got swept off my feet" comes from. One kiss and *bam.* Oh, what the fuck. Good-bye, Gina! Really nice to have met you and I enjoyed hanging out with you. Have a safe drive home. Kiss! WOW! It was amazing! Now what?

We kept in touch by e-mail, and eventually she came to LA with a few friends for a short vacation, but she had an idea brewing in her head. She had already exhausted all of her drumming possibilities in Exeter, and now she wanted to experience the music scene in LA. This was a big, life-changing move for her. She had no one supporting her with this bold idea. She was doing this all on her own, and I thought it was awesome. When she came back to LA the next time, she came with her son, Connor, and stayed for three months.

Gina eventually formed an all-girl band and started rehearsing five days a week and practicing whenever whe wasn't with the band. She was seriously committed to playing and performing and eventually played shows with her band, Kamikaze, at Molly Malone's and at the Mint. I saw both gigs and she just continued to blow me away. Gina totally kicked ass—she's small and really beautiful and sexy to watch, but at the same time she is very aggressive and physical when she plays. She can really beat the crap out of a drum set.

I was spending most of my time in LA and decided to rent a small apartment, and it made a huge difference because the recording budgets had gotten smaller and smaller. I was an in-town guy now; no one had to import me from Indiana.

When I had time, I showed Gina around and helped her get more situated in the LA music scene. When I introduced her to my friends and other musicians, I loved watching their faces when I told them that she was a devoted, hard-hitting drummer who could destroy a drum set. No one could believe it.

36

Chickenfoot

I was doing a session at Henson Studio in early 2006 when John Shanks came in and said, "Hey, man. How are you doing? Want to play on a Rod Stewart record I am co-producing with Clive Davis?" I said, "Are you fucking kidding me? He is one of my all-time favorite singers. . . . This is amazing, dude! You were in Rod's band a few years ago, and now you're *producing* him, which means both Clive *and* Rod approve of you? Holy shit, that is huge. . . . Congratulations!"

Rod was coming off of years of doing his "American Songbook" albums and was getting back into his rock roots on this album.

He was actually singing with the band live in the studio while we tracked, which he hadn't done in years. Rod is the boss, the lead singer, and the ultimate rock star, but he loves hanging out with the musicians, like he is just another dude in the band. He's one of the guys. That's rare. Ironically, the first song we recorded for the project was "Have You Ever Seen the Rain," a CCR song written by John Fogerty. The album debuted at #1 on the *Billboard* Top 200 Albums chart in 2009 with 184,000 sold in the first week!

After working with Rod, Desmond Child rang me up to come play drums on Meat Loaf's third installment of the *Bat Out of Hell* album series, this one being *The Monster Is Loose*, and the fourth record I'd made with Meat Loaf in fifteen years. Jim Steinman wasn't involved with Meat Loaf's records anymore, and Desmond was a great choice for a producer.

Meat Loaf has a unique way of describing what he wants me to play. He's very dramatic and emotional when he tries to convey what he wants.

He doesn't spell his ideas out clearly. He talks in concepts, like a movie director might do, but somehow I have always been able to figure out what he wants. And Desmond can also be emotional when he is trying to convey his ideas. Between the two of them, I felt like I was in a theatrical production, with all the special effects, but the end results were spectacular.

One of the things that makes producers—like Don Was and John Shanks—so amazing is they are great *listeners*. They always wanted to hear my ideas and encourage me to experiment and do my thing.

One of the best is Matt Serletic (Matchbox Twenty, Rob Thomas, Collective Soul). In 2001, I recorded Willie Nelson's *The Great Divide* with Matt—a record that featured collaborations and duets with pop and country superstars, including Rob Thomas, Lee Ann Womack, Kid Rock, Sheryl Crow, and Bonnie Raitt. Matt was president of Virgin Records USA at age thirty-four—he was beyond talented, he had a whole other thing going on, he was actually very "presidential," and I learned a lot from him.

Howard Benson is another one of my favorite producers—I did Puddle of Mudd's "Psycho" with him in 2007, which became a #1 hit for nine weeks. He also hired me to record tracks on Gavin DeGraw, Less Than Jake, the Starting Line, and Creed's Scott Stapp's solo records. Howard could mastermind songs into hit singles—he was like a fucking magician.

Another very focused producer I worked with around the same time as the Meat Loaf sessions was Todd Rundgren, as part of a reboot of new wave icons the Cars, in a group they'd dubbed the *New Cars*.

Lead guitarist Elliot Easton and keyboardist Greg Hawkes had teamed up with Todd and his bass player, Kasmim Sultan, to make a new album. Todd was stepping in on lead vocals to replace Ric Ocasek, who had become a successful record producer himself and had seemingly lost interest in fronting his old band.

Todd was 100 percent business, and I really liked working with him. He's a brilliant musician, artist, producer, and songwriter. He really knows his shit. But if you replace someone like Ric Ocasek, it has to make sense to the band, and especially to the fans. Todd was a good choice, but I feel that without Ric Ocasek there is no Cars.

They made an odd sort of record called *It's Alive!* I was only on two tracks—and the rest were live tracks of the New Cars playing the original Cars hits, plus a couple of old Rundgren tunes. It wasn't something that was likely to create a lot of excitement—with "legacy" acts you really need to bring the original band, or at least something close to it, and have a very real and loyal following, a la Skynyrd or Heart, for instance.

Honestly, I liked playing with them because the original Cars were the ultimate "two and four" band—their whole sound had been based on very simple beats (snare on the two and four, and not much else), and very simple but catchy guitar and synth hooks. In some ways it was a real test to see how much a simple zero-frills rock beat can really swing.

━◦━

In this business it's never good to turn down a gig if you can avoid it. Everything leads to something, even if it's not so obvious at the time. You really have to make your own luck. A lot of that just comes from being there and being enthusiastic. At this point in my career, for as many big names I played with, I was also doing sessions with up-and-coming bands trying to make it.

My discography for that year reflected an amazing diversity of artists and bands within a new generation of millennials, and a lot of indie folks just trying to break out. I played on Trevor Hall's *The Rascals Have Returned*, Huecco's self-titled debut from Mexico, Lennon's *Damaged Goods*, After Midnight, Canadian county star George Canyon, Lena Park, Philip Jones, Brittney Christian, Jesse McCartney, and Steve Richards out of LA; Chris Otepka out of Chicago; Dean Davidson in Philadelphia; Jane Jenson and Kold War out of Indianapolis; Nolan and Steve Rider out of NYC, and Rasul 2 out of Brooklyn; Marc Berley out of New Jersey; GB Leighton out of Minneapolis; and on and on.

And I was back in the studio that spring to work on Avril Lavigne's latest record. It was pretty much standard procedure for her to write some songs after the record was finished, just like when Mellencamp wrote "Crumblin'

Down" for the *Uh-Huh* record, after it was done. Some artists always feel that they could do better, and I admire that.

I think I was like a good-luck charm for her. I got called in to record "My Happy Ending" for her *Under My Skin* record two years earlier—after the record was already finished—and it became a #1 hit in the US and charted in twenty countries.

I was also playing with my peers, my heroes, and some legends: Vinnie Colaiuta and I were both the house drummers in 2006 for *Les Paul and Friends: 90th Birthday Salute* at the Gibson Amphitheatre in LA. We played drums for all of the artists honoring Les Paul, including Aerosmith's Joe Perry, Buddy Guy, Slash, Edgar Winter, Steve Lukather, Joe Satriani, Neal Schon, Merle Haggard, and Alison Krauss.

One of the coolest gigs I played that year was when I subbed a few shows for Matt Sorum on some Camp Freddy dates.

Camp Freddy is a badass LA all-star band that Matt—drummer of Guns N' Roses/the Cult/Velvet Revolver—had formed to go out and play corporate gigs around the world. It was an ingenious idea, to make some dough and have a shit load of fun playing without the pressure of real tours and scoring a hit.

Camp Freddy has been around since 2002 with regular members guitarists Dave Navarro (Jane's Addiction), Billy Morrison (the Cult, Billy Idol), Slash (Guns N' Roses, Velvet Revolver), Jerry Cantrell (Alice in Chains), Tom Morello (Rage Against the Machine, Audioslave, the E Street Band), bassist Chris Chaney (Jane's Addiction, Methods of Mayhem, Alanis Morissette), and a list of all-star vocalists, including Scott Weiland (Stone Temple Pilots, Velvet Revolver), Sebastian Bach (Skid Row), Sully Erna (Godsmack), Chester Bennington and Mike Shinoda (Linkin Park), Corey Taylor (Slipknot, Stone Sour), Greg Dulli (the Afghan Wigs), Chino Moreno (the Deftones), and Brandon Boyd (Incubus), among others. They played greatest hits from all their respective catalogs, as well as classic rock 'n' roll covers, and audiences just ate it up. It was a party, a dream band, and a rock 'n' roll retrospective all at once. Mostly it was guys playing for the sake of playing, and fans loved seeing their rock heroes come onstage one after another. It was like a monster from outer space, something to witness in complete awe.

One of the Camp Freddy gigs I played was at the House of Blues on Sunset, for a Sunset Strip festival honoring Ozzy Osbourne. Donovan Leitch and Corey Taylor from Slipknot were the main lead singers that night, along with special guests like Steve Stevens from Billy Idol's band playing guitar.

We performed a ton of Ozzy Osbourne tunes, and eventually Ozzy climbed up onstage and sang "Crazy Train," "Paranoid," and "Iron Man." It was a real LA scene—and if you were there, you would never forget it.

In some ways, Camp Freddy was a lot like Chickenfoot, another real-life super group I played with about four years later. I know that the word "super group" gets thrown around sometimes, but seriously—you had half of Van Halen, the drummer from the Red Hot Chili Peppers, and Joe Satriani, who is one of the best guitar players on the planet. It was a sick lineup.

Chickenfoot was all about having fun, jamming, laughing, but still doing your job, kicking ass and playing great music. The name Chickenfoot sort of symbolizes that fun attitude. The bottom line is that name is not to be taken seriously; it's supposed to be funny.

I think they got started just jamming at Sammy Hagar's place in Cabo—and I am sure the tequila was flowing. It was Sammy and Michael Anthony from VH on bass, and Chad Smith from the Chili Peppers, and then they had the idea to call in Satriani—who not only plays great, but looks great. He has a shaved head and goes in for big sunglasses. You can see why I am a fan.

Carter, Chickenfoot's manager, had called me a couple of years ago panicked because Chad had torn a bicep. Chickenfoot was on tour in Europe and trying to decide whether they should get a replacement drummer, postpone some shows, or just cancel the rest of the European leg of the tour. Carter wanted to see if I was available in case they needed me to fly out immediately. Chad ended up doing the rest of the shows with one arm because *that* is Chickenfoot! They decided having Chad play with one arm—and keeping the vibe going—was more important than getting a great replacement drummer with two arms. Now that's a band that sticks together.

Flash-forward two years—I got a call from Mick Brigden, who was now managing Chickenfoot. Carter, shockingly, had succumbed to cancer. It was devastating to everyone who knew him, and I was winded just hearing the news, but Mick got right to business. He didn't have much of a choice.

"Are you available to go on tour with Chickenfoot?"

Chad had a conflict with upcoming Chili Peppers dates, and he recommended me as the guy to fill in. Mick suggested I talk to Sammy on the phone to get things rolling.

Sammy called me and said, "Look, I don't really want to do this if it's not fun. Chad is a big personality, and he's a big powerful drummer, but he swears you're the guy to take his place."

> **Chickenfoot/Red Hot Chili Peppers Drummer Chad Smith**: I have known Kenny from back in the Mellencamp days when the Peppers were in Sydney, Australia, and I got into my hotel room finding a note under my door, saying, "Don't be too loud with your boyfriend. I'm right next door. Love, Kenny." I knew he was the man for the job. Of course his hard-hitting musical style would fit in perfectly.

There were lots of drummers who wanted this gig—Tommy Lee, Abe Laboriel, Jr., Jason Bonham, and Matt Sorum, among them, all great drummers, all great guys.

Not only was Chickenfoot stacked with legit superstars, it was a party on wheels. I told Sammy, "Look, Chad's a hard hitter; I'm a hard hitter. Chad's a rock drummer who plays funk; I'm a rock drummer who plays R & B and funk. We're really similar in that regard. Chad's a big personality; I'm a big personality. Chad is definitely way funnier than me—but I'm bald and beautiful."

The bottom line is, if Sammy and I hadn't gotten along on that first phone call, I never would have been invited to jam with the guys. Sammy wasn't kidding when he said it had to be fun—these guys all had other gigs. They didn't have to do this. This band was like their vacation from their other bands.

As usual, to get ready to play with them, I wrote out charts on all the songs from both of their albums (their second album, by the way, is called *Chickenfoot III*, which shows you just how deadly serious they were). For starters, I wanted to embrace what Chad did. . . .

> **Michael Anthony**: Kenny came in and he had written out all the drum parts. That's what he does when he comes in for a session, and I remember him and I sitting there before Joe and Sammy came in, and I'm looking at him, and he's got his music stand and is putting all the charts up, and I go, "Kenny, you know as soon as you know all that, you're tearing all that shit up and throwing it out, right? Because that isn't what this band's about. We want Kenny Aronoff. We don't want a Chad clone. You gotta be you. We wanted him to be part of the band, as opposed to Chickenfoot with a hired gun on drums. Once he got really comfortable with that, he probably got almost as close to being as crazy as Chad as you can get. And it was great—now it was like, Alright, Kenny, just do your own thing!

After about five seconds of playing, I was blown away by the feel of these guys, especially Joe Satriani. Guitar players a lot of times will rush, but Joe is impeccable in the pocket. He had a reputation as a lead guitarist, but his rhythm playing was flawless.

> **Joe Satriani**: Kenny's extremely different from Chad when it comes to where he places his groove. Kenny brings power, a solid velocity, and feel at the same time to his playing—that is what I would always notice when I'd see him playing with other bands, live or on TV—I'd be thinking, Man, that guy lays that snare and propels the band with his hi-hat like nobody else. That's very different from Chad, who propels the band with his kick and brings the band back with the snare, but sort of dances around with the hat. Kenny's style of drumming is quite unique, actually, and he definitely goes a little bit crazy with us—when he's playing with Fogerty, he's got a very strict set of guidelines that he's got to stick to—with us, it's "Go crazy!"

The first time I performed live with Chickenfoot was in Cabo, Mexico, at Sammy's club for his annual weeklong birthday bash. Gina flew down with me and we had the best week. In the early morning, we would wake up and watch the cruise ships come into the bay from our balcony, which was littered with the detritus of the night before. Sammy had his own brand of tequila, and you can only imagine the partying that went on.

As soon as the shops on the street would open up, for some reason (Sammy's tequila, perhaps?) they always played Mellencamp's "Hurt So Good"—doubly funny for me.

Sammy's club holds 800 fans, possibly more if they are crazy drunk on tequila and really jammed in, which they always were, and every night for his weeklong bash it was a different group of musicians playing with Sammy.

The floor is totally packed, but there's a catwalk looking over the floor, which connects the stage to the dressing room, and there is some great stuff going on between the audience and the bands when they are up there going back and forth. It is a very cool setup.

Backstage, there was always a huge party going on—lots of musicians, of course, and Sammy would pick songs from this giant list, deciding what everyone was going to play. When I was up, he chose a couple of Van Halen songs and "Rock 'n' Roll" by Led Zeppelin.

I take John Bonham's original drum parts very seriously. Why wouldn't you? It would be sacrilege to get up onstage and not do it *right*. Which means studying it, and breaking it down, and learning that shit properly.

You might think you know the songs, but I guarantee unless you really study them, like a bug under a microscope, you don't. It's that way with a lot of songs—you name it, "Johnny B. Goode," any Beatles or Stones song, anything that gets played a lot, the guitar player and the drummer *think* they know it, but most of the time all they're doing is approximating their *memory* of it from hearing it on the radio, or playing it when they were in high school, and then it just ends up sounding like another bar band. This shit is important—you have to get it right. Even if you think it is super simple. Right now, somewhere in the world, there is a drummer playing "Honky Tonk Woman" totally fucking wrong because they think all it is, is this very basic beat, and they didn't bother to learn the subtleties and the little hi-hat tricks, never mind the little lick at the beginning, which is the perfect Charlie Watts drum riff.

Drum beats are not interchangeable. On "Rock 'n' Roll" you have to hit the eighth notes on both the snare *and* the hi-hats at the same time. And the hi-hats have to be open *exactly* right. It's a killer pattern, based on the intro to "Keep a Knockin'" by Little Richard, which is this completely insane takeoff on New Orleans R & B, but also has a really cool double-shuffle Chicago blues thing happening. It's not easy to play like that, not quite straight, not quite swinging. You've got to drive it with both hands, and the bass drum dances around the two and the four—but you can't lay it down too hard. There is a lilt and a swagger to it. You have to feel that inside shit, and you have to nail the tempo. Too fast or too slow and it dies.

John Bonham was a musician. He was bold enough to grab things from the past—Max Roach and Louis Bellson, and of course Gene Krupa—and know where it was all headed. He put a lot of ingredients together. He was a soul music obsessive. He had swing and style, but also great musical ideas. He was in the right place at the right time with Zeppelin, but he was the vessel that carried them as well. If I had to pick one guy, my favorite rock 'n' roll drummer of all time, it would be him. And he cared about his sound—it was *huge*. Without precedent. He was definitely involved with recording his drums. It wasn't all Jimmy Page, who was a brilliant producer, but Bonham had his head into all of it. This is what separates great drummers from the good ones.

When we played it down in Cabo, Sammy kept looking back at me and giving me the strangest looks. I wasn't really sure what it meant, but afterwards, as we were walking back to the dressing room across the catwalk, he said, "What the fuck was that? I never heard that played like *that* before. Man, that felt like the record! I never heard it played *right* before! That was fucking awesome!"

He knew. A lot of singers would have just gone along with whatever— honestly you can do a pretty good job just by faking it, but that's never going to cut it with people who *know*. Sammy was very tuned in. He totally blew me away. He was a very accomplished musician, far beyond being just an entertainer.

Chickenfoot was maybe the greatest band I've ever played with. It felt like I was in Led Zeppelin and Van Halen all in one, and along with being musically satisfying, it was without a doubt the most fun and stress-less tour I've ever been on. I had to *ask* for a sound check!

Everything was always tight and spot-on, because everyone is a badass in Chickenfoot, but there was a real looseness there, too, a *tight looseness* that is all about swagger and being a badass, like the Stones, and it was *fucking awesome.*

The show was ninety minutes long, and Sammy took us out to dinner almost every night when we weren't playing, and every night after the show we'd have a sit-down dinner together as a band. This was like a throwback to being in high school. It felt new. It was like a gang. We were a unit with four established stars, and that reflected in our playing onstage and in all the photo sessions, the interviews, the first-class accommodations—but, really, it was just some kids blowing off steam. Kids who played like motherfuckers, and the audiences saw and felt that.

The Chickenfoot "Different Devil" tour went across the US, Canada, and Europe in 2012 and ended at the Greek Theater in LA on June 15. Sammy was amazing with the audience. He talked to them as if we are all hanging out in his house drinking some of his tequila. He's all about vibe and fun. He's come up on my drum riser and hit the drums, and I would talk to the audience on my microphone. We were having a party onstage and kicking ass at the same time. The musicianship was amazing. Everybody was encouraged to stretch out.

One night in Boston, Chad had a night off from the Chili Peppers tour and he flew to Boston from NYC to come see us play. I played the show and Chad did the encore and the audience went ape shit. No one saw it coming, and I loved watching the crowd go ape shit when Chad jumped up onto my drums and started playing. It was so cool for the fans, and . . . me, because I was a fan! Which, sometimes, at least, is what it's all about. It would suck to stop being a fan.

37

Great Balls of Fire
and the Kennedy Center Honors

By 2007, it was finally time to open my own recording studio in Los Angeles. I had seen the writing on the wall by that point. With the landscape for album budgets shifting, there wasn't money to fly me all over the country to make records as much anymore. And since so much of the record-making process had transitioned to digital recording by then, in theory, I had the ability to record drum tracks for anyone anywhere in the world without ever having to leave town. All the artist or band had to do was e-mail me MP3s, or send me the Pro Tools files of their songs over the Internet; or they could come to my studio with their hard drive, and I could record five to twenty tracks of drums and percussion, depending on the vibe they were looking for.

After so many years working with so many top-flight producers, I knew a lot about recording drums and the process of getting a song to *sound great* on the radio. That was the ultimate goal, right? I knew what drums to use, how to tune them, what mics to use and where to place them, what pre-amps and EQs to dial in to get the desired sound for that particular track I was recording. I knew what to play to *get* a song on the radio. It wasn't just about me and the drums; it was about the song and the artist. I knew how to solve problems and get results. In my studio I still like to hire an engineer to record my sessions. That way, I can focus on the song and recording my drums. But having my own studio has made it affordable for artists or bands that do not have record deals to have me play drums on their records.

Uncommon Studios LA is super simple: I have two rooms—a drum room and a control room. And what's convenient about that location is that the building next door is Drum Paradise, where all of my studio and touring gear is stored—that's like nine different drum kits, over a hundred snare drums, 250 cymbals, and lots of percussion, enough choices to be creative and always get it right. I give the artists the takes they want, and I go in and put on my producer hat when I'm listening to the playback and make whatever adjustments are necessary to make the drum tracks and the song sound great together.

This is what I do whenever I am home, off the road, and not recording in the big studios with bands or artists. Basically, when I am not working, I am working.

—◦—

Things just got bigger and bigger in 2008, starting in February when I performed at the Fiftieth Annual Grammy Awards with John Fogerty, honoring Little Richard and Jerry Lee Lewis. Even John was blown away by being there with Richard and Jerry Lee—they were his heroes, and, of course, he had a big hit with "Good Golly Miss Molly," which was one of Little Richard's biggest hits.

When you do a live TV show like this one, the producer lets us know exactly how much time we have to perform. It was John's job to work out the medley for everyone and make sure it was exactly the right length of time. The medley started with the Fogerty band playing one of his recent compositions, "Coming Down the Road," and after a double chorus, we stopped abruptly and Jerry Lee Lewis started his most famous song, "Great Balls of Fire." That segued right back into two choruses of John's "Coming Down the Road," with another stop at the end, which set up Little Richard to play "Good Golly Miss Molly."

We had rehearsed this medley by ourselves, timed it with a stopwatch, and then rehearsed the medley with Jerry Lee Lewis, which went great. And right about the time we finished, in walked Little Richard and his entourage of musicians.

Little Richard is still completely outrageous. He is like a god. When he

300

enters the room, he is like King Tut or something, dressed in a crazy outfit and with a total air of royalty. He is very sweet, but he wants you to know that he is, as he likes to say, The *Beeeeeyoooooteeeeeeful* Little Richard.

We watched them start to unpack their instruments and didn't know exactly what was going on. I saw John look a bit concerned, and his wife, Julie (who is also his manager), immediately got on the phone and called Grammy producer Ken Ehrlich to sort things out. John very nicely walked over to Little Richard and politely said, "I have some pretty good players here myself. Why don't we just use my band?"

Little Richard didn't like that—he went off on John. I think he was ranting about an old lawsuit between Creedence and Specialty Records, which owned Little Richard's catalog, and about how many people in the music business ripped his music off and made millions of dollars, starting with the Beatles, and how he wasn't going to play with someone else's band just so they could get the credit again. John loved Little Richard, and John knew as much about being ripped off as anyone, so he took what he said very seriously, respectfully listening while his wife, Julie, continued to try and get Ken Ehrlich on the phone. Ken is the master at solving problems, so we weren't too worried, and the bottom line was that he wanted to have John Fogerty's band back up all three artists, because we sounded great, and logistically we weren't going to swap out bands during the show. Plus we were rehearsed and ready to go, polished down to the second for live TV.

Richard was still going on about how he felt, when Jerry Lee Lewis decided to play peacemaker. Everyone was surprised to see Jerry Lee trying to reason with Little Richard, the guy was definitely not known for his diplomacy.

Plus, traditionally, Little Richard and Jerry Lee have hated each other, or at least that's what we had heard. They'd do oldies tours together and they'd fight over who got to close the show, and they'd refuse to have their pictures taken together. It was real old-school stuff, bad blood going back sixty years. Richard once called Jerry Lee "the King of Stupidity."

Jerry Lee was smiling now and got up from his piano and whispered something in Little Richard's ear and sat down, still smiling. For some reason, that caused Richard to calm down and everything went great from then on, without a hitch. For all I know, Jerry Lee threatened to kill him. It would not have been out of character. This is the guy who once set his piano on fire with lighter fluid because he had to open for Chuck Berry.

◄o►

In 2008 was also when I got my first call to perform at the Kennedy Center Honors, which is like the Grammys, *SNL*, all of my tours, everything put together. This is the pinnacle of everything I have ever done. There is *nothing* more prestigious, more intense, and more about *perfection* than these shows, where some of the world's cultural icons (it isn't just music) are honored. It felt like being in the Super Bowl.

This was not a relaxed gig. Next to the presidential inauguration it is the most high-pressure gig I've ever done—but I loved every second of it and felt honored to be doing it.

Musical director Rob Mathes and the producers of the show handpicked the band member by member—you have to be able to play every style of music and keep a smile on your face and get along with everyone under this incredible scrutiny.

It's definitely another level of performing. It's one artist after another, a fourteen-camera shoot and live recording in front of an audience of dignitaries and stars (not to mention our president and a huge television audience), and it has to be beyond flawless, even with constant changes and relatively little rehearsal. I remember Sting giving me notes a second before we had to perform a medley of Springsteen songs, a last-second idea for part of the song "The Rising." Just as the curtain was going up, I wrote on that section of my chart, *don't fuck it up.* The pressure to play *perfectly* is intense.

The first year I performed at the Kennedy Center Honors, I played in the segments that honored the Who and George Jones. For the Who part of the show, I played with Dave Grohl, Chris Cornell, Rob Thomas, Joss Stone, and Bettye LaVette; and for the George Jones honors, I played with Garth Brooks, Alan Jackson, Brad Paisley, Randy Travis, and Shelby Lynne.

I had to go from Keith Moon crazy to Nashville calm—I remember talking to Dave Grohl about having to play like day and night on the same stage, starting with flailing on the drums for the Who numbers, hitting as hard as I could with reckless abandon, and then moving on to that soft country style, no rim shots on the snare, just keeping time, supporting the singers.

> **Rob Mathes:** Your band's only as good as your drummer, and if you have the best band in the world but the drummer's lacking in any way, already people come into a situation—and this is crucial, and is my life and will always be my life—but when you lead a house band, almost any artist you work with expects the worst. They're going to try to get as many of their artists on the gig as possible. They don't want to deal with a house band. They just want to come in and bring their own people, so with somebody like me—who has a good reputation in the music business but is not a celebrity like Paul Shaffer or Questlove—I'm only as good as the musical solutions I get from the people I work with. And what I pride myself on with the Kennedy Center Honors is that people can come in and I can write the charts out for them, but if they have any issues, I can do quick changes and then I have a band that's going to blow you away and is going to be so powerful and as dedicated to whoever's music we're playing as any band ever put together, and Kenny's the definition of that.

> **Billy Corgan:** I think it's great that over time Kenny has gotten his due, that when you see him on, like, the Kennedy Center [Honors], you don't go, like, "Who's that?" He belongs there.

After that first Kennedy Center Honors in 2008, Rob Mathes told me the gig was mine, and I kept getting calls year after year from Rob to honor an incredible lineup of the musical artists who were being celebrated, along with actors and artists, writers, all sorts of cultural heavyweights. But my job was to bring the beat.

For Bruce Springsteen's honors, in 2009, I performed with Melissa

Etheridge, Sting, Jennifer Nettles, Ben Harper, and my old boss, John Mellencamp. For Sir Paul McCartney and Merle Haggard, in 2010, I performed with Steven Tyler, Dave Grohl, Norah Jones, James Taylor, Mavis Staples, and Kid Rock to honor Sir Paul, and then Willie Nelson, Sheryl Crow, Vince Gill, Brad Paisley, Jamie Johnson, Miranda Lambert, and Kris Kristofferson for Merle Haggard's part of the show. For Neil Diamond, in 2011 (also honoring musicians Sonny Rollins, and Yo-Yo Ma), I got to play with Lionel Richie, Smokey Robinson, and Jennifer Nettles. For Led Zeppelin, in 2012, I performed with Lenny Kravitz and Kid Rock. I really wanted to play with Heart, who killed it with "Stairway to Heaven," performing with a full chorus and orchestra, but Jason Bonham had the inside track. For Billy Joel and Carlos Santana, in 2013, I performed with Don Henley, Garth Brooks, Brendon Urie, and Rufus Wainwright for the Billy Joel part of the honors, and then with Steve Winwood, Sheila E., Tom Morello, Fher Olvera, Juanes, and Orianthi for Carlos Santana. And for Sting, in 2014, I performed with Lady Gaga, Bruno Mars, Bruce Springsteen, Herbie Hancock, and Esperanza Spalding—plus I got to hang out with my old buddy Tom Hanks, who was also being honored that night (along with Al Green, Lily Tomlin, and Patricia McBride). In 2015, they let George Stevens go after thirty-seven years of producing, and sadly Rob Mathes went with him. But that's the business.

◄○►

Soon after the Grammys with Little Richard and Jerry Lee, I found myself back in Russia—this time with John Fogerty—standing in front of the Kremlin at sound check for a gig where it turned out that we were performing for, among other dignitaries and Communist Party muckety-mucks, Vladimir Putin.

We got out there and did our show like we always do, maybe even a little better because we were genuinely excited to be playing there. Once upon a time in Russia, they put people in jail for playing rock 'n' roll.

No one in the crowd clapped after any of our songs. After forty-five minutes of rocking our asses off, there was silence. I mean, *nobody did any-thing.* It was like playing for ghosts or zombies. And we were killing it! I was thinking they had booked the wrong band and everyone was just confused.

The irony was, as I found out later, Putin had not only been instrumental in bringing us over, but he'd personally made up our set list. Go figure. But he was a huge Creedence fan.

Finally, after we played through the hits, the whole audience got up and started dancing and clapping and finally having some fun—they'd all been waiting for Putin to clap or get up and dance. Once he was having a good time, everyone else was, too. I would hate to think what would have hap-pened if he *didn't* like us.

38

Hail to the Chief

The presidential inauguration in Washington, DC, for newly elected Commander in Chief Barack Obama was clearly the highlight of 2009.

The stage was set up in front of the Lincoln Memorial looking down toward the Washington Monument. In a tent next to the Lincoln Memorial, where we rehearsed, I had to wear long underwear and a snow parka and a ski hat with drummer's gloves to stay warm. During the actual show, it finally warmed up to thirty-two degrees—it was nine degrees when we did the stage rehearsal and sound check the night before with Jon Bon Jovi and Bettye LaVette.

The night of the inauguration, I performed with Garth Brooks, John Mellencamp, Beyoncé, Stevie Wonder, Mary J. Blige, Sheryl Crow, Jon Bon Jovi, Bettye LaVette, Willie Nelson, James Taylor, Josh Groban, Herbie Hancock, Heather Headley, John Legend, Jennifer Nettles, Usher, Shakira, will.i.am, and many others. More or less, I played the drums for everyone who performed that night, except Bruce Springsteen and U2.

For the live performance, I wore long underwear and drum gloves, but no hat because I think it's better to freeze and look cool than be warm and look like a dork, even though I was wearing layers like a little kid who had been dressed by his grandmother on a snow day. The horn players' horns froze—trombones locked in place, sax keys iced up. I have no idea how the guitar players played their freezing cold metal strings. The joke was we had heaters the size of my laptop, but in that cold they were basically useless.

On the day of the show, they had this huge mega-screen facing the stage so that the people talking could read the screen while looking into the cameras, and the singers who needed it could see their lyrics. I had the people writing the script put cues on the screen ("Kenny Aronoff counts off NOW!") so there would be no surprises for the singers who were just walking on.

That's why gigs like this are never just about playing great. It's about understanding the flow of the entire show, knowing what comes next, knowing when to count off and end songs. I wouldn't be there if the producer and the musical director didn't think they could count on me to do my job flawlessly and solve problems on the fly.

This was a big night—no less so because this would be the first time I had performed with John Mellencamp since leaving the band fourteen years ago, and I was actually looking forward to seeing him and playing "Pink Houses" with him again. I thought "Pink Houses" was one of the best songs we had ever recorded, and when we played it that night, it was the highlight for me because it brought back so many positive and powerful memories; and especially on such a special night, it almost brought tears to my eyes. Not quite, but almost.

I called John on the phone before he came to DC to touch base before we saw each other in person onstage.

"Hey, John. This is Kenny." He had a delayed reaction before he said, "Oh. Hi, Kenny . . ."

I got right to it. "Look, I wanted to call you for two reasons. One, I wanted to let you know that it's fucking freezing cold onstage, and, two, you're all alone up there. The house band is down below where you are standing." All he cared about was if he was performing after Joe Biden gave his speech.

I told him I didn't know because I hadn't seen the script yet, but he asked me to find out, which I did. Then he said, "Are you still playing with a lot of cymbals?" I laughed and said, "Hell yes. When you get to the double chorus at the end of 'Pink Houses,' you stop singing while I start hitting all my cymbals and go nuts on my double bass drums."

"Listen, fucker, if you hit those cymbals, I'm going to come down there and take them off the kit!" I laughed and told him, "Please come on down. I'll get more camera time!"

It was really cool to reconnect with John, and we had a good hang in his dressing room for forty-five minutes before the broadcast.

Just as good was during a break from rehearsing for the show, I went into the greenroom looking for coffee, and Tom Hanks walked in. When he saw me, he said, "Kenny! I didn't know you were going to be here. That's awesome!" We talked for a while, and when he was doing his sound check up at the podium here on the big stage in front of the Lincoln Memorial, someone told me he said into the microphone, "Hey, everybody, I just saw Kenny Aronoff and he's going to rock your socks off tonight!" That was his sound check. Thank you, Tom Hanks!

◄◦►

I loved seeing Mellencamp, but that part of my life, Indiana, was over, done, finished. I loved living in Bloomington. I spent more than half my life there. I love Indiana. I love the people there. You can take me out of Indiana, but you can't take Indiana out of me.

I finally sold my beautiful house in Bloomington and spent three days, eighteen hours a day, packing up the entire place. It took two gigantic moving trucks to move my stuff.

There were over a hundred snare drums, five drum kits, a ton of studio gear, marimba, hundreds of cymbals, hardware, road cases, and lots of percussion, all of which I moved by myself to a temperature-controlled storage unit. I had a huge attic with dozens of file cabinets filled with charts, business docs, just a massive amount of stuff that represented thirty years of my career behind the drums. After I loaded the trucks, I locked the door, put the keys in the plant box, and drove off. Driving away to catch an airplane back to LA was extremely emotional for me. I had spent forty amazing years of my life in Bloomington, but it was time to move on.

The year wound up with one of the more dreamlike experiences of this whole trip: playing with the Doors.

I got a call from my buddy T-Bone Wolk, who was Daryl Hall's musical director. He invited me to join him and Daryl for a very special segment of *Live from Daryl's House*, to be filmed in a house in the Pacific Palisades with the remaining members of the Doors—guitarist Robbie Krieger and keyboardist Ray Manzarek.

We played three Doors songs—"Break on Through," "Roadhouse Blues," and "Light My Fire,"—which took me right back to being fifteen years old when the Doors were a huge part of my life. Back then I had worshipped them—they were the perfect band to foment a young rebel.

After the Doors' mini-set, we played some Daryl songs. I can't remember what we played exactly, but he is a total badass. He may be a pretty boy, but he is without a doubt one of the greatest white soul singers in history.

Playing the Doors stuff was unreal. Playing the fast drum intro to "Break on Through" was like getting on a roller coaster—listen to it, you probably never realized how fast it is, the tempo is just crazy. It was like the Doors take on a Latin thing, and there is a lot of cross-sticking—another example of maybe you *think* you know a song because you've heard it so many times, but really, you don't. As always, I did my homework and was prepared. When the keyboard came in, it was like a freight train. So cool.

"Light My Fire" was like religion to me when I was in high school. I used to play it every day, all day long. We all did, and it was being played constantly on the radio. My brother, Jon, and I had a band, and Jon learned it note for note on his Vox Continental organ, just like the one Ray had. When we played "Light My Fire" at dances, people got up immediately and danced frantically.

"Light My Fire" starts with a hit on the snare drum, and then the band comes in together. I even practiced that one hit over and over again. When you are doing it for real, you have to be in the moment. You want to enjoy it, which is why I keep preaching *repetition*. It's just one hit on a snare drum, but the next thing that happens is *the Doors are playing* "Light My Fire." It's hard to fuck up, but I wasn't taking any chances. Ray and Robbie seemed very happy.

The Doors songs went down perfectly, and while Daryl was singing his songs, Ray asked someone for some white wine. "I want some white wine and it needs to be *really* cold. The shittier the wine, the colder it needs to be!" I had a feeling that the wine was never going to show up, and from my experience, this was not going have a happy ending. Ray seemed like he was losing his patience as time went by. We kept playing and filming, and there was still no wine. I was laughing, but it wasn't funny—why couldn't some-one get the guy a glass of wine? I'm not going to speculate, but the wine never came and Ray finally got up and left. No wine, no Ray.

39

Dad

On January 17, 2011, I woke up like any other day and headed in to the first of a three-day recording session with Atlanta Braves first baseman Nick Swisher. My drum tech was late getting to the session ahead of me to set up, which made me nervous because that meant it could potentially hold the whole session up.

I know it sounds weird, but I get called to do these records that professional athletes make with producer Loren Harriett. Athletes love to hang with musicians, and I am a big sports fan, so I love making records with these super jocks. I recorded an album with Bernie Williams from the Yankees (great jazz guitar player) and Boston Red Sox pitcher Bronson Arroyo—he was on the team that won the World Series in 2004. He was really into doing grunge stuff, Pearl Jam, STP, Nirvana, Foo Fighters—he just wanted to make a record, and he sang great.

After one session I asked Bronson to throw some pitches to me in the parking lot, which ended up being a big mistake. I wanted to step into his world for a second and experience what it would be like to catch a major league baseball player's pitches. Wow! His pitches *seemed* so consistent—except for the last second where they would curve up, down, left, or right. It's incredible to see the ball actually move. My main concern was the only thing between me and those fast curveballs was a flimsy glove. He said his pitches were slower than usual, but still going at least seventy miles per hour, which was about as fast as a changeup. How does anyone hit these pitches? Crazy. I finally caught one ball in the wrong place on my hand, and that's when I stood up and said *enough*.

At the Swisher's session, I was recording with *some* of the best session guys in LA, top players like Tim Pierce, Matt Rollins, and Lee Sklar, and as I was rushing to get sounds, I didn't notice I had two missed calls from my mom. When I saw her missed calls, it immediately set off an alarm—she knows that if I don't pick up, it means I am working and I'll call back as soon as I can. She never calls me two times in a row like that, never.

I stepped outside of the studio to call her back, and she said, "I don't know how to tell you this, but your dad has passed away. He dropped dead today in Florida from a heart attack. Your father is gone. . . ."

What do you say after your mom tells you that your dad just dropped dead? I was in shock, but really I was thinking about my mom and what she was going through. They had been married for sixty-two years. She was emotionally devastated, of course, but she held it together. She is a strong lady.

I knew my dad's time was limited—he had a heart attack when he was fifty-six and had been living with degenerative heart disease ever since. He was walking around with a pacemaker and defibrillator in him. It was just a matter of time.

They had just gone down to Sarasota, Florida, which was where they went to beat the cold winters in Western Massachusetts. My mom came in looking for him after she'd been out doing some errands. She hadn't seen him because he'd fallen, and the sofa was blocking her view of his body, and when she finally discovered him, she couldn't move him. She called 911, and even though all the doctors would later tell her there was nothing she could have done to save him, that his heart stopped before he'd even hit the ground, for a long time she still blamed herself for not being there when he fell.

I walked back into the control room and said, "Listen, guys, I'm very sorry that I've held the session up, but my dad just passed away this morning." No one expected to hear me say that. We talked for a bit about my dad, and then I said, "Let's get back to work."

Dad and I had shared our last *time* together the morning after Christmas Eve, just a few weeks before—we found ourselves alone in the kitchen at 4 a.m. looking for late-night snacks and wound up having a long talk. I could tell that he knew I was in a good place. I'd made a commitment to Gina. We were married soon after that (we had a small but decidedly rock 'n' roll wedding at the Sunset Marquis in Hollywood with Glenn Hughes [from Deep Purple] and his wife, Gabby, and Kerrie and Paul Geary [former drummer for Extreme] as our witnesses).

I had simplified my personal life and had made some big changes. My father saw that I was more present, grounded, more connected to everyone around me. I knew he was saying good-bye. I could tell, and it was like he knew he could leave this earth knowing that Kenny was doing great.

He gave a short personal speech to each one of us that night at dinner. I knew he knew his days were numbered, but he projected strength right to the very end. I still feel his strength every day. It's weird because it doesn't feel like he ever died. We always had a strong bond, and I feel like we still have that connection, and that made it possible for me to do the session that day. He made me feel that everything was going to be okay.

My father had requested to be cremated and to have us walk around and spread his ashes all over the property where we grew up in Stockbridge, which we did later on that year. I kept a small vial of ashes and wore it around my neck, and the weird thing is I kept losing that vial—in restaurants, in cars, in the studio—and it always came back to me. Throughout this whole time, Gina kept waiting for me to break down, but I have to admit, I felt peaceful and more joy than sadness, because I didn't—and still don't—feel like he's gone at all. I can't talk to him on the phone, and I can't see him in person, but he's as present for me as he ever was.

40

Meet the Beatles

The first album I ever bought was the Beach Boys' *Surfin' U.S.A.* when I was ten years old, and then when I was eleven, I bought the Beatles' *Meet the Beatles*. The Beatles, first on *The Ed Sullivan Show* and then in their movie *A Hard Day's Night*, inspired me to become a drummer in a rock 'n' roll band. My first band, the Alley Cats, played primarily Beatles and Beach Boys songs.

In 2014, *fifty years later*, I got to work with Brian Wilson of the Beach Boys in the studio and play live with Ringo Starr and Paul McCartney. Thanks to Don Was for both of those experiences!

When I got the call from Wesley Seidman, Brian Wilson's engineer, to come down and work with Brian, I fucking flipped. This was not just another session. A lot of people in *this* business get jaded, but I'm as enthusiastic as I was when we started when I was eleven. Brian Wilson? Fuck yeah!

Brian was in the studio finishing up his latest solo album, *No Pier Pressure*. Wesley had suggested to Brian and the producer that I should come down and play just on one specific track that he felt needed the Aronoff touch. I got a demo ahead of time, and as I always did, I made out a chart of the demo note for note. When I walked in, I remember Brian was sitting at the console in the control room looking straight ahead out into the live room where I'd be playing.

My instincts were to give Brian space and just talk to the producer about the song, because Brian was quiet and reserved, but I also knew he was listening to everything I was saying to the producer. I said, "Listen, I have a chart that I made from your demo, and if you like, why don't I start by playing the song like the demo first. Then if you want me to try some different ideas, I have those, too."

The challenge for me when I make records is to sound like *me*, but at the same time I want to do something imaginative, something new and different—but not to the extent that I fuck up the song. There's a fine line there. My point here was to communicate to them that I respected what they sent me, but if they wanted me to try anything else to just let me know. I wanted Brian to know that I could adapt to anything he wanted me to try, and that I was there to serve him creatively.

So I went out there, got drum sounds, and started recording. First, the producer made some suggestions, but eventually Brian started hitting the talk-back button and chiming in, and he said he wanted me to do more fills on the snare drum and not so much on the toms. It was very cool that Brian felt comfortable talking to me. He is famously withdrawn; this was a very big deal. I figured out what kind of snare fills he wanted and started playing them. He spoke up again and said, "Start the fill earlier. . . and play it longer." So I played the fill for almost a whole measure going into the first chorus, and he said, "Yeah, yeah, I like that, I like that!" Eventually I used that signature fill going into all the choruses.

I went into the control room to listen to the playback, and the producer said, "Great! I'm happy. What do you think?" Then Brian looked up at me and said, "I think we're good." And as happy as I was that he liked the take, I still wasn't happy with the fills and felt they could be a little bit cleaner, a little bit more in the pocket.

I said, "You know what, I want to go back and redo all the fills and make them really perfect because they are such a signature part of the choruses." Man, when I said that, Brian really got excited. "Yeah, yeah, that's a great idea. Do that, Kenny, do that." He is also a famous perfectionist, and it seemed like he was happy that I wasn't in a rush to leave and wanted to make my parts perfect. He was happy enough to call me back four weeks later to record three more songs.

The next time I recorded with him, it was just me, Wesley, Brian, and his wife. Brian was now the producer and it went great. The key was to constantly keep the session moving, keep recording, let Brian tell me what he liked or didn't like, and keep him inspired and excited to be in the studio. Like I've said before, *I listen, I learn, and I lead, but I'm not the boss.*

From the Beach Boys to . . . the Beatles!

Coming off the heels of the Brian Wilson session, I played on what would be *three* separate stages I'd share with my first drum hero, Ringo Starr, beginning at the El Rey Theatre in LA, where the David Lynch Foundation was honoring Ringo with the Lifetime of Peace and Love Award.

I got to anchor a superstar house band that included Don Was on bass (he was also the musical director), Peter Frampton and Toto guitarist Steve Lukather on lead guitars, and Tom Petty and the Heartbreakers keyboardist Benmont Tench, backing up lead performances by Joe Walsh, Ben Folds, Brendan Benson, Ben Harper, Bettye LaVette, and Dave Stewart from the Eurhythmics, and, of course, Ringo Starr. I got to play three songs with Ringo, and I'm still buzzed just writing about it.

Not only is Ringo a very loving and kind person, but sitting next to him and playing double drums triggered all of my childhood memories of listening to Ringo and the Beatles over and over again, fantasizing about playing with them, of *being* them, dreaming of touring and making records.

Well, here I was doing it. When Ringo came up onstage before the show, during the house band's sound check, he said, "Aronoff, Aronoff, Aronoff, all I hear is Aronoff! Aronoff, everywhere I go in LA, I hear about this Aronoff guy! And I get it now, I get it. . . ."

Ringo is an incredibly gifted drummer. I still am mesmerized by Billy Cobham, but back when I started I didn't appreciate the simpler, less-is-more style of drumming that guys like Ringo and Charlie Watts played, or even John Bonham playing "Kashmir," or Phil Rudd playing AC/DC's "Back in Black."

Mellencamp eventually cured me of that, and I realized just what an amazing musician Ringo truly is. He has style, a feel, and a sound all his own. He brought a lot to the Beatles—he's a true creative *and* serves the song. He's a team player.

Three weeks later, after the show at El Rey, I was back onstage with Ringo for the Fifty-Sixth Annual Grammy Awards. We did his solo hit "Photograph," and I was so high from just being there that I almost forgot that I had to play with the Highwaymen (Kris Kristofferson, Willie Nelson, Merle Haggard, and Blake Shelton) forty-five minutes later. Even better, the next day was another performance with Ringo . . . *and* Paul.

This was the cherry on the cake, the jewel in the crown. I mean, this was the money shot of my whole career: *The Beatles: The Night That Changed America* special on CBS, where I actually got to play alongside two Beatles at the same time!

Here it was—the completion of my dream, fifty years to the day after they were on *The Ed Sullivan Show*, when I turned to my mom and told her ridiculously that I wanted to be in the Beatles. Now I was hanging out backstage like I was one of them.

Before the show I had a great moment with Don Was, Ringo, and Paul. Paul talked about how they had no idea they were going to be performing for 72 million people on *The Ed Sullivan Show* that night. They just thought it was another TV show. He said that right before he walked onstage, someone said, "How does it feel to be playing to 72 million people?" What a thing to say to a kid right as he is walking onstage.

Paul reminisced about a time when he and John Lennon were first in Liverpool, just trying to make it. They went into the local music store, and the square dude guy behind the counter, wearing a suit and tie, showed them a minor sixth chord for the first time, and Paul said, "Hey, John, look at this. What's that chord he's playing?" Paul said they used it in "Michelle," and I believe he said they never used it again. It was fucking magic, hearing Paul and Ringo talk about when they were kids, just laughing and being regular. Paul said he actually felt old back then at the age of twenty-four, smoking fags and trying to look cool.

That night, along with Ringo and Paul, I got to play with Stevie Wonder,

Alicia Keys, John Legend, Keith Urban, John Mayer, Brad Paisley, Pharrell Williams, Jeff Lynne, Joe Walsh, Danny Harrison, and Dave Grohl.

One thing Ringo did that was really cool was during the sound check—he objected to the way they'd had the band split up into two sections, on the far sides of the stage, and as soon as he saw that, he stopped the stage crew and said, "Wait a minute, I don't want to be that far from the band. I want the band to move in close with me." Producer Ken Ehrlich immediately made it happen. He made the set change for Ringo.

I was so happy to hear Ringo say that. He was all about being in the group. Zero attitude. He wanted everyone close together the way he had played his entire life. He nailed the essence of what it meant to be in a band, whether you were rehearsing in a bunker in Indiana, or playing for 72 million people. It was about being on a team, a gang, doing it all together.

I got to play "Boys," "Yellow Submarine," and "A Little Help from My Friends" with Ringo, and then we all got to jam with Ringo and Paul together on "Hey Jude" for the big encore.

One of the highlights for me that night was performing "Something" with Joe Walsh. It is a very slow song. When played correctly it is so rewarding, but if you play it too fast it sounds completely amateur and it sucks.

Joe is a perfectionist, and we discussed the exact tempo and feel he wanted at rehearsal. The amazing thing to me, and this is rare, is that he played that exact same feel and tempo during the show, even with all the excitement in the air—artists tend to want things faster during a show. It's natural to speed things up with all of that adrenaline.

During the song I played these two buzz rolls on the rack tom, and then the floor tom on beats three and four, just the way Ringo had recorded it. It's nearly impossible to hear those buzz rolls clearly on the recordings, but the reason I knew to play them like that was because Don Was had sent me the isolated drum track from that song, and I studied it like a maniac.

It really was masterful drumming, simple but unexpected, really serving the song, taking it to the next level. When I watched the show on TV later on, the camera showed Ringo looking at me at that exact moment, and he air-drummed those rolls as I played them. He had a big smile on his face. It was like getting an A on the most important exam I ever took. I nailed it.

After the last number I walked offstage, past this roped-off section where Ringo and Paul were sitting with their wives and Sean Lennon and Yoko Ono and George Harrison's family, and they were all clapping. As I walked by, Ringo grabbed my hand and said, "Kenny! You did an amazing job!" Approval from a Beatle—what else was there to live for?

EPILOGUE

I Am Kenny Aronoff

The greatest reward I have received from playing the drums is to see the joy and emotions on the faces of people in front of the stage. It's never about me or the band—it's about *all of us*: the musicians onstage and the audience are a community, sharing joy, love, fun, happiness, a celebration, and we give to each other, an intimate back and forth.

Songs define people's lives. They remind us of specific moments in our lives, when we were younger, important life experiences, a person we love or loved, holidays, places we have been, smells, sounds, sites—everything. I've had people say to me: "I got laid listening to John Mellencamp's 'Jack and Diane' in my car in a cornfield in Kansas," or "Wow, man, I got married listening to Belinda Carlisle's 'Heaven on Earth'," or "Jon Bon Jovi's 'Blaze of Glory' was the first time I ever made out with my chick," and on and on with songs I've played on. Somehow I got to be part of the sound track to so many lives, and that is a genuine blessing.

I am so glad I kept calendars and weekly planners that documented every session and live gig I have ever done. Otherwise, I wouldn't have been able to write this book with any accuracy. I had forgotten that I had done so much in certain years, and I was surprised when I learned that records that I thought were no big deal had actually sold 8, 10 million, and even 22 million copies. I have played on over 300 million records sold, not including singles or digital downloads. I had no idea Celine Dion's record *Falling Into You* had sold *32 million copies worldwide*. That's a lot of records. People must have really loved that album! And through the process of looking back at my life, I learned a lot about who I am and finally answered the question "Why

Kenny Aronoff?" It's a question Jonathan Mover asked me in an interview many years ago.

―◦―

My uncle Nat was a fearless, self-made man who built an empire from nothing, a Golden Gloves boxer, a World War II navy pilot, the guy who did one-handed push-ups while smoking a cigar. He asked me when I was twelve years old, "Hey, kid, do you know what the most important thing in life is?"

I was so intimidated by this guy, and as my eyes focused on his gold wristwatch, I stammered, "Uh, money?"

He slammed his hand into my shoulder, almost knocking me over, and said, "No, stupid . . . time! Time is the most valuable thing in life."

I didn't get it at all. I just wanted to go back outside and play with my brother.

I used to think time was about *playing steady time* when I played the drums, or *being somewhere on time,* like getting to school, or having a certain amount of time to do something, like eating lunch or doing my homework.

But now I know. Life is all about time . . . and the question is, how do you want to spend it?

As soon as I started playing drums in a band, when I was eleven years old, I thought, I have to do this the rest of my life, and at age sixty-three I'm still saying, "I have to do this the rest of my life!"

Are you beginning to see a pattern emerge?

I never planned for this. I was going to be playing timpani with a symphony orchestra somewhere, or playing triple bass drums in a prog-rock band. How was I to see myself with the kings of Detroit rock, the titans of Americana—pop stars, country royalty, and the Rolling fucking Stones? How did this happen?

Build it and they will come! The resume I sent the Smashing Pumpkins was forty pages long. Now it is like 400—and it doesn't come close to telling the whole story. You know me now. Hopefully you know me a little bit like my friends do.

I hope I've been able to share with you the most important secret that I have learned: that there is no secret. Self-discipline, hard work, setting goals, communication skills, repetition, staying healthy, and staying relevant. It helps to get lucky, but you can make a lot of luck by *kicking* ass and not *being* an ass. And I love playing the drums. I mean, I really love it. And I get paid for it, which is simply bliss.

Fortunately, it hasn't slowed down. It can't. I can't! I have to make every date. I have to try harder to be a better Kenny Aronoff. After over fifty years of playing, the journey is just beginning.

Last week I was rehearsing with John Fogerty to do the halftime show at the Orange Bowl. This week we are in Vegas for a three-week run. We're still rehearsing "Proud Mary," still doing marathon sound checks, still trying to make it even better. Fogerty is never satisfied, but neither am I, and I love it.

After the first few Vegas shows, we had a day off, and John wanted to get the hell out of town. I have no idea what the rush was. One second I'm onstage, the next I'm in in the back of a Town Car, wrapped in towels, totally soaking with sweat, trying to change on the way to the airport. The driver is a gay woman who recognizes me from a Melissa Etheridge tour and wants to talk, but meanwhile I'm trying to dry myself off, get my jeans on, and not forget my phone or shoes.

Fifteen minutes later we're in the sky. It's real rock star shit, jumping on a private jet—the gig is over at 9:30 and at 11:30 I am walking through the door to have a glass of wine in my own home, in another state, still trying to come down from the show. It's the grown-up version of touring. But that's okay, because like I said at the beginning, the sexy part is what happens when we are up onstage playing. I'd trade all of the women and parties and wild times to have the sticks in my hands and a snare drum between my legs, onstage or in a studio with Mellencamp, Fogerty, Ringo and Paul, Lynyrd Skynyrd, Leonard Bernstein, you name it. Chickenfoot. Bob Dylan. The Alley Cats.

This book is about being a rock star, whether you're raising a family, self-employed or go to the office, whatever. It's about being the best you can be at whatever you do in life, for you, your family, the team, or whomever so that your family and your boss or coworkers or employees keep coming back to you with respect, with love, with a sense that you are not one of a million people who showed unrealized potential, or just didn't care. You have to keep trying. If you get anything out of this book, that's it—your business, whatever it is, might not last. But that doesn't mean your life is over. Check back with me in ten years and see where I'm at. If I am breathing, I'll be kicking ass.

SELECTED DISCOGRAPHY

Over the course of my thirty-six-year career, I've been fortunate to work with many amazing artists—signed and unsigned—in the studio and onstage. I've drummed on over 6,000 tracks (including 1,000 not yet released) since 1980. I have played on over 300 million records sold (not including singles or digital downloads) and on more than 1,300 RIAA-certified Gold, Platinum, and Diamond albums. Here is a selected list of those recordings.

1980s

Gregg Alexander—*Michigan Rain*
The BoDeans—*Home*
Belinda Carlisle—*Heaven on Earth*
Belinda Carlisle—*Runaway Horses*
Bill Carter—*Loaded Dice*
Marshall Crenshaw—*Good Evening*
Drive, She Said—*Drive, She Said*
The Graces—*Perfect View*
John Eddie—*Hard Cold Truth*
Randy Handley—*I Picture You*
Jefferson Airplane—*Jefferson Airplane*
Holly Knight—*Nature of the Beast*
Seth Marsh—*Whole Lotta Noise*
James McMurtry—*Too Long in the Wasteland*
John Cougar Mellencamp—*American Fool*
John Cougar Mellencamp—*The Lonesome Jubilee*
John Cougar Mellencamp—*Nothin' Matters and What if It Did*
John Cougar Mellencamp—"Rave On," *Cocktail* sound track
John Cougar Mellencamp—*Scarecrow*
John Cougar Mellencamp—*Uh-Huh*
John Mellencamp—*Big Daddy*
John Mellencamp—"I Saw Mommy Kissing Santa Claus," *A Very Special Christmas*
Michael Penn—*March*
Paul Pesco—*Make It Reality*

Mitch Ryder—*Never Kick a Sleeping Dog*
Brian Setzer—*The Knife Feels Like Justice*

1990s

Jann Arden—"Leave Me Now," "I Know You," "Holy Moses," "Wishing That," "Hanging by a Thread," *Happy?*
Jann Arden—*Living Under June*
Steve Bailey and Victor Wooten—*Bass Extremes, Vol. 2*
Jim Beard—*Song of the Sun*
Edoardo Bennato—*Se son rosie fioriranno*
Tab Benoit—*What I Live For*
John Berry—*Standing on the Edge*
Blessid Union of Souls—*Blessid Union of Souls*
The BoDeans—"Closer to Free," *Go Slow Down*
The BoDeans—*Joe Dirt Car*
Bon Jovi—*Cross Road*
Jon Bon Jovi—*Young Guns II* sound track
Jon Bon Jovi—*Destination Anywhere*
The Boneshakers—*Shake the Planet*
Tom Borton—*Dancing with Tigers*
Garth Brooks—*Garth Brooks In . . . The Life of Chris Gaines*
Cactus Brothers—*24 Hrs., 7 Days a Week*
Tony Carey—*Cold War Kids*
Belinda Carlisle—"Hate the World," "Little Black Book," *Live Your Life Be Free*
Bob Carlisle—*Bob Carlisle*
Bob Carlisle—*Collection*
Mary Chapin Carpenter—*Party Doll and Other Favorites*
Mary Chapin Carpenter—*Stones in the Road*
Deana Carter—"What Makes You Stay," *Hope Floats* sound track
Cinderella—*Still Climbing*
Philip Claypool—*A Circus Leaving Town*
Philip Claypool—*Perfect World*
Johnny Clegg and Savuka—*The Best of Johnny Clegg and Savuka: In My African Dream*
Johnny Clegg and Savuka—*Heat, Dust, and Dreams*
Joe Cocker—"Could You Be Loved," *Across from Midnight*
Joe Cocker—"Human Touch," *One Step Up/Two Steps Back: The Songs of Bruce Springsteen*
Joe Cocker—*Organic*
Mark Collie, Aaron Tippin, and Jeff Wood—"Fire Down Below," *Fire Down Below* sound track
Shawn Colvin—*Cover Girl*
Patricia Conroy—*You Can't Resist*
Tommy Conwell and the Young Rumblers—*Guitar Trouble*
Cox Family—*Just When We're Thinking It's Over*

Marshall Crenshaw—*Life's Too Short*
Marshall Crenshaw—*Live . . . My Truck Is My Home*
Rodney Crowell—*Jewel of the South*
Kacy Crowley—*Anchorless*
Shannon Curfman—*Loud Guitars, Big Suspicions*
Catie Curtis—*Catie Curtis*
Mary Cutrufello—*When the Night Is Through*
Billy Ray Cyrus—"The Fastest Horse in a One Horse Town," *NASCAR: Runnin Wide Open*
Jesse Dayton—*Raisin' Cain*
Billy Dean—"Once in a While," *8 Seconds* sound track
Stacy Dean Campbell—*Hurt City*
Neil Diamond—*Lovescape*
Celine Dion—"I Want You to Need Me," *All the Way . . . A Decade of Song*
Celine Dion—"It's All Coming Back to Me Now," *Falling Into You*
Celine Dion—"Where Is the Love," "Miles to Go (Before I Sleep)," *Let's Talk About Love*
Bob Dylan—*Under the Red Sky*
Lenita Erickson—*Lenita Erickson*
Melissa Etheridge—*Breakdown*
Melissa Etheridge—"Nowhere to Go," "I Could Have Been You," "Change," *Your Little Secret*
Billy Falcon—*Pretty Blue World*
John Fogerty— "Rambunctious Boy," "Rattlesnake Highway," "Hot Rod Heart,"
    "Joy of My Life," "Bring It Down Jelly Roll," *Blue Moon Swamp*
John Fogerty—*Premonition* (album and DVD)
Kim Fox—*Moon Hut*
Glenn Frey—"Part of Me, Part of You," *Thelma & Louise* sound track
Glenn Frey—*Solo Collection*
Glenn Frey—*Strange Weather*
Hearts and Minds—*Hearts and Minds*
Greta Gaines—*Greta Gaines*
Lisa Germano—*Excerpts from a Love Circus*
Lisa Germano—*Geek the Girl*
Lisa Germano—*Happiness*
Lisa Germano—*Inconsiderate Bitch*
Vince Gill and Little Feat—"What Do You Want the Girl to Do," *Indecent Proposal*
    sound track
Indigo Girls—*Nomads Indians Saints*
Indigo Girls—"Joking," *Rites of Passage*
Patty Griffin—*Flaming Red*
Hall & Oates—*Change of Seasons*
Corey Hart—*Attitude & Virtue*
Corey Hart—*Bang!*
Corey Hart—*Corey Hart*
Corey Hart—*Jade*

Corey Hart—*The Singles*
The Highwaymen—*The Road Goes On Forever*
Homeless Heart—*Shoeless*
Chris Isaak—*San Francisco Days*
It's Now or Never: The Tribute to Elvis—Travis Tritt "Lawdy Miss Clawdy," Tanya Tucker
    "Teddy Bear," Dwight Yoakam "Mystery Train," Melissa Etheridge "Burning Love,"
    Marty Stuart "Don't Be Cruel," Billy Ray Cyrus "One Night," and Faith Hill "Trying
    to Get to You"
Joe Jackson—"Right," *Heaven & Hell*
Vinnie James—*All American Boy*
Waylon Jennings—*Waymore's Blues, Part II*
Waylon Jennings—"You Don't Mess Around with Me," *Maverick* sound track
Jewel—"Have a Little Faith in Me," *Phenomenon* sound track
Elton John—"You've Got to Love," "I Swear I Heard the Night Talking," "Easier to Walk
    Away," and "Made for Me," *To Be Continued . . .* (box set)
Elton John—"You Gotta Love Someone," *Days of Thunder* sound track
Josh Joplin Group—*Useful Music*
Junkyard—*Sixes, Sevens, and Nines*
Mary Karlzen—*Yelling at Mary*
B. B. King (duet with Joe Cocker)—"Dangerous Mood," *Deuces Wild*
B. B. King—"Dangerous Mood," *King of the Blues* (box set)
Dave Koz—"Let Me Count the Ways," "Flat Feet," "That's the Way I Feel About You,"
    "My Back Porch," *Off the Beaten Path*
Jamie Kyle—*The Passionate Kind*
Ann Lewis—*La Adelita*
Lyle Lovett—*I Love Everybody*
Lyle Lovett—"You Can't Resist It," *Switch* sound track
Lynyrd Skynyrd—*Edge of Forever*
Amanda Marshall—*Amanda Marshall*
Amanda Marshall—"This Could Take All Night," *Tin Cup* sound track
Amanda Marshall—"Shades of Grey," *Tuesday's Child*
Ricky Martin—*Ricky Martin*
Julie Masse—*Circle of One*
Will T. Massey—*Will T. Massey*
Mac McAnally—*Knots*
Delbert McClinton—*Never Been Rocked Enough*
Delbert McClinton—"The Wanderer," *One Hot Summer* sound track
James McMurtry—*Candyland*
David Mead—*Luxury of Time*
Meat Loaf—*Bat Out of Hell II: Back Into Hell*
Meat Loaf—"A Kiss Is a Terrible Thing to Waste," *Songs from Whistle Down the Wind*
Meat Loaf—*Welcome to the Neighborhood*
Sue Medley—*Inside Out*

Sue Medley—*Sue Medley*
John Mellencamp—"Baby, Please Don't Go," *Blue Chips* sound track
John Mellencamp—*Dance Naked*
John Mellencamp—*Human Wheels*
John Mellencamp—"It Don't Scare Me None," *Falling from Grace* sound track
John Mellencamp—"Jailhouse Rock," *Honeymoon in Vegas* sound track
John Mellencamp—*Mr. Happy Go Lucky*
John Mellencamp—"R.O.C.K. in the USA," *The Concert for the Rock and Roll Hall of Fame*
John Mellencamp—*Sounds of the Season*
John Mellencamp—"Teddi's Song (When Christmas Comes)," *Christmas of Hope*
John Mellencamp—*The Unplugged Collection, Volume 1*
John Mellencamp—*Whenever We Wanted*
Jo Dee Messina—*Jo Dee Messina*
Robert Mirabal—*Mirabal*
Robert Mirabel—"Witch Hunt," *Tribal Fires: Contemporary Native American Music*
Eddie Money—*Love and Money*
Eddie Money—*Ready Eddie*
Eddie Money—"Rock and Roll Doctor," *Rock and Roll Doctor: A Tribute to Lowell George*
Eddie Money—*Shakin' with the Money Man*
Billie Myers—*Growing, Pains*
Tsuyoshi Nagabuchi—"Captain of the Ship"
Tsuyoshi Nagabuchi—*Japan*
Miyuki Nakajima—*10 Wings*
Nationalgalerie—*Indiana*
Willie Nelson, Shenandoah, Steve Wariner, Kris Kristofferson, Collin Raye, and David
    Ball—*Come Together: America Salutes the Beatles*
Karen Newman—*Moment in the Wind*
Randy Newman and Bonnie Raitt—"Life Has Been Good to Me," "Feels Like Home,"
    Faust
Stevie Nicks—"Somebody Stand by Me," *Boys on the Side* sound track
Stevie Nicks—*Street Angel*
Aldo Nova—*Blood on the Bricks*
Michael Penn—*Free-for-All*
Brother Phelps—*Any Way the Wind Blows*
Billy Pilgrim—*Billy Pilgrim*
Iggy Pop—*Brick by Brick*
Iggy Pop—"Candy," "Home," *Nude & Rude: The Best of Iggy Pop*
Presidents of the United States of America—"George of the Jungle," *George of the Jungle*
    sound track
Bonnie Raitt—"Feels Like Home," *Michael* sound track
Bonnie Raitt and B. B. King—"Right Place Wrong Time," *Air America* sound track
Revolver—*Calle Mayor*
James Reyne—"Any Day Above Ground"

Buddy Rich Big Band— "Straight, No Chaser," *Burning for Buddy: A Tribute to Music of Buddy Rich*

Buddy Rich Big Band—"Big Swing Face," *Burning for Buddy: Volume II*

Rolling Stones—*Bridges to Babylon*

Jimmy Ryser—*Jimmy Ryser*

Jimmy Ryser—*Let It Go*

Sanne Salomonsen with Little Feat—*Language of the Heart*

Richie Sambora—*Undiscovered Soul*

Adam Schmitt—*World So Bright*

John Schwab—*Crack of Dawn*

Pattie Scialfa—*Rumble Doll*

Randy Scruggs—"Both Sides Now," *Crown of Jewels*

Bob Seger—"Take a Chance," "The Real Love," "Sight Seeing," "The Mountain," *The Fire Inside*

Bob Seger—*It's a Mystery*

Masanori Sera—*Return*

Michelle Shocked—*Arkansas Traveler*

Shenandoah—*15 Favorites*

Sister Whiskey—*Liquor and Poker*

Slash and Michael Monroe—"Magic Carpet Ride," *Coneheads* sound track

Patty Smyth—"No Mistakes," "Sometimes Love Just Ain't Enough," *Greatest Hits*

Patty Smyth—*Patty Smyth*

Patty Smyth—"You Hung the Moon," *8 Seconds* sound track

Rod Stewart—"Faith of the Heart," *Patch Adams* sound track

Rod Stewart—"Leave Virginia Alone," *A Spanner in the Works*

Marty Stuart and the Staple Sisters, B. B. King and George Jones, Conway Twitty and Sam Moore, Gladys Knight and Vince Gill, Aaron Neville and Trisha Yearwood, Chet Atkins and Alan Toussaint, Patti LaBelle and Travis Tritt, Natalie Cole and Reba McEntyre—*Rhythm, Country and Blues*

Henry Lee Summer—*Way Past Midnight*

That Thing You Do! sound track

Richard Thompson—*Watching the Dark: History of Richard Thompson*

Travis Tritt—*The Restless Kind*

Bonnie Tyler—*Bitterblue*

Various Artists—*Colors: A Musical Tribute to Ryan White*

Dave Uhrich—*Change*

Paul Westerberg—"Dyslexic Heart," *Singles* sound track

Tony Joe White—*Lake Placid Blues*

Hank Williams, Jr.—*A.K.A. Wham Bam Sam*

Hank Williams, Jr.—*Hog Wild*

2000s

American Idol—Season 4: The Showstoppers

Anastacia—*Anastacia*

Anastacia—"Welcome to My Truth," *Pieces of a Dream: Best Of*

Trey Anastasio—*Shine*

Jann Arden—"Could I Be Your Girl," "Insensitive," "Unloved," "Good Mother," *Greatest Hurts: The Best of Jann Arden*

Bronson Arroyo—*Covering the Bases*

AstroGin—*Dynamic Trash*

Jimmy Barnes—*Double Happiness*

Edorado Bennato—*Afferrare una stella*

Tab Benoit—*Best of the Bayou Blues*

Black Lab—*See the Sun*

The BoDeans—*Homebrewed: Live from the Pabst* (CD, DVD)

The BoDeans—*Still*

Bon Jovi—*100,000,000 Bon Jovi Fans Can't Be Wrong* (box set)

Boneshakers—*Monster Blues*

Michelle Branch—*Covered, A Revolution in Sound*

Michelle Branch—*Hotel Paper*

Michelle Branch—"All You Wanted," *The Spirit Room*

Buffalo Nickel—*Long Play 33 1/2*

George Canyon—*Somebody Wrote Love*

Belinda Carlisle—*Original Gold*

Mary Chapin Carpenter—"Stone in the Road," "Shut Up and Kiss Me," *The Essential Mary Chapin Carpenter*

Jason Michael Carroll—*Growing Up Is Getting Old*

Anzu Christina—*I Like Me*

Cinderella—*Gold*

Cinderella—"Blood from a Stone," *Rocked, Wired & Bluesed: The Greatest Hits*

Kelly Clarkson—*Breakaway*

Joe Cocker—*Gold*

Joe Cocker—*Greatest Love Songs*

Joe Cocker—*Respect Yourself*

Joe Cocker—"Sail Away," *Ultimate Collection*

Paul Colman—*Let It Go*

Confederate Railroad—*Rockin' Country Party Pack*

Alice Cooper—*Dragontown*

Rodney Crowell—*Small Worlds: The Crowell Collection 1978–1995*

Billy Ray Cyrus—*Home at Last*

Aaron Neville "Life on the Layaway Plan," Marc Boussard "When You Lose Somebody," *Dark Streets: Original Motion Picture Soundtrack*

Dean Davidson—*Drive My Karma*

Diana DeGarmo—*Blue Skies*

Gavin DeGraw—"Cheated on Me," "Cop Stop," "Young Love," Medicate the Kids," "Relative," "Let It Go," *Gavin DeGraw*

Jennie DeVoe—*Ta Da*

Dirty Children—*Shut Off the World*

Celine Dion—"It's All Coming Back to Me," *My Love: Essential Collection*

Haylie Duff—"A Whatever Life," *Stuck in the Suburbs* sound track

Hilary Duff—"Crash World," *A Cinderella Story* sound track

Hilary Duff—"Fly," "Underneath This Smile," "Who's That Girl," "I Am," "Someone's Watching Over Me," *Hilary Duff*

Hilary Duff—*Most Wanted*

Betty Dylan—*Abdicate the Throne*

Betty Dylan—*Heart Land*

John Eddie—*Who the Hell Is John Eddie?*

Melissa Etheridge—"Refugee," "Christmas in America," "I Need to Wake Up," *Greatest Hits: The Road Less Traveled*

Melissa Etheridge—*Live . . . and Alone*

Melissa Etheridge—*Lucky*

Melissa Etheridge—*Lucky Live* (DVD)

Melissa Etheridge—*Skin*

Evan and Jaron—"The Distance," *Serendipity* sound track

Rose Falcon—"Fun" (drums and producer), *Rose Falcon*

Fan_3—*Geek Love*

John Fogerty—*The Blue Ridge Rangers Rides Again*

John Fogerty—*Deja Vu (All Over Again)*

John Fogerty—"Almost Saturday Night" (live), "Rockin' All over the World," (live), *The Long Road Home: The Ultimate John Fogerty–Creedence Collection*

John Fogerty—*Revival*

4Runner—*Getaway Car*

Dexter Freebish—*Tripped Into Divine*

Glenn Frey—"Part of Me, Part of You," *The Best of Glenn Frey: The Millennium Collection*

Gloriana—*Gloriana*

Gratitude—"Last," "Feel Alright," "If Ever," "Dream Again," *Gratitude*

Pat Green—*Lucky Ones*

John Gregory—*Pictures from Home*

John Gregory—"Ride of Your Life," *What a Girl Wants* sound track

Andy Griggs—*Freedom*

Andy Griggs—*Sharp Dressed Men: A Tribute to ZZ Top*

David Grissom—*10,000 Feet*

Travor Hall—"Other Ways," *Shrek the Third*

Trevor Hall—*The Rascals Have Returned*

The Heligoats—*The End of All Purpose*

The Highwaymen—*The Road Goes On Forever* (reissued with bonus tracks and DVD)

Rebecca Lynn Howard—*Forgive*

Huecco—"Tacones baratos," "Mis 100 gitimas mananas," "Tereta," "Apache," "Me guemas," *Huecco*

Zachary Hunter—*In Your Dreams*

SELECTED DISCOGRAPHY

Michael Hutchence—*Michael Hutchence*
Indigo Girls—*Retrospective*
Indigo Girls—*X2*
Tony Iommi— "Black Oblivion," *Iommi*
Tony Iommi and Glenn Hughes—*Fused*
Mick Jagger—*Goddess in the Doorway*
Jane Jensen—*My Rockabye*
George Jones—"Patches," with B. B. King, *My Very Special Guests*
Phil Jones—*The Art of War*
Emory Joseph—*Labor & Spirits*
Andy Kim—*I Forgot to Mention*
Inaba Koshi—*Peace of Mind*
Krokus—*Hoodoo*
Bruce Kulick—*Audio Dog*
Bruce Kulick—*BK3* (limited edition EP)
Avril Lavigne—*The Best Damn Thing*
Avril Lavigne—"My Happy Ending," "Fall to Pieces," *Under My Skin*
Lee Seung Hwan—*Monglong*
G. B. Leighton—*Shake Them Ghosts*
Lennon—*Damaged Goods*
Lennon—*5:30 Saturday Morning*
Less Than Jake—*In with the Out Crowd*
Jon Peter Lewis—*Break the Silence*
Like a Storm—*End of the Beginning*
Lynyrd Skynyrd—*Edge of Forever*
Lynyrd Skynyrd—*Then and Now*
Lynyrd Skynyrd—"Workin'," *Thyrty: 30th Anniversary Collection*
Lynyrd Skynyrd—*Twenty*
Tim Mahoney—*3 Different Views*
Mars Arizona—*All Over the Road*
Ricky Martin—*Sound Loaded*
Jesse McCartney—"Because You Live," *The Princess Diaries 2: Royal Engagement* sound track
Jesse McCartney—"Anybody," *Right Where You Want Me*
Meat Loaf—*Bat Out of Hell III: The Monster Is Loose*
Meat Loaf—*Couldn't Have Said It Better*
John Mellencamp—"I Don't Know Why I Love You," *Conception: An Interpretation of Stevie Wonder's Songs*
Jo Dee Messina—"Heads Carolina, Tails California," *Greatest Hits*
Krystal Meyers—*Krystal Meyers*
MiG—*MiG*
Leslie Mills—*Different for Girls*
Robert Mirabal—*Music from a Painted Cave*
Robert Mirabal—*Music from a Painted Cave* (VHS and DVD)

SELECTED DISCOGRAPHY

Eddie Money—"There Will Never Be Another You," *The Essential Eddie Money*

Alanis Morissette—*So-Called Chaos*

M2M—*The Big Room*

Leigh Nash—"Need to Be Next to You," *Bounce* sound track

Willie Nelson—*The Great Divide*

Willie Nelson (with Lee Ann Womack)—"Mendocino County Line," *Songs*

Willie Nelson, Eric Clapton, Steven Tyler, Shania Twain, Sheryl Crow, Kris Kristofferson, Ray Charles, Toby Keith, Norah Jones, Kenny Chesney, Lyle Lovett, Shelby Lynne, Ray Price, Diana Krall, Elvis Costello, and Leon Russell—*Willie Nelson & Friends: Live and Kickin'*

Willie Nelson & Friends—*Live and Kickin'* (DVD)

The New Cars—"Not Tonight," "More," *It's Alive!*

Jamie O'Neal—*Brave*

Orianthi—"Now or Never," *Bratz* sound track

Jake Owen—*Easy Does It*

Jake Owen—*Startin' with Me*

Les Paul and Friends—"Somebody Ease My Troublin' Mind," "How High the Moon," "Bad Case of Lovin' You," "Caravan," "Good Morning, Little Schoolgirl," "69 Freedom Special," *American Made, World Played*

Les Paul and Friends—"The Walls Came Tumbling Down," "Slippin' Into Darkness," "Freedom Special," *A Tribute to a Legend*

Iggy Pop—"Home," "Candy," *A Million in Prizes: The Anthology*

Puddle of Mudd—"Famous," "It Was Faith," *Famous*

Marion Raven—*Here I Am*

Revolver—*Grandes éxitos*

Steve Richard—*Steve Richard*

J. R. Richards—*A Beautiful End*

Jason Sadites—*Weve*

Nate Sallie—*Ruined for Ordinary*

Santana—*All That I Am*

Owen Sartori—*Another Beautiful Day in the Cube*

Owen Sartori—*Selections from the Cube*

Philip Sayce—*Peace Machine*

Zoe Scott—*Beautiful to Be Alive*

Earl Scruggs and Melissa Etheridge—"The Angels" (Melissa Etheridge), *Earl Scruggs and Friends*

Tommy Shaw—"Happy Xmas (War Is Over)," *Metal Christmas and a Headbanging New Year* (various artists)

Tommy Shaw, Steve Lukather, and Marco Mendoza—*We Wish You*

Jed Sheldon—*Gravity*

Silvercrush—*Stand*

Ashlee Simpson—"Autobiography," "Shadow," "Love Makes the World Go Round," "Surrender," "Nothing New," *Autobiography*

The Sky Kings—*From Out of the Blue*
The Starting Line—"21," "Island," "What You Want," *Direction*
Tommy Shane Steiner—*Then Came the Night*
Rod Stewart—all songs except "Everything I Own," *Still the Same . . . Great Rock Classics of Our Time*
Gary Stier—*The Albatross*
Stryper—*Murder by Pride*
Marty Stuart—"The Weight," *Compadres: An Anthology of Duets*
Michael Sweet—*Truth*
Rob Thomas—*Cradlesong*
Richard Thompson Band—*More Guitar*
Thunderado—*Thunderado*
Trick Pony—*On a Mission*
Trick Pony—*Trick Pony*
Travis Tritt—*The Rockin' Side*
Travis Tritt—*The Lovin' Side*
Travis Tritt—*The Storm*
Walter Trout—*The Outsider*
Two Fires—*Ignition*
Various Artists—"I Saw Her Standing There," *Butchering the Beatles: A Headbashing Tribute*
Jaci Velasquez—*Mi Corazón*
Jeremy Vogt Band—*Villains and Vocoders*
Charlie Watts and Jim Keltner—*Charlie Watts/Jim Keltner Project*
Paul Westerberg—"Dyslexic Heart," (originally released on the *Singles* motion picture sound track), *Besterberg: The Best of Paul Westerberg*
Bernie Williams—*The Journey Within*
Bernie Williams—*Moving Forward*
Robbie Williams—"A Man of All Seasons," *Johnny English* sound track
Anna Wilson—*The Long Way*
Lee Ann Womack—"Mendocino Country Line," *Greatest Hits*
Lee Ann Womack—"Something Worth Leaving Behind," *Something Worth Leaving Behind*
Lucy Woodward—*While You Can*
Yuridia—*Entre Mariposas*
Zucchero—"E' Delicato," *Fly*

2010–

Trace Adkins—*The King's Gift*
The Aerolites—*The Aerolites*
Gregg Allman—*All My Friends: A Tribute to Gregg Allman* (CD and DVD)
American Idol Artists—various recordings for iTunes downloads
Ben Ashley—*These Black Snakes*
Alex Band—*We've All Been There*

Jimmy Barnes—*Rage and Ruin*

Noah Benardout—"I'll Grown Old," "Down in the Trenches," "Come Close to Me," "When I Go to See You," "Take a Ferry," "Shoes," "Haley"

The BoDeans—*I Can't Stop*

The BoDeans—*Indigo Dreams*

Bobby Brown—*The Masterpiece*

Owen Campbell—*The Pilgram*

Greyson Chance—*Hold On 'Til the Night*

Thelma Cheechoo—*Stay*

Rodney Crowell—*Jewel of the South*

Rodney Crowell—*Let the Picture Pain Itself*

Beto Cuevas—*Transformación*

Billy Ray Cyrus—*Change My Mind*

Lee DeWyze—*Live It Up*

Celine Dion—*Essential Celine Dion*

Yazawa Eikichi—*Twist*

Flint Face—"Did I Stutter," *Hope*

Brandon Flowers—*The Desired Effect*

John Fogerty—*The Finder* (TV show theme)

John Fogerty—Miranda Lambert featuring Tom Morello, "Wrote a Song for Everyone," Keith Urban, "Almost Saturday Night," Shane and Tyler Fogerty "Lodi," John Fogerty "Mystic Highway," Kid Rock "Born on the Bayou," John Fogerty "Train of Fools," Bob Seger "Who'll Stop the Rain," Brad Paisley, "Hot Rod Heart," *Wrote a Song for Everyone*

Manola Garcia—"Todos amanos desesperademente," "Lo Queiro Todo," "Un giro teatral," "Estoy alegre," "Compasión y silencio," "Estamos Ahi," "Cabalgar la eternidad"

Paul Gilbert—"Back in the Middle," "I Got the Feelin'," "Goodbye Yellow Brick Road," "Shock Absorber," "Murder by Numbers," "My Girl," "Stone Pushing Uphill," *Stone Pushing Uphill Man*

Matt Gold—*Let It Out* (production and drums)

Michael Grimm—*Michael Grimm*

Ayumi Hamasaki—"Love Songs," "Sending Mail," *Love Songs*

Levon Helm—*Love for Levon: A Tribute to Levon Helm*

The Highwaymen—"The Devil's Right," "It Is What It Is," "Live Forever," *The Essential Highwaymen*

Jimi: All Is By My Side movie sound track—Waddy Wachtel, "Wha Shuffle," "Waddania," "Warm Milk," "Manish Boy," "Birdland," "Sgt. Pepper's Lonely Hearts Club Band," "Wild Thing"

JoHik—*The Game*

David Kershenbaum—*Little Miss Innocent* sound track

Kill the Alarm—*Against the Grain*

Bruce Kulick—"Between the Lines," *BK3*

David Lane—"Go for a Ride," *David Lane*

SELECTED DISCOGRAPHY

Bettye LaVette—*Interpretations: The British Rock Songbook*

Avril Lavigne—"Falling Fast," *Avril Lavigne*

Seth Loveless—*Seth Loveless*

Bob Malone—*Mojo Deluxe*

Sean McCarthy—*Everything Has Past*

Meat Loaf—"A Kiss Is a Terrible Thing to Waste," *The Very Best of Meat Loaf*

Adam Michaelson—"Long Slow Vacation," *Elephants, Walls and Fences*

Miyuki Nakajima—*Drama!*

Steve Ouimette—*Epic*

Al Pacino—*Danny Collins* sound track

Los Perfekt—*Aria*

Planes movie sound track

Pou Piam—*On the Rocks*

Jimmy Rankin—*Tinseltown*

Jason Sadites—*Broken*

Philip Sayce—*Innerevolution*

Scott Stapp—*Proof of Life*

Ryan Star—*11:59*

Rod Stewart—*Another Country*

Rod Stewart—*Time*

Supersonic Blues Machine—*West of Flushing, South of Frisco*

Michael Sweet—*I'm Not Your Suicide*

Nick Swisher—*Believe*

Switchblade Glory—*Switchblade Glory*

Teenage Mutant Ninja Turtles movie sound track (theme song)

Mumiy Troll—*Paradise Ahead*

Walter Trout—*Common Ground*

TruWorship—*Radio the World*

TruWorship—*Songs from the Playhouse*

Velvet Saints—*Shadows*

Deborah Vial—*Stages and Stones*

Walk the Line: Johnny Cash Tribute at Austin City Limits—Brandi Carlile "Folsom Prison Blues," Kris Kristofferson "Big River," Same Beam "Long Black Veil," Buddy Miller "Hey Porter, Sheryl Crow "Cry, Cry, Cry," Willie Nelson "If I Were a Carpenter," "Highway Man," Shelby Lane, "It Ain't Me Babe," Iron and Wine, "The Long Black Veil," Rhett Miller, "Wreck of the Old 97s," Carolina Chocolate Drops, "Jackson," Kris Kristofferson "Sunday Morning Coming Down," Amy Lee "I'm So Lonesome," Ronnie Dunn "Ring of Fire," Lucinda Williams "Hurt," full ensemble, "Walk the Line," Matthew McConaughey, "The Man Comes Around," Shooter Jennings "Cocaine Blues," Andy Grammer, "Get Rhythm" Pat Monahan "Help Me Make It Through the Night"

Laura Warscher—"Little Lost Girls," *Take It or Leave It: A Tribute to the Queens of Noise*— *The Runaways* (various artists)

SELECTED DISCOGRAPHY

Leslie West—*Unusual Suspects*
Brian Wilson—*No Pier Pressure*
Kana Wormz—*Who Is Your Friend*

SELECTED CHRONOLOGY
OF LIVE PERFORMANCES

Next to the studio, the road has been a home away from home for nearly four decades. I've enjoyed the bliss of performing onstage from Bloomington, Indiana, to the Acropolis in Greece—not only playing rock 'n' roll but teaching, too. It's been an incredible journey. Here is a selected list of notable tours and other performances.

1980s
TOURS AND CONCERTS
John Cougar—*American Fool* Tour (USA and Canada)
John Cougar—*Nothin' Matters and What If It Did* Tour (USA and Canada)
John Cougar Mellencamp—*Late Night with David Letterman*
John Cougar Mellencamp—*The Lonesome Jubilee* Tour (USA and Canada)
John Cougar Mellencamp—*Scarecrow* Tour (USA and Canada)
John Cougar Mellencamp—*Uh-Huh* Tour (USA and Canada)
John Cougar Mellencamp, Brian Setzer, John Fogerty, and Bonnie Raitt—Farm Aid 1 (Champaign, Illinois)
John Cougar Mellencamp, John Prine, and Lou Reed—Farm Aid 3 (Lincoln, Nebraska)
Bo Diddley—Various Live Shows
Jefferson Airplane—USA Tour
Sam Kinison—Cable TV Special
Richard Thompson—USA Tour

MUSIC VIDEOS AND FILMS
John Cougar—"Hand to Hold On To"
John Cougar—"Hurts So Good"
John Cougar Mellencamp—"Check It Out"
John Cougar Mellencamp—"Cherry Bomb"
John Cougar Mellencamp—"Crumblin' Down"
John Cougar Mellencamp—"Lonely Ol' Night"
John Cougar Mellencamp—"Paper in Fire"
John Cougar Mellencamp—"Pink Houses"
John Cougar Mellencamp—"Rain on the Scarecrow"
John Cougar Mellencamp—"R.O.C.K. in the USA"

John Cougar Mellencamp—"Small Town"
Corey Hart—"A Little Love"
Jefferson Airplane—"Planes"
Jefferson Airplane—"True Love"

DRUM CLINICS
Tama Drum Clinics—USA (multiple tours)
Zildjian Drum Clinics—USA (multiple tours)

1990s
TOURS AND CONCERTS
BoDeans—USA Tour (multiple tours)
Jon Bon Jovi—A Tribute to the President (Ford's Theater, Washington, DC)
Camerata Chamber Orchestra—Concert Guest Soloist (Bloomington, Indiana)
Patricia Conroy—Canadian Music Awards
John Cougar Mellencamp—*Late Night with David Letterman*
John Cougar Mellencamp—*Saturday Night Live*
John Cougar Mellencamp, Was (Not Was), Joe Ely, Bonnie Raitt, Lou Reed, Iggy Pop,
     John Hiatt, and Bruce Hornsby—Farm Aid 4 (Indianapolis, Indiana)
Marshall Crenshaw—USA Tour
Melissa Etheridge—*Breakdown* Tour (USA and Canada)
Melissa Etheridge—*Late Show with David Letterman*
Melissa Etheridge—Promotional Tour (five shows, USA)
Melissa Etheridge—*The Rosie O'Donnell Show*
Melissa Etheridge— *Hard Rock Live* (VH1)
Melissa Etheridge—*Your Little Secret* Tour (USA)
John Fogerty—America's Millennium Concert (Washington, DC)
John Fogerty—*Blue Moon Swamp* Tour (USA)
John Fogerty—A Festival at Ford's (Ford's Theatre, Washington, DC)
John Fogerty—*Good Morning America*
John Fogerty—*Late Night with Conan O'Brien*
John Fogerty—*Late Show with David Letterman* (three shows)
John Fogerty—Farm Aid
John Fogerty—*Hard Rock Live* (VH1)
John Fogerty—*VH1 Storytellers*
Corey Hart—Promotional Tour (Canada)
The Highwaymen—USA Tour
Kris Kristofferson and Lorrie Morgan—*American Music Shop*
Late Night with David Letterman—(two shows as sub for Anton Fig in the World's
     Most Dangerous Band)
Late Show with David Letterman—(multiple shows as sub in Paul Schaeffer's CBS Orchestra)
John Mellencamp—*The Arsenio Hall Show* (multiple times)
John Mellencamp—Billboard Awards Show

SELECTED CHRONOLOGY OF LIVE PERFORMANCES

John Mellencamp—Bob Dylan Thirtieth Anniversary Tribute Concert (Madison Square Garden, New York City)

John Mellencamp—Carnegie Hall Concert (New York City)

John Mellencamp—Concert for the Rock and Roll Hall of Fame (Cleveland, Ohio)

John Mellencamp—Concerts for the Heartland (Flood Victims Benefit)

John Mellencamp—*Dance Naked* Tour (USA and Canada)

John Mellencamp—Farm Aid 5 (Dallas, Texas)

John Mellencamp—Farm Aid 10 (Louisville, Kentucky)

John Mellencamp—Fourth of July Concert (live broadcast, ABC TV)

John Mellencamp—*Late Show with Dave Letterman*

John Mellencamp—MTV/VH1 Live Concert for Cable TV Convention (Tipitina's, New Orleans, Louisiana)

John Mellencamp—MTV Movie Awards

John Mellencamp—*MTV Unplugged*

John Mellencamp—*Whenever We Wanted* Tour (USA and Canada)

John Mellencamp and Dwight Yoakim—Farm Aid 6 (Des Moines, Iowa)

Willie Nelson—Academy of Country Music Awards

Willie Nelson—Live at the Roxy (Los Angeles, California)

Willie Nelson—*The Tonight Show with Jay Leno*

Willie Nelson, B. B. King, Bonnie Raitt, Ray Charles, Bob Dylan, Paul Simon, Waylon Jennings, Marty Stuart, Kris Kristofferson, Travis Tritt, Emmylou Harris, and Lyle Lovett—Willie Nelson's Big Six-O Celebration (Austin City Limits, Austin, Texas)

Willie Nelson and Paul Simon—*Saturday Night Live*

Willie Nelson and Frank Sinatra—Benefit Concert for St. Jude's Hospital

Carl Perkins, Waylon Jennings, Billy Ray Cyrus, Suzy Bogguss, Kathy Mattea, John Hiatt, Vassar Clements, Earl Scruggs, Randy Scruggs, Leon Russell, Sammy Kershaw, Rodney Crowell, Mark Collie, Jimmie Dale Gilmore, and Radney Foster—*Red Hot + Country*: Live (Ryman Auditorium, Nashville, Tennessee)

Bonnie Raitt, John Hiatt, Foster & Lloyd, B. B. King, Was (Not Was), Chris Isaak, Syd Straw, Michael McDonald, and Emmylou Harris, John Fogerty, and Iggy Pop—Roy Orbison Tribute to Benefit the Homeless (Universal Amphitheatre, North Hollywood, California)

Linda Ronstadt and Peter Asher, Reimy, Takako Shirai, Ryudo Uzaki, Yoshihiro Kai—Greening of the World: John Lennon Fiftieth Birthday Concert (Tokyo Dome, Japan)

Richie Sambora—Gavin Convention (San Diego, California)

Richie Sambora—*Late Show with David Letterman*

Richie Sambora—*The Tonight Show with Jay Leno*

Bob Seger & the Silver Bullet Band—*It's a Mystery* Tour (USA and Canada)

The Smashing Pumpkins—*Adore* World Tour

The Smashing Pumpkins—*Late Show with David Letterman*

The Smashing Pumpkins—*Saturday Night Live*

The Smashing Pumpkins—Much Music Awards

The Smashing Pumpkins—VH1 Fashion Awards

Patty Smyth—*The Arsenio Hall Show*
Solo Performance—Stone Song Festival (Bloomington, Illinois)
Marty Stuart and the Staple Singers—*The Tonight Show with Jay Leno*
Various Artists—Elvis Presley Tribute Concert (Memphis, Tennessee)
Various Artists—Rhythm Country and Blues Concert (Universal Amphitheatre, North Hollywood, California)
Hank Williams Jr.—World's Largest Rodeo (The Astrodome, Houston, Texas)

MUSIC VIDEOS AND FILMS

Chet Atkins and Allen Toussaint—"Southern Nights"
Mary Chapin Carpenter—"Shut Up and Kiss Me"
Bob Dylan—"Most of the Time"
John Fogerty—"Blueboy"
John Fogerty—*Premonition* (DVD)
John Fogerty—"Walking in a Hurricane"
Corey Hart—"Bang"
Corey Hart—"92 Days of Rain"
The Highwaymen—"It Is What It Is"
George Jones and B.B. King—"Patches"
Patti Labelle and Travis Tritt—"When Something Is Wrong with My Baby"
Sue Medley—"Falling Star"
Sue Medley—"That's Life"
John Mellencamp—"Again Tonight"
John Mellencamp—"Human Wheels"
John Mellencamp—"Love and Happiness"
John Mellencamp—"Now More Than Ever"
John Mellencamp—"When Jesus Left Birmingham"
John Mellencamp—"Wild Night"
Sam Moore and Conway Twitty—"Rainy Night in Georgia"
Aaron Neville and Trisha Yearwood—"I Fall to Pieces"
Billy Pilgrim—"Get Me Out of Here"
Richie Sambora—"Hard Times Come Easy"
Sanne Salomonsen (with Little Feat)—"Haven't I Been Good to You"
The Smashing Pumpkins—"Perfect"
Marty Stuart—"Don't Be Cruel (To a Heart That's True)"

DRUM CLINICS

Tama Drum Clinics—USA and Canada (multiple tours)
Zildjian Drum Clinics—USA

2000s
TOURS AND CONCERTS

Bronson Arroyo—*Cold Pizza* (ESPN 2)

Steve Bailey and Victor Wooten Bass Camp—Bass at the Beach (Myrtle Beach, South Carolina)

BoDeans—USA Tour (multiple tours)

The Bombastic Meatbats—Japan Tour

Jon Bon Jovi and Friends—Two Shows (Sayreville, New Jersey)

Michelle Branch—Are You Happy Tour (USA, Europe, Australia, Japan, Hong Kong, and Canada)

Michelle Branch—*The Tonight Show with Jay Leno* (multiple times)

Michelle Branch—*MTV Beach House/Total Request Live*

Michelle Branch—*Live with Regis and Kelly*

Michelle Branch—*Good Morning America*

Michelle Branch—*Pepsi Smash* (WB Network)

Michelle Branch—*The Ellen DeGeneres Show*

Michelle Branch—*Last Call with Carson Daly*

Michelle Branch—*MTV Hard Rock Live*

Michelle Branch—*The View*

Michelle Branch—Radio Music Awards

Michelle Branch—*Monday Night Football* Halftime Show

Michelle Branch—Major League Soccer Cup 2003 Halftime Show

Michelle Branch—*Jimmy Kimmel Live!*

Michelle Branch—*Late Night with Conan O'Brien*

Michelle Branch—World AIDS Day/Staying Alive Concert (MTV)

Michelle Branch—Bogart Tour for a Cure Concert

Joe Cocker Tour—USA and European Tours (multiple tours)

Joe Cocker Tour—USA Tour (multiple tours)

Joe Cocker—*The Tonight Show with Jay Leno*

Joe Cocker—*Austin City Limits*

Chris Cornell, Dave Grohl, Rob Thomas, Joss Stone, Bettye LaVette, Garth Brooks, Alan Jackson, Shelby Lynne, Brad Paisley, and Randy Travis—2008 Kennedy Center Honors, honoring the Who (Pete Townshend and Roger Daltrey), George Jones, Barbra Streisand, and Morgan Freeman

Melissa Etheridge—*Breakdown* Tour (USA and Europe)

Melissa Etheridge—Concerts (Los Angeles and New York)

Melissa Etheridge—*Good Morning America*

Melissa Etheridge—*Last Call with Carson Daly*

Melissa Etheridge—*Late Show with David Letterman*

Melissa Etheridge—*Lifetime Television Presents Women Rock!*

Melissa Etheridge—*Live with Regis and Kelly* (multiple times)

Melissa Etheridge—*Lucky* Tour (USA, Europe, and Canada—multiple tours)

Melissa Etheridge—*The Tonight Show with Jay Leno*

Melissa Etheridge—*You Rock with . . .* (VH1)

Melissa Etheridge, Chaka Khan, k.d. lang, Michael Feinstein—Equality Rocks! Concert (Los Angeles, California)

Melissa Etheridge and Joss Stone—2005 Grammy Awards
John Fogerty—Australia Tour (multiple tours)
John Fogerty—Concert for Artists' Rights
John Fogerty—*Late Night with Jimmy Fallon*
John Fogerty—*Late Show with David Letterman* (multiple times)
John Fogerty—New Zealand Tour
John Fogerty—*Soundstage* (PBS)
John Fogerty—*The Tonight Show with Jay Leno* (multiple times)
John Fogerty—USA, Canada, and European Tour (multiple tours)
John Fogerty—*World Cafe* (NPR)
John Fogerty, Jerry Lee Lewis, and Little Richard—Fiftieth Annual Grammy Awards
John Fogerty, Natasha Bedingfield, Chrisette Michele, Ryan Shaw, and Musiq Soulchild—
    "Sounds of Change" Concert: Grammy Foundation Music Preservation Project
Daryl Hall, Ray Manzarek, and Robbie Krieger (The Doors)—*Live from Daryl's House* Webcast
Daryl Hall and Kevin Rudolf—*Live From Daryl's House* Webcast
Chrissie Hynde, Chaka Khan, Gloria Estefan, Lee Ann Womack, Michelle Branch, and
    Jennifer Love Hewitt—*Lifetime Television Presents Women Rock!*
Kris Kristofferson, Norah Jones, Dwight Yoakam, Alison Krauss, Jerry Lee Lewis, Kid
    Rock, Martina McBride, Brad Paisley and Montgomery Gentry—*I Walk the Line: A
    Night for Johnny Cash* (CBS TV Special)
Late Show with David Letterman (as sub in Paul Schaffer's CBS Orchestra—multiple shows)
Ricky Martin—*Late Show with David Letterman*
John Mellencamp, Melissa Etheridge, Sting, Jennifer Nettles, and Ben Harper—2009
    Kennedy Center Honors, honoring Bruce Springsteen, Mel Brooks, Robert De Niro,
    Dave Brubeck, and Grace Bumbry
Marco Mendoza—Los Angeles Concerts (La Ve Le Club, Studio City, California)
Robert Mirabal—*Music from a Painted Cave* (PBS TV Special)
M2M—Promotional shows (New York City)
Willie Nelson, Eric Clapton, Steven Tyler, Shania Twain, Sheryl Crow, Kris Kristofferson,
    Ray Charles, Toby Keith, Norah Jones, Kenny Chesney, Lyle Lovett, Shelby Lynne,
    Ray Price, Diana Krall, Elvis Costello, and Leon Russell—*Willie Nelson & Friends—
    Live and Kickin'* (USA Network TV Special and DVD)
Willie Nelson and Sheryl Crow—*Crossroads* (Country Music Television)
Willie Nelson and Sheryl Crow—Thirty-Fifth Annual CMA Awards
Willie Nelson and Lee Ann Womack—Academy of Country Music Awards
Willie Nelson and Lee Ann Womack—*The Tonight Show with Jay Leno*
Graham Nash, Dave Mason, Joe Ely, Delbert McClinton, the Crickets, Peter and Gordon,
    Bobby Vee, Wanda Jackson, Tommy Allsup—"50 Winters Later" Concert (Clear Lake,
    Iowa)
Pepsi Voice of the Next Generation (Zhejiang Satellite TV, China)
Joe Perry, Buddy Guy, Slash, Edgar Winter, Alison Krauss, and Steve Lukather—Les Paul
    and Friends: Ninetieth Birthday Salute
Vasco Rossi—Italy Tour

Philip Sayce—Japan Tour
Philip Sayce—USA Tour (multiple tours)
Lee Seung Hwan—Concert (Seoul, South Korea)
Styx—Two concerts (USA)
Various Artists—House of Blues All Stars of Rock and Roll Concert (Jackson Hole, Wyoming)
Stevie Wonder, John Mellencamp, Jon Bon Jovi, Beyoncé, Mary J. Blige, Garth Brooks, Sheryl Crow, James Taylor, Josh Groban, Herbie Hancock, Heather Headley, John Legend, Bettye LaVette, Jennifer Nettles, Usher, Shakira, will.i.am—We Are One: The Obama Inaugural Celebration at the Lincoln Memorial (Washington, DC)
VH1—"Save the Music" Presentation (New York City)

MUSIC VIDEOS AND FILMS

American Idol—TV Commercials
BoDeans—*Homebrewed: Live at the Pabst* (DVD)
Michelle Branch—"Are You Happy Now?"
Michelle Branch—"Breathe"
Melissa Etheridge—*Lucky Live* (DVD)
Robert Mirabal—*Music from a Painted Cave* (DVD)

DRUM CLINICS

Tama Drum Clinics—Australia, Canada, Italy, Poland, and USA (multiple tours)
Zildjian Drum Clinics—Argentina, Australia, Canada, Chile, China, Germany, Hong Kong, Italy, Japan, Malaysia, Philippines, Singapore, South Korea, Russia, Thailand, and USA (multiple tours)

2010–
TOURS AND CONCERTS

Trace Adkins and the Las Vegas High School Marching Band—American Country Awards (Las Vegas, Nevada)
BoDeans—USA Tour (multiple tours)
BoDeans, Mark Farner, Craig Fuller, Sam Moore, Micky Dolenz—Vallarta-Nayarit: Classic Rock Festival (Puerto Vallarta, Mexico)
The Bombastic Meatbats—Concerts (Los Angeles, California)
Jackson Browne, Sheryl Crow, Jack White, Bruce Springsteen and Tom Morello, Aaron Neville, Willie Nelson, Derek Trucks and Susan Tedeschi, Bonnie Raitt, John Doe, and Tom Jones—MusiCares honoring Bob Dylan
Brandi Carlile, Kris Kristofferson, Sheryl Crow, Iron and Wine, Amy Lee, Ronnie Dunn, Willie Nelson, Lucinda Williams, Matthew McConaughey, Shooter Jennings, Andy Grammer, Jamey Johnson, Pat Monahan—Walk the Line: Johnny Cash Tribute (Austin City Limits, Austin, Texas)
Chickenfoot—Different Devil Tour (USA and Canada)
Chickenfoot—*Jimmy Kimmel Live!*

Chickenfoot—*The Tonight Show with Jay Leno*
Chickenfoot—Promotional Tour (USA and Europe)
Chickenfoot—Sammy's Birthday Bash (Cabo San Lucas, Mexico)
The Drills—Concert (Austin, Texas)
An Evening with Kenny Aronoff (Butler University, Indianapolis, Indiana)
An Evening with Kenny Aronoff (Risk Management Nonprofit Organization, Chicago, Illinois)
An Evening with Kenny Aronoff (Coin Laundry Association, Oakbrook Terrace, Illinois)
An Evening with Kenny Aronoff (Drake University, Des Moines, Iowa)
An Evening with Kenny Aronoff (JCC Indianapolis)
An Evening with Kenny Aronoff—(Mahaiwe Theater, Great Barrington, Massachusetts)
An Evening with Kenny Aronoff—Sweetwater (Fort Wayne, Indiana)
An Evening with Kenny Aronoff—Wilbur Wright College (Chicago, Illinois)
Kenny and Friends—Baked Potato (Los Angeles, California—multiple shows)
John Fogerty—The Venetian (Las Vegas, Nevada)
John Fogerty Tour—USA Tour (multiple tours)
John Fogerty—Stage Coach (Indio, California)
John Fogerty—Orange Bowl Halftime Show
John Fogerty—Canada Tour (multiple tours)
John Fogerty—*The Voice*
John Fogerty—*Late Night with David Letterman*
John Fogerty—European and Scandinavian Tour (multiple tours)
John Fogerty—New Orleans Jazz Festival
John Fogerty—Howard Stern Sixtieth Birthday Celebration
John Fogerty—SXSW (South by Southwest) (Austin, Texas)
John Fogerty—South America and Russia Tour
John Fogerty, Carole King, Martina McBride, Jennifer Hudson, Arturo Sandoval, Pat Monahan, Willie Nelson, Merle Haggard, Mavis Staples, Emmylou Harris—Smith Center Grand Opening (Las Vegas, Nevada)
Billy Gibbons and Friends—Concert (Texas)
Goo Goo Dolls—USA Tour
Goodfellas (Steve Lukather, Steve Weingart, Fabrizio Grossi)—European Tour
Warren Haynes, Susan Tedeschi and Derek Trucks, Robert Randolph, Keb Mo, Sam Moore, Dr. John, John Hiatt, Brantley Gilbert, Pat Monahan, Taj Mahal, Gregg Allman, Trace Adkins, Vince Gill, Martina McBride, Eric Church, Jackson Browne—All My Friends: Celebrating the Songs and Voice of Gregg Allman
Don Henley, Garth Brooks, Brendon Urie (Panic at the Disco), Rufus Wainwright, Steve Winwood, Sheila E., Tom Morello, Fher Olvera (Mana), Juanes, Orianthi—Kennedy Center Honors honoring Carlos Santana, Billy Joel, Herbie Hancock, Shirley MacLaine, and Martina Arroyo
The Highwaymen (Merle Haggard, Willie Nelson, Blake Shelton, and Kris Kristofferson)—2014 Grammy Awards

SELECTED CHRONOLOGY OF LIVE PERFORMANCES

Chrissie Hynde, Joe Walsh, Gregg Allman, Dr. John—Paul Allen's Sixtieth Birthday Party (New Orleans, Louisiana)

Russ Irwin—Concert (Los Angeles, California)

Joan Jett—LA Fashion Show, 2016

Mayssa Karaa, Rami Jaffee, Luis Conte, Curt Schneider, Michael Fish Herring, Marcus Nand, Sharlotte Gibson, Angela Latham—When Music Matters (Abu Dhabi, United Arab Emirates)

Kid Rock, Sam Moore, Brad Paisley, Mavis Staples, Darius Rucker, Carrie Underwood, Jonny Lang, Reba McEntire, Garth Brooks—"All Together Now" Show at the Kennedy Center

Lenny Kravitz and Kid Rock—2012 Kennedy Center Honors, honoring Led Zeppelin, Buddy Guy, David Letterman, Dustin Hoffman, and Natalia Makarova

Lady Gaga, Bruno Mars, Bruce Springsteen, Herbie Hancock, Esperanza Spalding—2014 Kennedy Center Honors, honoring Sting, Tom Hanks, Al Green, Lily Tomlin, Patricia McBride

John Mellencamp, James Taylor, Sheryl Crow, Stephen Stills, John Fogerty, Keith Urban, Booker T. Jones, Norah Jones, Jackson Browne, Elton John, Leon Russell, T Bone Burnett, Crosby, Stills & Nash, Emmylou Harris, Patty Griffin, Lucinda Williams, Lady Antebellum, Ben Harper, Josh Groban, and Jack Black as the MC—MusiCares Person of the Year Tribute to Neil Young

Willie Nelson, John Fogerty, Mary J. Blige, Romeo Santos, Sgt. Christiana Ball, Captain Auer and Captain Smith—A Salute to the Troops: In Performance at the White House

Lionel Richie, Smokey Robinson, Jennifer Nettles—2011 Kennedy Center Honors, honoring Neil Diamond, Sonny Rollins, Barbara Cook, Yo-Yo Ma

Philip Sayce—Concert (Los Angeles, California)

Paul Simon and Edie Brickell, Willie Nelson, Alison Krauss, Cyndi Lauper, Rosanne Cash, Jamey Johnson, Raul Malo, Leon Bridges, Ana Gabriel, Buckwheat Zydeco, Luke and Micah Nelson—Library of Congress Gershwin Prize for Popular Song honoring Willie Nelson

Bruce Springsteen, John Fogerty, Dr. John, Cyril Neville, Allen Toussaint, Dave Malone, Big Chief Monk Boudreaux, Irma Thomas, John Boutté, George Porter Jr., Jason Isbell, Shannon McNally, Anders Osborne, the Blind Boys of Alabama, Chuck Leavell, Mavis Staples, Jimmie Vaughan, Ryan Bingham, Warren Haynes—The Musical Mojo of Dr. John: Celebrating Mac & His Music

Ringo Starr—2014 Grammy Awards

Ringo Starr, Paul McCartney, Jeff Lynne, Joe Walsh, Danny Harrison, Stevie Wonder, Pharrell Williams, Brad Paisley, John Legend, Alicia Keys, Dave Grohl, Keith Urban, John Mayer—The Beatles: The Night That Changed America

Supersonic Blues Machine with Special Guests Billy Gibbons, Robben Ford, Walter Trout, and Steve Lukather—2016 Netherlands, Norway, and European Tour

Steven Tyler, Sheryl Crow, John Fogerty, Willie Nelson, Brandon Flowers, Eric Church, Kris Kristofferson, Chris Stapleton, Aloe Black, Juanes, Pat Monahan, and Tom Morello—Imagine: John Lennon Seventy-Fifth Birthday Concert

STYX—USA Tour

Switchblade Glory—SXSW (South by Southwest) (Austin, Texas)

Steven Tyler, Dave Grohl, Norah Jones, James Taylor, Mavis Staples, Willie Nelson, Sheryl
Crow, Kid Rock, Vince Gill, Brad Paisley, Jamey Johnson, Miranda Lambert, Kris
Kristofferson—2010 Kennedy Center Honors, honoring Paul McCartney, Merle
Haggard, Oprah Winfrey, Bill T. Jones, and Jerry Herman

Deborah Vial—Concert (Dallas, Texas, and Maui)

Yamaha DTX Electronic Drum Kit Tour—USA Tour (multiple tours)

Zep Set—Concerts (Los Angeles, California)

MUSIC VIDEOS AND FILMS

Danny Collins—Movie starring Al Pacino (music and acting)

DRUM CLINICS

Tama Drum Clinics—USA Tours

Yamaha DTX Drum Clinics—USA, Scandinavia, and European Tours

Zildjian Drum Clinics—USA Tours

ACKNOWLEDGMENTS

This book would not have been possible without Jake Brown, whose idea it was in the first place to chronicle my improbable career. He took on the Herculean task of documenting thirty-five years of sessions and tours, hits, near misses—a literal odyssey of rock 'n' roll—not to mention collecting the interviews that pepper this book and make it so much more than just my story. Without Jake's patience, passion, and perseverance, this project would have been just a dream.

My collaborator—the author, editor, and musician Mike Edison—worked with me tirelessly, pushing me past my comfort zone, teaching me that talking isn't writing, and that cadence, meter, and groove go past the drum set and onto the page. He encouraged me to stop, take a breath, and look around, even as I was zooming to the next session. Mike is also a drummer and a badass whose own books chronicle his unique career playing rock 'n' roll against all obstacles, and his understanding of music, narrative, and the dynamics of working with other musicians were essential to this book every step of the way.

Thanks and gratitude to all the artists and bands that I have recorded and toured with, all the musicians I have worked with in Los Angeles, Nashville, New York City, Muscle Shoals, Austin, Indiana, and everywhere else in the world, both live and in the studio. I couldn't have done it without you, but none more than . . .

John Mellencamp who gave me my first break and taught me what it took to be a success in this business, working his ass off to be the best he could be. He taught me "the fear," and he showed me how to turn that into a career.

My undying thanks to John and to all the guys in the band. We were a band of brothers that lived together and shared so many memorable experiences, the kind that one can only experience in a great rock 'n' roll band.

Thanks to everyone who invited me to go out and tour or be on their records—Bob Seger, Billy Corgan, the Jefferson Airplane—what a trip! Ten years with Joe Cocker! Ten amazing years with the great Melissa Etheridge! Twenty-five years with the BoDeans (Kurt Neumann, Eric Holden, Sam Hawksley, Bukka Allen, Stefano Intelisano)! Twenty-one years with John Fogerty! (Thanks to John and all the guys in the band—James LoMenzo, Bob Malone, Devon Pangel, Shane Fogerty.) Thanks to Rob Mathes for seven years at the Kennedy Center Honors and, of course, President Obama's Inauguration. Thanks to Meat Loaf, Michelle Branch, Styx, Goo Goo Dolls, Corey Hart, Jon Bon Jovi, Chickenfoot, Vasco Rossi, the Rolling Stones, Supersonic Blues Machine Band (Fabrizio Grossi, Lance Lopez), and everyone else that made this story possible—thank you all for inviting me into your world.

Thanks to all the great producers I have worked with but especially my great friend Don Was, who I have been working with now for over twenty-seven years.

Gratitude and thanks to the Jacobs School of Music, Indiana University, Bloomington Indiana, UMass Amherst Department of Music, Aspen School of Music, Tanglewood Music Center—Fellowship Program, Vic Firth, George Gaber, Arthur Press, Peter Tanner, Alan Dawson, and Gary Chester, for an amazing education in music. Thanks to all the people and teachers who have given me life lessons.

Thanks to David Jenkins, Christopher Tolton, Thomas Clements, Ken Rutkowski, Keith Chambers, Deborah M. Loober, Scott Ross, Dr. Gordon, Dr. Abrams, and David Greenspon. Thanks to Dennis Mukai. Thanks to Neil Peart. Thanks to John and Missy Butcher and all the drummers I have taught lessons to at Indiana University and all around the world (you know who you are).

Thanks to all the engineers who made me sound great. To Tama drums, Zildjian cymbals, Vic Firth sticks, Evans heads, Remo heads, Meinl Percussion, Gator cases, Yamaha DTX electronic drums, BAE Audio, Shure, Royer, Mojave, and Lewitt. Porter and Davis and Alfred Publishing. And to *Rolling Stone*, *Modern Drummer*, *Drum*, *Rhythm*, *Drumhead*, and all the other drum magazines and publications around the world for your continued support and enthusiasm.

Thanks to the team at Backbeat Books—publisher John Cerullo was a great champion of this book, and senior editor Bernadette Malavarca kept a steady hand on the wheel and helped us find the finish line.

Thanks to my twin brother Jonathan for being so good looking, the perfect brother, and a badass at whatever he does; my sister Nina, a great listener, always supportive and a great hang, supplier of great wine and super smart! My son, Nikolai, for carrying on the Aronoff legacy of drumming, love, kindness, music and the arts, and for always searching.

My undying gratitude to everyone who ever came out to see me play, because, really, we could not have done any of it without you.

Thanks, and all my love, to my wife, Georgina Anouska Aronoff, for her love, laughter and fun and her beautiful everything, her support, her lifelong companionship . . . and her barking dogs!